OTHER BOOKS BY TRAILER LIFE

Trailer Life's RV Repair & Maintenance Manual
Edited by Bob Livingston

All-new, updated edition presents recreational vehicle owners with all the practical knowledge needed for diagnosing problems, making repairs, communicating with mechanics. Detailed troubleshooting guides for all RV systems, hundreds of comprehensive illustrations and photographs, step-by-step instructions for repairing, replacing, and maintaining systems.
8½ × 11, 336 pages
$29.95   ISBN 0-934798-12-5

The RV Handbook
Bill Estes

This new encyclopedia of information on the mechanical aspects of using a recreational vehicle contains chapters on improving engine performance, how to make an engine last longer, troubleshooting gasoline and diesel engines, RV handling, safety and weight ratings, how to choose a tow vehicle, understanding propane, electrical systems, and living without hookups.
7¼ × 9¼, 352 pages
$29.95   ISBN: 0-934798-32-X

Full-time RVing: A Complete Guide to Life on the Open Road
Bill and Jan Moeller

The answers to all the questions anyone who dreams of traveling full time in an RV may have can be found in this remarkable source book. *Full-time RVing* takes the mystery out of fulltiming and makes it possible to fully enjoy this once-in-a-lifetime experience.
7¼ × 9¼, 352 pages
$14.95   ISBN: 0-934798-14-1

The Good Sam RV Cookbook
Edited by Beverly Edwards and the editors of *Trailer Life*

Over 250 easy and delicious recipes, including 78 prize-winners from the Good Sam Samboree cook-offs around the country. Also contains tips, ideas, and suggestions to help you get the most from your RV galley.
7¼ × 9¼, 252 pages
$14.95   ISBN: 0-93478-17-6

These books are available at fine bookstores everywhere. Or, you may order directly from Trailer Life Books. For each book ordered, simply send us the name of the book, the price, plus $2.95 per book for shipping and handling (California residents please add 8¼% and Indiana residents, 5% sales tax).
Mail to:

Trailer Life Books, P.O. Box 4500, Agoura, CA 91376-9939

You may call our customer-service representatives if you wish to charge your order or if you want more information. Please phone, toll-free, Monday through Friday, 6:30 A.M. to 5:30 P.M.; Saturday, 7:30 A.M. to 12:30 P.M. Pacific Time, **(800) 234-3450.**

Dedication

To my parents,
Billy and Virginia Howells,
who instilled in me twin instincts:
pragmatism and pursuit of dreams.

THE RVer's MONEY BOOK

■ Bob Howells

TRAILER LIFE
BOOKS

Trailer Life Book Division

President/CEO: Joe McAdams
Senior Vice President/CFO: Lewis M. Caster
Vice President/Publisher, Book Division: Michael Schneider
Associate Publisher, Book Division: Joe Daquino
General Manager, Book Division: Rena Copperman
Assistant Manager, Book Division: Cindy Halley
Bulk Sales/Distribution Manager, Book Division: Judy Klein

The material quoted on page 178 is from *Blue Highways:
A Journey into America,* by William Least Heat Moon.
Copyright © 1982 by William Least Heat Moon.

Editor/Production manager: Rena Copperman
Production coordinator: Robert S. Tinnon
Senior editor: Martha Weiler
Cover design: Hespenheide Design
Interior design: Robert S. Tinnon
Cartography: Robert Lamarche
Additional typography: Viki Buysse
Indexer: Barbara Wurf
Cover separations: Western Laser Graphics

This book was set in ITC Garamond Light by Andresen Typographics, Tucson,
Arizona, and printed on 50-pound Amherst Ultra Matte by The Banta Company.

ISBN 0-934798-32-X

Library of Congress Cataloging-in-Publication Data

Howells, Bob, 1953–
    The RVer's money book / by Bob Howells.
        p.   cm.
    Includes bibliographical references and index.
    ISBN 0-934798-32-X : $29.95
    1. Mobile home living—Economic aspects.   2. Recreational
vehicles—Economic aspects.   I. Title.
HD7289.6.H69   1992
332.024 ' 91—dc20   91-29011
                                                                 CIP

Contents

■ ■ ■ ■ ■ ■ ■ ■ ■

Foreword

■ ■ ■ ■ ■ ■ ■ ■

While it's true that most of us have chosen the RV lifestyle because it's our preferred method of travel—the best way, regardless of cost, to get to all the places where we want to spend our time recreating—few of us would pass up the chance to save money on a new RV, camping fees, fuel or anything else we buy during our travels. As is often said of wealthy people, they didn't get that way by throwing away money.

Even though the average investment in the typical RV (tow vehicle and trailer, or motorhome) may be $40,000 to $60,000, few of us would pass up a $5 discount on camping fees. Few of us would forgo taking an extra five or ten minutes to look for a lower price on fuel if we thought we could find it by going a bit out of our way.

Saving money can be a significant part of the satisfaction we get from RVing—the same kind of satisfaction one might get from finding clothing, a home appliance or a lawn mower on sale. We may not need to look for ways to save money, but we do it anyway—either out of habit or simply because we enjoy it!

If all that sounds logical, then you would probably agree that this book should have been titled *The RV Fun Book*. The fun just gets better and better—from saving bucks on RV insurance to earning money on the road; from getting the best rates on RV service (and avoiding hassles) to economically taking care of your health.

Of course, this is not to say that all of us are well fixed. Some of us may have to stretch our Social Security and pension dollars to stick with this wonderful, adventurous lifestyle.

If you're already dedicated to RVing but would like to make it even more satisfying, your choice of reading matter couldn't have been better. You'll find *The RVer's Money Book* an excellent investment.

BILL ESTES
Associate Publisher
Trailer Life/MotorHome

Preface

■ ■ ■ ■ ■ ■ ■ ■ ■

I occasionally run across studies that contrast the cost of an RV vacation with a car/hotel or an air/resort vacation, for instance. RVing always wins.

I don't get too excited about such studies, though, and I don't cite any in this book. Sure, a typical two-week RV vacation will undoubtedly work out cheaper than a Concorde flight to Paris and a fortnight on the French Riviera. On the other hand, I'm sure I could find a nice deal on a flight to some lesser resort packaged with a stay in a pretty decent hotel for a most reasonable amount of money—less money, undoubtedly, than I could spend on an RV vacation if I really put my mind to self-indulgence.

These comparisons are somewhat bogus. For one thing, they leave out the cost of the RV itself. Let's face it: Buying or renting a recreational vehicle can be a considerable investment. But it's an investment millions have chosen to make. Their reasons are generally pretty similar to mine. I love traveling by RV because it affords me comfortable mobility, great independence, and a convenient, mobile base camp for the many activities I enjoy.

This book presupposes that you are similarly inclined, that you enjoy traveling by recreational vehicle (or contemplate some RV travels in the near future) because it's a great way to go, not because it's cheaper than a fancy hotel.

I firmly believe that most people who travel by RV do so out of choice, not out of necessity.

RVers are people who dare to fulfill their dreams of mobility and independence. Happily, once they make that choice, they can also choose to economize in myriad ways. One purpose of this book is to point out these ways, every step of the way, from the dealer's lot to an idyllic campsite and a thousand places in between.

But the real purpose of the book is to help you to indulge your dreams, to squeeze every possible enjoyment from your RV travels.

It's not about pinching pennies. It's about channeling them in the direction of maximum pleasure. That doesn't mean skimping. It does mean avoiding waste.

The RVer's Money Book is really about living as fully as possible and using money as an energy to fuel your travels through life.

Acknowledgments

■ ■ ■ ■ ■ ■ ■ ■ ■ ■ ■ ■ ■

This book wouldn't be possible without the resources and editorial staff of TL Enterprises. I particularly wish to thank Martha Weiler, John Thompson, Bob Longsdorf, Gail Harrington, Barbara Leonard, Gaylord Maxwell, Bob Livingston, Bill Estes, Rich Johnson, Sue Bray, Maxye Henry, and Beverly Edwards for their contributions. Many thanks to Bob Tinnon for his input and creative enthusiasm, and my appreciation to Rena Copperman and Michael Schneider for their faith and advice.

I also wish to thank the dozens of willing experts in numerous fields, including many stellar individuals in the RV industry, who graciously submitted to having their brains picked, and many others out there on the road, who so kindly shared their "secrets" with me.

CHAPTER ONE

Budgeting for RV Ownership and Travel

■ ■ ■ ■ ■ ■ ■ ■ ■ ■

You don't need to be sold on the attractiveness of the RV lifestyle. If you've opened this book, you either already own an RV, or you want to own one. The freedom of the open road, the wonderful sights to see, friendships to be made, unique experiences to enjoy . . . if you've not experienced these already, you are probably looking forward to them in the near future.

So let's get right down to business. How can you afford to buy the recreational vehicle that best allows you to enjoy all these wonderful things? Once you have the RV, how can you afford to travel in it as often as possible, in the most satisfying way?

In this chapter, we'll start with the status quo, your personal budget. How much do you make and how much do you spend? That answered, you'll know how much you can allot to the purchase and use of an RV.

Then we'll look at your RV-travel budget. What are your RVing expenses? The mere process of quantifying these factors will lead to some revelations; you might be able to afford more than you think, or, you might be shocked to see where all your money's going.

If, after filling out the worksheets in this chapter, you get the impression that you can't afford an RV, or you can't afford to travel as you would like, don't despair. The remaining chapters in this book will present thousands more revelations—tangible, practical, usually simple, ways to save a great deal of money.

Reading this first chapter will give you the tools to become your own business manager, to have a grasp of all the relevant figures.

In This Chapter:

- *How do I determine what I can afford to spend on my RV and RV travels?*
- *How do I assess my personal finances?*
- *How do I allocate my RVing budget?*
- *What will my costs be?*
- *What records should I keep?*

Reading the remaining chapters will help you become your own efficiency expert, adept at the kind of creative cost-cutting that will enable your "business"—that is, your RV travels—to go farther and be more successful and enjoyable.

YOUR INCOME

If you're going to structure a budget for home and travel, the obvious beginning is to know how much money you have coming in during the year (see Worksheet 1.1). Nothing else is relevant until you know this figure.

Consider every source of income: your regular take-home pay and/or pension, bonuses, stock dividends, interest on bonds or savings accounts, tax refunds you have coming, rental income, and profits from anything you might sell, such as your home.

Most of these figures will be estimates. Be realistic. Some figures could fluctuate significantly during the year, but it's best for your purposes here to use low estimates.

Be sure to deduct taxes *before* you enter any income figure. If you are self-employed, be sure to deduct self-employment tax.

YOUR FIXED EXPENSES

Putting aside money every month as a fixed expense is a key to building the nest egg that may one day enable you to RV . . . full time.

Your next step is to estimate your fixed expenses (see Worksheet 1.2). If you prefer to do this month by month, fine. That way you can see exactly what is due when, such as property taxes and insurance payments. But a key to managing your budget is to spread those big expenses over the course of the year, so that you account for a portion of those expenses every month. For example, if you have a big insurance payment due every March, budgeting one-twelfth of that payment every month insures that you can make the yearly payment without straining your budget. For this reason, Worksheet 1.2 calls for annual totals divided by twelve.

For now, leave your RV payments and insurance out of this ledger. We'll include those in your RV fixed-expenses budget.

Your fixed-expenses estimate includes everything predictable, including rent or mortgage payments, charitable contributions, memberships, and dues. It should also include planned-for medical expenses, such as annual checkups.

Include savings as an expense. This is especially important if you are still working. Putting aside money every month as a fixed expense is a key to building the nest egg that may one day enable you to RV extensively, even full time. Financial experts recommend that you maintain at least two months' income in an emergency savings fund to cover unexpected expenses. That fund should be readily accessible, or liquid. See Chapter Eighteen, "Handling Your Finances on the Road," page 197, for some liquid savings suggestions.

Income Worksheet

INCOME SOURCE	YEARLY AMOUNT
Salary and wages #1	_____
Salary and wages #2	_____
Bonuses	_____
Social Security	_____
Interest	_____
Dividends	_____
Commissions	_____
Rental income	_____
Gifts	_____
Tax refunds	_____
Profit from sales	_____
Annuities	_____
_____	_____
_____	_____
_____	_____
_____	_____
_____	_____
_____	_____
_____	_____
_____	_____
_____	_____
_____	_____
_____	_____
_____	_____
Total spendable income	_____
(÷ 12 = monthly income)	_____

Worksheet 1.1: Your Income

Fixed-Expense Worksheet

EXPENSE	YEARLY AMOUNT	MONTHLY AMOUNT (YEAR ÷ 12)
Housing (Principal, interest, taxes, and insurance)	_____	_____
Rent (Condominium association membership, if applicable)	_____	_____
_____	_____	_____
_____	_____	_____
Insurance		
Life	_____	_____
Health	_____	_____
Dental	_____	_____
Auto (other than RV)	_____	_____
_____	_____	_____
_____	_____	_____
Savings		
Emergency fund	_____	_____
Permanent fund	_____	_____
Investments	_____	_____
Debts, obligations		
Auto loan	_____	_____
Installment payments	_____	_____
Bank charges	_____	_____
Alimony	_____	_____
Child support	_____	_____
Personal, charitable		
Church	_____	_____
Other charities	_____	_____
Union/professional dues	_____	_____
Service organizations	_____	_____

Worksheet 1.2: Fixed Expenses

If you're retired, you will probably reduce, maybe even eliminate, your monthly savings figure. Now's the time to enjoy the fruits of your labors!

YOUR FLEXIBLE LIVING EXPENSES

Once you know what your *fixed* expenses are, you'll know how much you have left for *flexible* living expenses (see Worksheet 1.3). Then, when you deduct both fixed and flexible living expenses from your annual income, you'll have the amount available for your RV budget.

Estimate your flexible expenses by reviewing your checkbook, bill stubs, and receipts from the past year.

Many of these flexible expenses may not seem so flexible—you'll always have food, clothing, and medical costs. You may not be able to eliminate many of these expenses, but you can control most of them.

Remember, any reductions you can make in your flexible expenses can go directly into your RVing fund. Don't accept these flexible totals as fixed obligations. Put yourself on a household budget that calls for cutting back on these expenses.

How do you cut back? The specifics of reducing your household budget are beyond the scope of this book, yet in many of the following chapters you'll find hundreds of suggestions for reducing travel expenses that are directly applicable to household expenses. Chapter Fifteen, "Shopping: For the Road, on the Road," and Chapter Sixteen, "Food: Dining In, Dining Out," are examples.

Pay special attention to your credit-buying habits. Interest and service charges you are paying on charge-account and bank-card purchases is money that could be yours.

Remember, if you're planning extensive RV travels, some of your home living expenses will be reduced. For example, if you live in the north and plan to spend February in the Sun Belt, you can lower your home-heating figure.

Any reductions you can make in your flexible expenses can go directly into your RVing fund.

Dollar-saving Tip

Treat your home as a business with a budget, and justify every expense. Those that can't be justified should be reduced or eliminated.

DETERMINING YOUR AVAILABLE RVING BUDGET

Now it's time to calculate the totals. On Worksheet 1.4, enter your net annual income figure and then subtract your fixed-expenses figure from it. Next, subtract your total flexible expenses. What's left over is the *available* amount of money you have for your annual RV budget. Naturally, you don't have to use the entire figure for RVing. The portion of the figure you wish to devote to your travels is a personal decision. But if you've been thorough in filling out Worksheets 1.1 through 1.3, you should be confident in this figure. All your other expenses should have been accounted for, so you can safely use this money for your RV payments and travels.

Flexible Living-Expense Worksheet

EXPENSE	YEARLY AMOUNT	MONTHLY AMOUNT (YEAR ÷ 12)
Home		
Heating oil	_____	_____
Gas	_____	_____
Electricity	_____	_____
Water	_____	_____
Telephone	_____	_____
Refuse disposal	_____	_____
Repairs	_____	_____
Improvements	_____	_____
Garden	_____	_____
Transportation (non-RV)		
Gas and oil	_____	_____
Maintenance	_____	_____
Public transportation	_____	_____
Food and dry goods		
Groceries	_____	_____
Restaurant meals	_____	_____
Paper products	_____	_____
Laundry products	_____	_____
Toiletries	_____	_____
Clothing		
_____	_____	_____
_____	_____	_____
_____	_____	_____
_____	_____	_____
_____	_____	_____
_____	_____	_____

Worksheet 1.3: Flexible Living Expenses

Flexible Living-Expense Worksheet (Continued)

EXPENSE	YEARLY AMOUNT	MONTHLY AMOUNT (YEAR ÷ 12)
Entertainment and recreation		
Non-RV travel	_____	_____
Movies and theater	_____	_____
Home entertainment	_____	_____
Gifts	_____	_____
Education, hobbies, postage		
Classes	_____	_____
Books	_____	_____
Magazines and newspapers	_____	_____
Hobby supplies	_____	_____
Stationary and postage	_____	_____
Services		
Gardener	_____	_____
Pool maintenance	_____	_____
Professional (CPA, legal, etc.)	_____	_____
Medical		
Doctor	_____	_____
Dentist	_____	_____
Prescriptions	_____	_____
Other		
_____	_____	_____
_____	_____	_____
_____	_____	_____
_____	_____	_____
_____	_____	_____
_____	_____	_____
Total	_____	_____

Available RV-Budget Worksheet

Enter your annual income from Worksheet 1.1:   _____

Subtract your fixed expenses from Worksheet 1.2:   _____

Subtotal   _____

Subtract your flexible expenses from Worksheet 1.3:   _____

Amount available for your RV budget: _____

Amount you allocate to your RV budget   _____

Worksheet 1.4: Available RV Budget

If you view your RV and your RV travels as a business, the money you allocate from this total is your operating budget. Worksheets 1.5 and 1.6 will indicate how that money will be spent.

As stated previously, if your RV-budget figure seems low, don't despair. This book will show you how to stay within your budget and still enjoy your travels.

If you don't currently own an RV, you can still estimate . . . expenses.

Allocating Your RVing Budget

Now it's time to see just where your RVing budget will go. If you already own an RV, you should know your fixed expenses. If you keep good records, you'll also know your flexible expenses. Otherwise, estimate them. But begin recordkeeping as soon as possible so you can accurately know these expenses (see page 12).

If you don't currently own an RV, you can still estimate all these expenses. A few phone calls to a bank, RV dealer, and your insurance agent will help you estimate your fixed expenses. Friends whose family size and lifestyle are similar to yours can help you estimate your flexible expenses. If you don't know any RVers, contact the national office of an RV club and ask them to refer you to some club members in your area who might help.

Fill out Worksheets 1.5 and 1.6, using your present situation and your past experience, or by using input from experts. Then, after you read the rest of this book, fill them out again. If you apply lessons from every chapter of the book, you will be able to drastically reduce your RVing expenditures, both fixed and flexible. Why? Because it's almost certain that you are spending too much money for everything!

You might also be able to add to your income ledger (see Chapter Nineteen, "Earning (and Volunteering) Your Way." The net result? More money to spend on RVing, which will cost less money (per week, month, or year) than in the past. That means you can extend your travels further, upgrade your RV, or enjoy the fruits of your budgeting in any way you wish.

Your Fixed RV Expenses

Your fixed expenses should include your RV loan payment, if applicable, and such unavoidable expenses as insurance and storage (see Worksheet 1.5). If you belong to a membership campground, include your annual dues, as well as any other RV-related memberships.

While you might have a difficult time reducing your fixed household expenses, your fixed RV expenses can almost certainly be reduced by following some of the strategies outlined in this book. Chapter Three tells you how to negotiate the best deal possible on

Fixed RV-Expense Worksheet

EXPENSE	YEARLY AMOUNT	MONTHLY AMOUNT (YEAR ÷ 12)
Expense		
Loan payment	_____	_____
Extended warranty	_____	_____
Registration	_____	_____
Insurance	_____	_____
Emergency road service	_____	_____
Storage	_____	_____
Campground membership	_____	_____
Club memberships	_____	_____
Camping passports, (Golden Eagle, KOA, etc.)	_____	_____
Total:	_____	_____
_____	_____	_____
_____	_____	_____
_____	_____	_____
_____	_____	_____
_____	_____	_____
_____	_____	_____
_____	_____	_____
_____	_____	_____
_____	_____	_____
_____	_____	_____
_____	_____	_____
_____	_____	_____

Worksheet 1.5: Fixed RV Expenses

Flexible RV-Expense Worksheet

EXPENSE	YEARLY AMOUNT	MONTHLY AMOUNT (YEAR ÷ 12)
Travel		
Campsite fees	_____	_____
Admission charges	_____	_____
Entertainment	_____	_____
Fishing and hunting licenses	_____	_____
Tolls	_____	_____
Vehicle		
Gas and oil	_____	_____
Repairs	_____	_____
Preventive maintenance	_____	_____
Tires and batteries	_____	_____
LP gas	_____	_____
Supplies (toilet chemicals, etc.)	_____	_____
Food and Supplies		
Groceries	_____	_____
Restaurant meals	_____	_____
Entertaining	_____	_____
Kitchen supplies	_____	_____
Cleaning supplies	_____	_____
Laundry supplies and expenses	_____	_____
Personal		
Phone	_____	_____
Postage	_____	_____
Mail forwarding and message services	_____	_____
Film and processing	_____	_____
Books and directories	_____	_____
Toiletries	_____	_____
Total	_____	_____

Worksheet 1.6: Flexible RV Expenses

your RV, Chapter Six will show you how you can save on financing—even if you already have a loan, and Chapter Seven will show you how to reduce your insurance costs.

Your Flexible RV Expenses

Once you have estimated your fixed expenses, you'll know how much you have left for the expenses of day-to-day travel. For the sake of consistency with the other worksheets, Worksheet 1.6 is divided into annual and monthly totals. However, you may wish to break these figures down to weekly or daily totals, especially if you travel only a short time per year.

Unless you're a fulltimer, you should include medical expenses in your household budgets.

Be sure to fill out this worksheet again after you put into practice the money-saving suggestions outlined in the remaining chapters of this book.

RECORDKEEPING

Meticulous recordkeeping does not come naturally to most people. But if budgeting for your RV purchase and travels is a concern, recordkeeping is crucial. It's the best way to assure that you're not spending more than you have coming in or more than you've allotted to your RV budget. The simplest way to record your expenses is to keep a running tally, day-by-day, of every expenditure (see Figure 1.1). At the end of a week or month, transfer the totals to a ledger (see Figure 1.2).

You can also record your daily expenditures onto a ledger sheet, available at any stationery store. This way your expenses are automatically recorded into categories. Label the columns on the ledger sheet with the categories listed on Worksheet 1.6, or other categories that you prefer. You can combine certain categories to accommodate the number of columns on the ledger sheet.

Whatever method you select, you must be diligent about recording everything. If you don't record your outlays immediately, at least hold onto your receipts and set aside time every evening to record the totals.

The mere act of recording expenditures has a de facto way of making moneysaving a matter of habit. Recording each purchase or transaction makes it "official"; you know it will come under the watchful scrutiny of your RV business manager—that is, yourself or your spouse. You'll begin to question certain expenses and eliminate others.

You'll soon find that by keeping records, you're not so much imposing a discipline on yourself as gaining new enlightenment. You'll know exactly where your money's going so that you can better

---

— $ —

Dollar-saving Tip

Record every expenditure; to be able to save money, you must know how you spend it.

The mere act of recording expenditures has a de facto way of making moneysaving a matter of habit.

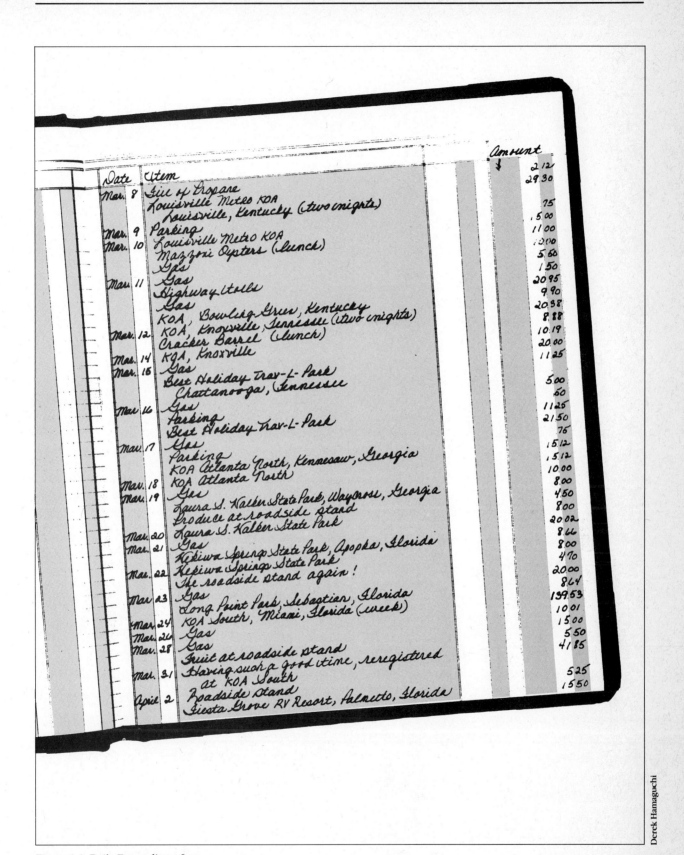

Figure 1.1: Daily Expenditure Log

Month	Travel	Vehicles	Food	Enter-tainment	Household	Fixed Payments	Misc.	Monthly Total:
Jan.								
Feb.								
Mar.								
Apr.								
May								
June								
July								
Aug								
Sept.								
Oct.								
Nov.								
Dec.								
Yearly Total:								

Figure 1.2: Expenditure Ledger Sheet

channel it exactly where you want it to go. You take control of your money and your life in a new way—a way that helps you have the things you really want and need. It's really not as much an awful discipline as a wonderful liberation.

CHAPTER TWO

Shopping for an RV

■ ■ ■ ■ ■ ■ ■ ■ ■ ■

T ake your RV shopping seriously. It is, after all, likely to be the second largest personal investment you'll ever make next to the purchase of your home. Many of your RV-shopping considerations are purely personal. No book, no magazine, no dealer can tell you what type of RV will meet your family's needs and lifestyle. But every decision you make—RV type, floorplan, accessories—is really a money decision. It doesn't matter if you get a great deal: If you're unhappy with your RV purchase, you've wasted your money.

Be methodical. Be thorough. Do your homework. Even if you're a seasoned RVer, don't assume you know all you need to know. Many seasoned buyers are really seasoned suckers, too proud to ask all the right questions, too likely to make kneejerk decisions.

As you know, RVs are sophisticated machines. Innumerable questions arise; you should ask them. Bewildering terminology will be tossed about; you should learn the language before you deal. There are hundreds of RVs to choose from; you must learn how to narrow the field to make an intelligent decision.

Some decisions are inevitably emotional ones, based on an inner sense rather than practical criteria. You may simply like the lines of a certain unit, or a color scheme, just as many new-car buyers are swayed by "new-car smell." Save the olfactory and visceral decisions for later. "There's just something about this one that I like" is not an uncommon reaction, but defer it until after you've done some serious comparisons. Let emotional factors serve as a figurative cointoss, a tiebreaker, *after* you've taken the practical steps to evaluate your needs, study the market, and narrow your choices.

The following practical steps will lead you to the threshold of a gut decision. But it will be an informed gut decision, one that will please both your inner self, your family, and your budget.

In This Chapter:

- *How do I select the right RV for my tastes and needs?*
- *How do I evaluate my purchase from a money-saving point of view?*
- *Can I save by shopping at an RV show?*
- *What are the financial advantages of trailers versus motorhomes?*
- *What do I get for my RV money?*
- *What about sharing an RV purchase?*

KNOW YOURSELF

Whether you're an experienced RVer or a potential first-time buyer, if you're reading this section you probably have the bug—the "New-Rig Bug." And that can be a dangerous affliction. Before you succumb, ask yourself some questions, and answer honestly.

The Do-I-Really-Need-a-New-RV Quiz?

How Much Will I Use the RV?

Dollar-saving Tip

Don't let an emotional decision get you in over your head.

Consider how the RV will fit into your lifestyle. How much free time do you have? If you only get away for an occasional weekend, you can probably enjoy a smaller rig that would become claustrophobic on longer trips. You can probably endure a bit of inconvenience, such as cranking up a folding trailer or stepping on toes in a crowded floorplan. Or, you might consider sharing ownership of an RV (see boxed copy below).

If you intend to take several weeks of vacation every year, you'll need more space, not only for yourself, but for your things. Look for a unit with good storage for chairs, barbecue, fishing tackle, and other vacation items.

If you travel several months a year, you must think of your RV as a home substitute. Minor inconveniences become major annoyances on long outings. Crowded floorplans, noisy or underpowered engines, lack of air conditioning—these can make your travels unpleasant. Remember, it's a *recreational* vehicle you're buying. It's for recreation, for having fun. If you're not going to enjoy being in your RV, you've wasted your money.

Shared Ownership: A Money-Saving Alternative

Unless you plan to travel full time, your RV will undoubtedly be idle much of the year. Why not work out an arrangement to share ownership with friends or relatives?

The specifics of the arrangement must be worked out individually. You can talk to a loan officer about sharing payments on the loan (that way both parties can take advantage of the tax deduction on interest). Or one party can simply pay the other a half share every month, or, if you're paying cash, half the cash price. Put the agreement down on paper, and have each partner sign and date it.

You might include in that agreement, or a separate one, an allowance for a predetermined number of weeks of use per partner a year. An agreement should also cover maintenance costs.

You can save, not only on up-front costs and maintenance, but also on insurance and storage. Choose your partners carefully, but if all the agreements are in writing, shared ownership is a great way to cut the cost of RV ownership in half—or more.

Again, be realistic about the time you'll spend traveling. Base your answer on real life, not the life you dream about having someday. RVs do tend to provoke dreaminess, which tends to provoke bad decisions. "Gee, wouldn't it be nice if someday we could travel around in a luxury motorhome?" Sure, it would be nice, but if right now you're busy with a career that gives you two weeks of vacation a year, you probably don't need a top-end motorhome. Consider your circumstances as they *are*. Base your decision on the future only if it's firm: For example, you know you're retiring within the year and want to travel half-time.

What Kind of Camping Do I Favor?

If you're an avid fisherman who enjoys out-of-the way places, your main satisfaction comes from outside your RV, not from luxury appointments. You can probably do without some frills, but you do want something capable of handling rough roads, like a truck camper. But you may also have special self-containment requirements if you think you might camp far away from hookups and dump stations for long periods of time.

If you prefer resort-style camping for long periods at a time, in campgrounds with good roads, full hookups, and large sites, maneuverability isn't all that important to you; a large RV may suit you nicely.

Perhaps you're not sure what kind of camping you'll do, or possibly every type has some appeal. That's okay. The beauty of most RVs today is versatility. Big motorhomes can usually handle graded dirt roads into national forest campsites. Folding trailers are welcomed at the most luxurious resorts. But it's still a good idea to close your eyes and visualize just how you *think* you'll use your new RV. The point is not to spend money for more than you need, nor to be overly frugal and be unhappy with your purchase after a time.

> Critical decisions about type, size, and floorplan depend on who will most commonly travel in the RV.

Who Will Use It?

Critical decisions about type, size, and floorplan depend on who will most commonly travel in the RV. Again, you must be realistic. If you have teenagers, their interest in traveling with the "old folks" may be waning. Or, they might be quite happy to camp next door in a tent, which could save you a considerable amount of money. If you have little ones, remember that they require *more*, not less, space than older children. Kids under four need room to roam; your twelve-year-old is probably less fidgety and more independent.

If you travel with friends, privacy may be important; you don't want friends stepping over friends to use the bathroom.

Some RVs are more labor intensive than others: Folding trailers require cranking up and folding out. Mini motorhomes require a climb up to the fixed cabover bed. Determine in advance whether you or your traveling companions are up to such tasks.

What Can Do Double-Duty?

An RV that can serve two purposes may save you a lot of money, or at least justify the money you are spending.

First, consider what you already own. If you have a mid-size sedan, you can pull a lightweight trailer. If you have a full-size truck, it can likely carry a camper or pull most sizes of trailers. If this is the case, the passenger vehicle you already own can serve as your RV powerplant. Why pay for another expensive powerplant in the form of a motorhome? Even if you must purchase a tow vehicle, that purchase may make financial sense; the tow vehicle can also serve as a second or even primary family vehicle.

Second, consider imaginative uses of an RV, whether trailer or motorhome. It might be able to serve as a guest room, and you won't need to add on to your house for such a purpose. You might even be able to move into a smaller house; the RV can handle the occasional visits from children and relatives.

RVs frequently do double-duty as vacation cabins, either on property you own, in a time-share campground, or any favorite campground that will accept long-term parking. A trend is growing among snowbirds: Purchasing park-model trailers and leaving them in their favorite Sun Belt campgrounds. The snowbirds then commute to their trailers by cars or in small, economical RVs. Wherever you put it, even the most expensive park-model trailer is probably cheaper than any livable building you could construct.

Third, think about your family vehicle fleet. If you have a rarely used second vehicle, you could sell it and apply the money toward a motorhome, which could then be pressed into service occasionally as a second vehicle.

Where Will I Store It?

While storage may seem like one of your last considerations, it should be one of your first. Many municipalities have restrictive RV-parking ordinances. You must inquire whether it is legal to park your RV on the street or in your driveway. If it is legal, how large an RV can you store at home? If it is not legal, what accommodations will you need to make? You might need to build a gate to store it in a side or back yard, or you may need to store it at a commercial lot. You must factor in these costs to the total expense of buying and maintaining an RV.

While storage may seem like one of your last considerations, it should be one of your first.

GET INFORMED

Once you have answered these questions, you should have a general idea of what type RV you think you want. Now it's time to arm yourself with as much information as possible. Learn all you can about the advantages and disadvantages of each type of RV. Study floorplans. Read test reports. Talk to RV owners.

Take all these steps before you ever talk dollars with a dealer. In fact, being informed enough to make the right RV selection is *more* important than driving a good bargain. Not only will you choose the right size and configuration, you'll also select a reliable manufacturer whose units are less likely to break down and more likely to earn you a higher resale price. The following are some sources of information on RVs and the RV lifestyle.

> Learn all you can about the advantages and disadvantages of each type of RV. Study floorplans. Read test reports. Talk to RV owners.

RVIA

The Recreation Vehicle Industry Association (RVIA) can provide some basic information on the various RV types (see Appendix, page 249). The RVIA can also tell you whether or a not a certain manufacturer is a member of the association; RVIA members must meet standards established by the American National Standards Institute (ANSI) for fire and safety features, as well as electrical, plumbing, and LP-gas systems.

Don't expect the RVIA to recommend particular makes or models. It is an industry association representing members who make all types of RVs and suppliers who make RV components and accessories. For the consumer, it is most useful as a clearinghouse for basic RV information.

Magazines

Magazine test reports on RVs can provide useful reference material, but should never substitute for your own evaluation. A great number of the factors they evaluate are subjective. A floorplan that worked well for the tester might be a disaster for you. Be aware that some magazine articles are merely previews or profiles and only offer straightforward factual information. The listing of features can be useful, but look for mention in a test report of the author's actual use of the rig. Did he spend some time in it, and put it through its paces?

If so, read the test article for performance evaluations: Did the unit handle well? Was it balanced? Was it adequately powered? How did it hold up in crosswinds and to passing trucks? Was the visibility good? Was it noisy? Did it climb grades well? In other words, look for the author's evaluation of aspects that you may not be able to evalu-

Dollar-saving Tip

Write to the RV magazines for copies of test stories on an RV you're considering. They're available for a nominal charge.

ate yourself in a short test drive. His or her opinion on construction and finishing can also be valuable.

Trailer Life and *MotorHome* are the leading national RV magazines. *Trailer Life* evaluates all types of RVs, including tow vehicles and motorhomes; *MotorHome* limits its reports to self-powered vehicles. *Family Motor Coaching* and *Highways* are also national magazines published for members of RV clubs, the Family Motor Coaching Association and the Good Sam Club, respectively. Both offer RV evaluations. Some smaller, regional publications and club newsletters also evaluate RVs.

A list of all publications, including regionals, for RVers and campers is available from RVIA.

Buyers' Guides

Annual RV buyers' guides can give you an overview of nearly every RV manufactured. They do not offer any evaluations or test results. They do list specifications, construction details, floorplans, brands and specifications of accessories, and suggested retail prices. They can be useful for making comparisons, but again, should supplement your first-hand evaluation. Buyers guides also list addresses and/or furnish reader service cards, whereby you can obtain brochures on the RVs that interest you.

Buyers' guides are published by Trailer Life and Woodall's (see addresses in Appendix, page 246).

RV Owners

People who have shelled out their hard-earned money for an RV and have put it to the only really valid test, that is, extensive use, can be an invaluable source of information.

RVers generally love to talk and are an opinionated lot, so you can ply them for lots of information. If you're undecided about what type of rig to buy—trailer, motorhome, camper—be prepared for an overload of opinion. Much of it will be thoughtful and based on experience, but remember: Your choice has to be for *your* particular needs and preferences.

If you've narrowed your decision to a few brands of a particular type, the input of present owners can be invaluable. How to find them? If you don't have friends who happen to own these RVs, you can contact a local RV club and ask if anyone in the club is familiar with a certain unit. Many of the national clubs listed in the Appendix on page 247 can refer you to local chapters. You can also visit nearby campgrounds and ask questions of the RV owners there. A good RV dealer will be happy to refer you to a few of his customers. These

People who have shelled out their hard-earned money for an RV . . . can be an invaluable source of information.

are certain to be satisfied customers, of course, but most will be open in sharing their major likes and dislikes about the RV.

Ask the Right Questions. Whomever you speak to about experiences with a particular RV, be sure to ask specific questions, such as:

- What did they pay?
- Has the RV lived up to their expectations?
- What difficulties have they had?
- Have all the components worked reliably?
- If a motorhome, have they run into problems with lack of power?
- If a trailer, what tow vehicle do they use, and has it proven to be adequate for the size and weight of the trailer?
- Has warranty service been handled promptly?
- What has pleased them the most? The least?

RV Shows

RV shows allow you the luxury of conveniently looking over a number of RVs at one time in one place. You'd have to comb a lot of dealer lots to see the selection of RVs showcased at one regional show. Most RV shows are held in the fall and winter. Contact RVIA for a list of shows nationwide (see page 249 for address).

Can you make a deal at a show? Absolutely! Dealers count on shows as a direct source of sales. At one time shows were more for public relations than for dealing, but that has changed; shows have become extensions of the dealers' lots. A purchase agreement signed at a show is more valuable to a dealer than your intent to return to his lot someday. The dealer has a certain number of RVs in mind he needs to sell to directly justify his expenses for transporting units and exhibiting at the show. Since he *wants* to sell RVs, you can make this work for you.

Try to visit a show during slow times, such as a weekday morning. You can spend more unhurried time shopping and get better attention from salespeople.

Wait until the end of the show to talk business with a dealer. Although the selection may be more limited then, the dealer will also be more willing to bargain. (Be sure to read Chapter Three before negotiating with a dealer at a show; the same principles apply at a show as on the dealer lot.)

Be careful: Shows work well for dealers because a subtle frenzy tends to build among buyers at a good RV show. If the exhibitors have done their job well, hordes of buyers are positively drooling over the opportunity to buy a dream RV. Don't get swept up in this frenzy. You can almost certainly cut as good a deal on the lot as at the show. The same dealer and the same units will be waiting for

Can you make a deal at an RV show? Absolutely!

Dollar-saving Tip

Take advantage of a dealer's willingness to bargain toward the end of an RV show.

Wait until the end of the show to talk business with a dealer.

you on the lot when you return in a rational state of mind. Only agree to purchase at a show if you've done all your homework and followed the principles outlined in Chapter Three, so you *know* you're getting a good deal.

Take a Manufacturer's Tour

Among the best ways for RVers to become more knowledgeable about RV construction is to watch the process take place. Many manufacturers offer tours of their plants, during which visitors can observe construction techniques and learn what materials are used. You can often ask RV engineers questions about even the finest points of RV manufacturing. Your dealer can tell you if the manufacturer of the unit(s) you are interested in offers tours.

TRAILERS VERSUS MOTORHOMES: A FINANCIAL PERSPECTIVE

This is a money book, not a buyer's guide to RVs. The many comparative advantages and disadvantages of each RV type is not our concern here, but rather the *financial* advantages and disadvantages of

---

Travel Trailer Financial Advantages

If you already own a tow vehicle, travel trailers offer a considerably lower purchase price for equivalent space and livability features. Otherwise, a good tow vehicle and travel trailer combination typically add up to about the price of moderately priced motorhome.

- Travel trailers depreciate less than motorhomes. Some luxury travel trailers depreciate very little. Motorhomes depreciate very quickly.
- Chassis wear and tear is less on a trailer and is generally limited to axles, tires, and brakes. The service and replacement of these, of course, is less expensive than on a motorhome.
- Insurance is much less on a travel trailer. (See page 75.)
- Gas mileage is generally about the same for the trailer combo versus a motorhome of similar livability. But once the trailer is parked in a camp-

site, driving around for errands or sightseeing is less expensive in a tow vehicle than a motorhome, unless you tow a small car with your motorhome. But remember that towing a vehicle behind a motorhome means you must maintain two powerplants—that is, two vehicles on which to change oil, tires, etc., and you must insure two motor vehicles. (Insuring a small car is far more expensive than insuring a trailer.) These expenses will most likely offset the gas mileage advantage of the small car.

These comparisons generally hold true for all types of travel trailers and motorhomes, as long as you compare equivalent livability: for example, a mini motorhome versus a medium-size travel trailer, or a micro-mini motorhome versus a small travel trailer. Folding trailers defy comparison; they're just plain cheaper to purchase and maintain than any other type of RV.

each. As we've stressed again and again, the most important financial consideration is buying an RV that suits *your* needs. Some decisions have nothing to do with money: If you hate the idea of towing anything, don't buy a trailer. If you love the idea of sitting in your living room while you drive, or being able to rest in the back while the pilot steers you down the road, buy a motorhome. Motorhomes are delightful, easy-to-handle creatures. But we're not talking about convenience or delight; we're talking about money, and for many people, the nod must be given to travel trailers from a financial perspective.

WHAT DO YOU GET FOR YOUR MONEY?

As with nearly any product, there's a strong price-to-quality correlation among RVs. But what you're paying for is often not clearly evident. The following are generalizations, but should give you an idea of what you pay for as you advance through the price ranges of the various RV categories. One generalization applies to all RV categories: You pay more for a larger RV. And with a larger RV come larger capacities: refrigerator, water heater, LP-gas, holding tanks, all of which you pay for.

If you hate the idea of towing anything, don't buy a trailer.

Travel Trailers

Low end: A wood frame, or what is known is in the RV business as "stick-and-staple" construction; aluminum-siding exterior; artificial wood cabinetry and paneling; manually operated appliances, such as a hand-lighted water heater or rarely, a manual water pump; in some cases an icebox rather than refrigerator; square-cornered windows; low-quality upholstery; maybe some rough edges on the woodwork.

Mid-range: Wood or aluminum framing; laminated walls; fiberglass or polystyrene insulation; some fiberglass exteriors; radius-corner windows; genuine-wood trim inside, although paneling may be artificial; more elaborate appliances; three-way, or automatic, refrigerator; some brass hardware and fixtures; better-quality upholstery; artificial stained-glass door trim.

High end: Wood or welded aluminum frame; rarely, laminated sidewalls; fiberglass or polystyrene insulation; more fiberglass exteriors; formed fiberglass end-caps, rather than wrapped-around siding; more trim on wall-to-roof junctions; construction joints tighter; improved suspension system; assembly screws and nails concealed better; wiring and plumbing more neatly bundled and routed; more style to the body; genuine-wood paneling and trim inside; top-end appliances; high-quality upholstery; stained-glass trim; composite counter tops; fully automatic devices such as automatic-ignition water heaters; better and more kitchen accessories, such as food processors; higher-quality fixtures and hardware throughout.

Motorhomes

Low end: Livability features equivalent to low-to-medium travel trailers. Construction varies less among motorhomes; some low-end motorhomes have wood reinforcing, but all have some sort of steel or metal frame. Traditional gas-powered chassis with front engine.

Mid-range: Livability features equivalent to medium-to-high-end travel trailers; all-metal cage construction; some laminated (fiberglass-on-lauan paneling) sidewalls; some diesel-powered drivetrains; some rear-engine diesels; improved suspension systems, such as tag axles; air-bag suspension.

High end: Livability features equivalent to high-end travel trailers; superior suspension systems—air bags, tag axle, rubber-block suspension, anti-sway bars; expensive diesel engines, in general, more sophisticated designs inside and out; higher quality.

Truck Campers

Low end: Like low-end trailers, these may have stick-and-staple frame; inexpensive aluminum siding; lack of self-containment features such as toilets and showers.

Mid-range: Livability equivalent to low-end travel trailers; wood-frame construction.

High end: May still have wood-frame construction, but interior is nicely done; fully self-contained; top-quality appliances.

Folding Trailers

Low end: Minimal or no livability features (such as no portable toilet, sink, or water system); icebox.

Mid-range: Minimal livability features, such as a manual water pump, portable toilet; stove; optional furnace; power converter.

High end: Freshwater toilet; oven; shower; demand water system; optional air conditioning.

Camping Van Conversions

The range of interior features through the various price levels is similar to other RVs: the more expensive units have real wood and are fully self-contained; they also have better seats and upholstery. Less expensive units may lack water heaters, freshwater toilets, and showers. Chassis and exterior construction, though, vary little with the price.

Money Matters You Should Compare

Many of the comparisons you'll make as you shop for an RV are subjective, peculiar to your tastes and circumstances. The following considerations, though, are money matters that you should keep in

---

Beware the Gypsy Dealer

Death forces sale of brand new travel trailer, never been used. Cost new $16,000, will sacrifice for $9,000.

Must sell. New travel trailer never used. Illness in family. Bought for $15,000, will sell for $8,000.

The scam is as old as the RV business itself: fly-by-night dealers or individuals selling substandard trailers for supposedly bargain prices.

Newspaper ads usually herald the arrival of gypsy dealers—typically on the cusp of the summer vacation season:

The theme in the ads above are typical—death or other misfortune allegedly forces the owner to sell at an amazingly low price. Or gypsy dealers will display the trailers in a campground or prime RV vacation area, offering a terrific markdown, when in reality the "dealer" purchased the trailer at about half the selling price. Unfortunately, a few unscrupulous trailer manufacturers are in on the scam.

Few gypsy trailers carry the RVIA seal, which indicates the manufacturer has complied with industry standards for construction and safety. The manufacturers know every trick for cutting costs: They buy endsheets of aluminum—in essence,

scraps—and slap them together. A number of side seams is a giveaway. Construction is basic stick-and-staple. Wiring may be substandard, even dangerous. Yet the trailer *looks* like a trailer. It *is* a trailer. So more suckers fall for the scam every year.

Some service centers are so weary of servicing these substandard coaches that they have instituted a service boycott. They simply won't work on units they recognize to be gypsy brands.

A few gypsy brands even come with a warranty. However, dealer networks do not exist for these brands, so you'd have to go to the manufacturer for warranty work.

If you suspect a gypsy scam, contact the Recreation Vehicle Dealers Association (see Appendix, page 249). RVDA can refer you to its regional or state organizations, which are usually up to date about gypsy operations in their area and can advise you whether or not the trailer is a gypsy brand.

mind when you compare RVs. They are fairly objective, and should be weighed equally with your personal criteria. We'll cover additional money matters in Chapter Three, when you've narrowed your choices and are ready to deal.

- *Total cash outlay.* Pretty obvious, but be sure to include the price of a tow vehicle or towed vehicle if relevant.
- *Factory warranty.* Most trailer manufacturers offer a twelve-month warranty, but motorhome warranties vary.
- *Insurance costs.* Your insurance company can give you a quote on any RV or vehicle-trailer combination you're considering. (See Chapter Seven for more on insurance.)
- *Reputable brand.* This may be slightly subjective, but if the manufacturer has been around for some time, it has pleased enough customers to stay in business. A dealer should be able to provide this information. Also ask if the brand has changed hands; an old brand bought out by a new company may not have the same quality control. If it's a new brand, investigate the company. Find out the background of the manufacturer; he might be an experienced RV builder with strong financial backing who has started a new company. If so, a new brand might not be so risky. If a dealer hesitates to provide information on the manufacturer, contact the RVIA to determine if the manufacturer is a member in good standing.
- *Service network.* Does the brand have a number of dealers nationwide (or at least in the region you most travel) who are authorized to perform warranty service?
- *Service record.* Here you'll have to rely on the experience of other RVers, but their input is important. If they report few problems, the manufacturer's quality control is probably good.
- *Resale value.* How does the brand hold its value compared to other makes? Ask your dealer or financial institution to show you the RV appraisal guides (published by Kelley and the National Automobile Dealers Association) to determine how quickly various models depreciate.

CHAPTER THREE

Dealing with Dealers

■ ■ ■ ■ ■ ■ ■ ■ ■ ■ ■

Of the thousands of ways to save money listed in this book, the deal you make on a new RV (and its financing) is the most important. Key decisions you make at the dealership can either save or cost you thousands of dollars. Sure, it's important to save money every day, in every possible way, taking every discount, every free night of camping, every early-bird dinner you can find. Pennies do add up. But unwise decisions made before you ever drive off the dealer's lot can cost you more in an instant than you can save in years of penny-wise travel.

It's not unusual to feel intimidated by dealers and their sales-people. They speak a language that is not your everyday tongue: the language of RVs; of features and construction; and the language of financing, interest rates, service contracts, and insurance.

There's another language they speak, although not out loud (at least not to you): *profit*, the language that keeps a dealership in business. You can be sure they know very well all the nuances of this silent tongue. So do bankers. All those friendly people who shake your hand so warmly are also trying to increase their profit as much possible. It can indeed be an intimidating state of affairs, but not if you read this chapter carefully and follow its advice.

Keep one overriding thought in mind as you home in on your RV purchase. You are the customer. The dealer or the bank or the credit union needs you. If at any time you feel pressured or confused, if you nod knowingly at gobbledygook you really don't understand, or if you find yourself making an on-the-spot decision you're really not ready to make, put the brakes on. Ask questions, even "stupid" ones. Or walk away, clear your head, and return the next day, or the next

In This Chapter:

- *How do I find a good dealer?*
- *How can I speak the dealer's language?*
- *How do I determine what I can afford?*
- *How do I negotiate the best deal?*
- *How do I spot a shoddy dealer?*
- *What advice do dealers themselves offer?*
- *What about "back-end" deals?*
- *Should I buy a service contract?*

week. Never jump into a decision just to maintain harmony. Don't bluff savvy if you're actually confused. Never be afraid to change your mind. The stakes are too high for you to make a rushed or uninformed decision about any aspect of your RV purchase.

SHOPPING FOR A DEALER

Although you should certainly shop at more than one dealership, deciding on a dealer with whom to do business, even preliminary business, is as important as deciding the make and model of RV you want to purchase. How do you find a good one? Follow these principles:

Look Locally First

The advantages of doing business with a local dealer are many: for convenient follow-up service, for major repairs, for the mere fact that he's a member of your community. Your relationship with your RV dealer will very likely be a long-term one. With a local dealer, you can establish a rapport that may save you a great deal of money, as well as time and aggravation.

Also, if you purchase out of town or out of state, and then rely on a local dealer for warranty service, you can't expect first-class treatment. The dealer will inevitably serve his or her own customers first. The exceptions are dealers who run their service departments to make warranty service a profit center; some do. But with most dealers, it's not really spiteful, just human nature; your repair order goes to the bottom of the pile. You won't get those "freebies," little make-goods and adjustments that a local dealer almost always performs graciously for his customers. So, if at all possible, seek out dealers within a reasonable radius of your home.

Two exceptions make it more reasonable to deal with distant dealers such as those high-volume dealers who advertise toll-free numbers:

1. If price is definitely your major priority, or
2. You are a fulltimer or near fulltimer, and having a local dealer isn't relevant.

How Long Has the Dealer Been in Business?

Dealers should willingly tell you how long they've been around. You can get confirmation from the Recreation Vehicle Dealers Association if they are RVDA members (see Appendix, page 249). Or you can ask the county or city agency that issues business licenses. A

> Your relationship with your RV dealer will very likely be a long-term one.

dealer's longevity is not in itself a sign of a quality dealership; some find an endless supply of suckers to stay in business. This is why the next factor is so important.

Investigate the Dealer's Reputation

Referrals are probably the best way to check on a dealer's reputation. If you don't have friends who can refer you to a dealer, ask local members of RV clubs. National RV clubs, listed in the Appendix, page 247, can refer you to local chapters. Ask members who have dealt with a particular dealer how he did business. Was he fair? Did he use high-pressure tactics? Has he willingly performed warranty services?

You can ask the dealer himself for names of customers to whom he has sold RVs. These no doubt will be customers who would vote for the dealer for mayor, but there's nothing wrong with hearing good things about the person to whom you're considering shelling out $50,000.

> Referrals are probably the best way to check on a dealer's reputation.

Talk to the Better Business Bureau

Ask the local BBB if there have been complaints against a particular dealer. A lack of complaints on file is not a guarantee of a dealer's honesty, but the presence of complaints should serve as a warning to you.

Check Out the Parts Department

Make sure the dealer's parts department carries a good inventory of replacement parts and add-on accessories for your particular RV. You don't want your vacation delayed while the dealer orders you a widget from across the country.

Meet the Service Manager

If you buy from this dealer, you'll undoubtedly get to know the service manager quite well. You may as well qualify him from the outset. RV-service people have to be mechanics, plumbers, electricians; a good RV mechanic is not simply a grease monkey. Ask the service manager his background, what his service policies are, how long his mechanics have been working for him, and whether they've recently attended a service school operated by the manufacturer whose brand you're interested in.

One service manager told me, "We never let a customer lose a vacation. If you're leaving tomorrow, we'll borrow a part from another trailer if need be." You have to like that attitude; you can't be certain of his absolute expertise, but you can get a good feeling for the dealership by talking to the service manager.

Ask about Checkout and Showout

Determine how the dealer checks out the units before he or she waves goodbye to a customer. Good dealers will tell you exactly how they prepare and check every working system on the rig, from engine to generator to water system to each appliance.

They should have customer-showout routines or pre-delivery inspections (PDI), very patient walk-throughs and explanations of every feature. Many dealers suggest their customers spend a night in the rig (after the purchase) parked right on the lot, using as many systems as possible and going over any problems the next day. The dealer should also have someone carefully go over driving techniques and safety. If you've never towed a trailer, you should have a thorough checkout on hitching, driving, turning, and backing up.

Some dealers have ongoing seminars and travel slide shows. These may not be as important to you as making a good buy, but they do indicate a concerned, aware dealer who is likely to treat you well after the purchase.

BEFORE YOU NEGOTIATE

By now you have a good idea what RV you're interested in, and you've found a dealer or two with whom you might want to do business. Before you start talking purchase price on any unit, follow these steps:

Know What You Can Afford

Most of the factors that go into determining what you can afford are discussed in Chapters One and Two. Let's assume you've studied all these factors, that you know the role your RV will play in your lifestyle, that you've allowed for operating expenses, insurance, and money left over to enjoy the quality of life and travel you desire. Now you are ready to determine the RV purchase price you can afford.

If you're a cash buyer, you call the shots, not a lending institution. You must determine how much you can spend without overly depleting your nest egg, especially if you count on interest or dividends from that fund as an important part of your monthly income. If you plan to dip into your nest egg for $30,000, for example, ask your banker or broker how much your interest or dividend income will be reduced. If you can live with that figure, you can afford the $30,000.

> **I**f you've never towed a trailer, you should have a thorough checkout on hitching, driving, turning, and backing up.

> **Y**ou must determine how much you can spend without overly depleting your nest egg.

If you plan to finance your RV, you should approach it as a lending institution will. You probably have an idea how much you can afford to pay each month. But first, get a piece of paper and write down your monthly net income. Use your current income, not what you hope to be making. You have to be realistic. (Obviously, if that income is going to diminish, you must take that into account.)

Next, add up your debts—your mortgage payment, other installment loans, your credit-card debt—all the monthly payments you make. Now add to that figure the monthly payment you think you can afford. Will your total monthly debt still be under 50 percent of your net income? If so, you have a good chance of getting a loan for that amount. Some lenders are more conservative, and use a 45-percent figure; they contend that your monthly debt should not exceed 45 percent of your income. More eager lenders may go as high as 60 percent. These lenders probably have a high repossession rate. They may let you go too deeply into a hole, and you could lose your rig. (This is shameful, but true. Some lenders will require a large down payment, then lend you more money than you can afford, and they *know* it. When you fall behind, they'll have your down-payment money *and* your RV.)

Once you've determined a monthly payment you can afford, you must then decide over how long a period you want to make those payments. Then you can ask a bank or credit union how much money that payment will buy over the amount of years you've set. That figure is your *loan cash*.

Add to that loan-cash figure the sales tax and title fees you're expected to pay (any dealer or lender can tell you these figures) plus the highest down payment you can afford—at least 15 percent will be required. Also add in the wholesale value of your trade-in (see "Get the Best Price for Your Trade-In," page 36), assuming you owe no debt on your trade-in, or add in the money you've received for selling your rig yourself. That total is your *available cash*. That is what you can afford to pay for an RV (see Figure 3.1).

Know What You Want

Once you've read Chapters One and Two and done other research, you should know exactly what you want and what you can afford. For example, you can tell the salesperson that you're interested in brand X, 28 feet long, with front-kitchen floorplan. This saves time and game playing. If you put yourself in the hands of the salesperson with only the vaguest notion of what you want, you're in for a dizzying trip through RVs that you either aren't interested in or can't afford. Be firm about your basic inclination. Be open to seeing units of similar design and price, but don't let yourself be "switched," a sales method that relies on titillation to get you to spend more than you want.

Some lenders . . . contend that your monthly debt should not exceed 45 percent of your income.

Dollar-saving Tip

If price is your priority, high-volume dealers can save you money. Most of the larger ones advertise in RV magazines.

How to Determine What You Can Afford

Affordable monthly payment _____ × _____ years @ _____ % = _____ Loan cash

Loan cash _____

+

Tax and title fees (approximately) _____

+

Down payment (20% of approximate price
— highest figure you can afford) _____

+

Wholesale value of trade, minus what you
still owe, or cash from sale of old RV _____

Available cash: The purchase price =
you can afford to pay _____

Figure 3.1: What You Can Afford to Pay for an RV

Know What You Can Tow

If you're shopping for a trailer, don't rely on the dealer to tell you what you can tow with your tow vehicle. Trailer dealers *should* be conversant in the intricacies of tow ratings, axle ratios, and so forth, but many aren't, and they'll be happy to sell you a large (and expensive) trailer that is much too heavy to tow behind your vehicle.

If you exceed your tow vehicle's tow rating, you're headed for expensive engine and transmission repairs. Obtain the manufacturer's trailer-towing brochure for your tow vehicle or for every tow vehicle you're considering. If these are not available from your car or truck dealer, write the manufacturer. If no towing brochure is available, read the owner's manual carefully.

If you are buying both a new trailer and a new tow vehicle, you must decide on the trailer first, so you can shop for an appropriate tow vehicle, one rated to tow that trailer. Make the trailer *decision* first, but not the trailer *purchase*. You should purchase the tow vehicle first, so you can test-tow the trailer before you buy.

Never buy a trailer without towing it first. In addition to the critical factor of weight, you should evaluate handling, balance, bounce, power for accelerating, and power for pulling grades.

If you are cutting it close—if your tow vehicle is just barely rated for the trailer you want—check the weight of the trailer yourself. Factor in an estimate of the weight of supplies you may carry, as well as the weight of water (8.2 pounds per gallon) and propane (4.25 pounds per gallon). Then weigh the trailer at a commercial scale.

The RV Handbook, by Bill Estes, has an excellent chapter on choosing a tow vehicle that you should read for more technical information before making this important decision. Remember, mating a tow vehicle with a trailer is not just a matter of convenience and comfort. A bad decision could cost you thousands of dollars in repairs.

> You should purchase the tow vehicle first, so you can test-tow the trailer before you buy.

Shop at More than One Dealership

Even if you're impressed with a particular dealership, you should investigate at least one or two others. Compare the factors outlined on pages 28–30. And, of course, compare the prices. Even if you have to venture farther away from home than you really want to, knowing what other dealers are selling their units for is important leverage in negotiating—which we'll get to shortly.

Shop for Financing in Advance

Shop around for the best financing arrangement you can make *before* you negotiate with a dealer. If he or she can offer an equal or better financing arrangement, fine. But you should know in advance how much you can finance and what the going interest rates and terms are. This advice applies even if you are contemplating a cash purchase. Some financing deals are too good to pass up; you might be money ahead by electing a credit purchase. Financing is discussed in detail in Chapter Six.

THE NEGOTIATION

Okay, you've made your choice. You know what you want. You're ready to talk price. Now the fun begins. Actually, it *can* be fun. Dealers expect you to negotiate. If they have done their jobs well, you like them and you're eager to buy. Now it's time for *you* to do *your* job well. It's time to drive a fair bargain. Here's how:

Look at the Manufacturer's Sticker Price

RV dealers, unlike car dealers, are not required to post the manufacturer's suggested retail price for their rigs and options. But good dealers will. If they don't, ask to see it. If they won't produce the sticker, ask why. (It's true that some manufacturers don't provide stickers.) If their answers seem evasive, be very cautious about doing further business with these dealers.

Beware of a tactic some unscrupulous dealers use. They will put their own sticker on the RV, marked well up from the manufacturer's suggested retail price, and then "generously" discount that figure. They can thereby dupe some customers into paying full retail—and thinking they got a bargain. Make sure the sticker is the manufacturer's, not the dealer's.

The sticker price is, of course, useful only in comparing prices and as a starting point for negotiation. But you should always be able to see it.

Keep Profit Margin in Mind

The dealer must make a profit on every RV he sells, with rare exceptions, so you can be sure the sticker price includes a dealer's profit. How much? Unfortunately, that's a carefully guarded secret in the RV business. In the car business, you can easily learn what the dealer cost is for any vehicle, by checking such sources as *Edmund's Car Prices Buyer's Guide.* No such books exist for recreational vehicles. Rules of thumb are tricky, too. Built-in profit margin varies. Some units may be slow movers, and the dealer may be willing to come way down in price. If you followed a rule of thumb, you might end up paying *more* than you need to.

It's obvious that the sticker price includes profit when you see an identical RV selling for 20 percent off list at one dealership. And

M̲ake sure the sticker is the manufacturer's, not the dealer's.

Dollar-saving Tip

I̲f no manufacturer's sticker is available, comparing prices with other dealers is all the more important.

even when such a discount is offered up front, there's usually some room for negotiation. Paranoid dealers who don't want customers to know about profit margins have little respect for the buying public; *everybody* knows the sticker price includes profit, and this profit margin is the subject of negotiation.

Now, some customers think dealers get 40-percent profit on new RV sticker prices. This isn't true, with rare exceptions. If you open negotiations by offering 40 percent off the sticker price, you may be off on a bad foot. A typical markup is in the neighborhood of 25 to 35 percent. The markup is on the high side for more expensive RVs, and lower for less expensive RVs. "Loan codes" in the back of the *Kelley Blue Book* indicate dealer cost and markup on some new RVs.

A smart buyer uses markup knowledge subtly. For one thing, you can't be *sure* exactly what the dealer's markup is on any particular unit. Also, if you play the tough guy and tell the dealer, "Look, I know you make 35 percent on this sticker price," and you try to grind him down to dealer cost, you're not really playing the negotiating game. You may or may not make a deal, but you'll end up paying for your toughness in other ways. The dealer will do his best to be less lenient on financing, insurance, service contract, and the like. You certainly won't be his favorite customer. It'll probably take a very long time to get that leaking holding tank fixed!

Unless they run very high-volume operations, dealers probably need 20 percent as fair profit to run their dealerships, to pay their overheads. You don't *have* to grant them that, and in many cases they will come down well below 20 percent if they need to move a unit. Rules of thumb are just too broad to apply in a blanket manner.

So at this point in the negotiations, you're just keeping profit margin in mind. Your opening salvo is to ask for a price. Read on.

> A typical markup is in the neighborhood of 25 to 35 percent. . . . A smart buyer uses markup knowledge subtly.

Ask for the Dealer's Best, Fair Price

You can eliminate a lot of game playing early on by asking the dealer for the best price he or she can give you on the RV you want. If you're dealing with a salesperson who hesitates to answer, ask to speak to the owner or manager. (The salesperson probably isn't authorized to give you the lowest figure anyway.) Ask for a straight answer that isn't dependent on irrelevant factors, such as, "Well, if you buy *today,* I can give it to you for . . ." You aren't going to buy today. You're going to leave the lot with that price as a comparison figure.

Get at Least Two More Quotes

Next, ask at least two other dealers for their best, fair price. Go out of town if necessary. Remember, though, that an out-of-town dealer can offer a lower price because he assumes he won't have handling costs

Seldom do dealers quote their true best prices in the opening round.

after the sale. Although manufacturers reimburse dealers for warranty service, part of the expense of keeping a customer happy is borne by the dealer. And if the dealers don't have that expense, they can undercut dealers who do.

Be certain you're comparing apples to apples—that you obtain quotes on identical units equipped with identical options. It's best to do this in person, where you can get the quote in writing. If you get a quote from a dealer far away, perhaps one who advertises a lot with an 800 number, you may not be getting a true quote for an identical unit. And you won't have any way of holding the dealer to that quote (unless you ask them to put it in writing and mail or fax it to you). But many of these businesses won't put anything in writing until you get there. Beware of such a situation.

Still, getting quotes from other dealers is critical ammunition in negotiating with the dealer from whom you want to buy.

Negotiate from Your Best Price Quote

Once you have a few quotes, go to the dealership you want to do business with and tell them you'd prefer to buy from them if they can match or come close to your best quote. Small local dealers probably can't match the quote you obtained from a distant dealer with an 800 number, but they almost certainly can come down from the "best" prices they quoted earlier. Seldom do dealers quote their true best prices in the opening round.

Now is the time to weigh again all those factors we discussed earlier. If you are truly impressed by this dealer, if he or she has a solid reputation, good service, a good parts department, and is conveniently located, the deal he or she offers, even if it's a bit higher than another, is probably the best deal for you.

Get the Best Price for Your Trade-in

Dollar-saving Tip

Know what your trade-in is worth.

If you're trading in at the same time you're purchasing an RV, you naturally want to make the most you can on your trade-in. Of course, the best way to do this is to sell it yourself (see Chapter Five). If you can't be bothered with selling it yourself, ask the dealer for the best fair price for your trade-in.

Should you hide your trade-in at the outset? Dealers don't like that. You can tell the dealer that you're thinking about trading in, but you'll decide later. No matter what, keep the negotiation for the new RV separate from the negotiation for your trade-in.

An excellent way to get a fair price for your trade-in is to offer it to a few dealers. Tell the dealer with whom you're negotiating that you've shopped around and have a pretty good idea what your rig is worth, but don't give him a figure. That should get you a good, honest appraisal.

You should have already checked the appraisal guides for prices on your trade-in. These appraisal guides, one published by Kelley and the other by the National Automobile Dealers Association, list prices for used RVs. You can ask your banker for this information. The dealer will not offer you high blue-book value because he must make a profit on the resale of your rig. He is going to offer you a wholesale price (probably less) for your RV, and will sell it at retail. If you sell it yourself, *you* get the retail price.

Don't fall for some inflated price figure for your trade-in. Don't listen to talk about trade-in "allowance." You want an appraisal, not an allowance. If your salesperson tosses out a figure you know to be more than it is worth wholesale, that is, well above blue-book value, you can be sure that he's simultaneously padding the price of the new unit.

You can't expect to negotiate a near-wholesale price on a new RV and at the same time receive a retail price on your old one. Ask for a fair price on the old one; if it's way under blue book, don't accept it. But save most of your negotiating energy for the new one.

Don't Deal in Terms of Monthly Payments

Determining the monthly payment you can afford is critical in deciding on a total purchase price you can afford (see Chapter One and pages 30–31). *But determining a monthly payment is a financing arrangement that has nothing to do with negotiating the purchase price of the vehicle.*

If you shop by telling a salesperson you want to buy an RV for $450 a month, he'll juggle the financing around so that you'll be paying exactly that—but the total purchase price will be much more than you really need pay. You've effectively bowed out of the process of negotiating. The salesperson is now dictating the purchase price—it may even be above the sticker price! You've padded his profit.

BUYER BEWARE

The following are warning signs that a dealer may not be a straight shooter. You might get a good deal from him, but if you run across any of the following tactics or practices, be very, very careful in proceeding:

Has High-Pressure, "Buy-Today" Attitude. Maybe you've come to expect high pressure from your dealings with automobile dealers. But good RV dealers and salespeople are happy to nurture a customer. They should patiently show you as many RVs as you want to see, answer your questions, and allow you time to think and browse. Don't fall for "today only" lines. If a salesperson asks, "What will it

Don't listen to talk about trade-in "allowance." You want an appraisal, not an allowance.

Dollar-saving Tip

Always negotiate total price, not monthly payment.

Don't fall for "today only" lines.

take to get you to drive out of here today in one of our RVs?" you should answer, "I am not buying today, but I might buy tomorrow. Right now I need some straight answers and your best price."

Badmouths Other Dealers.   You're smart enough to make up your own mind. Unscrupulous dealers sometimes spread bad information about their competitors.

Cannot Offer Financing.   If a dealership can't offer financing (even if you don't want it), it may mean they don't have a good relationship with local banks. Their business may be on thin ice.

Cannot Produce Title.   Some shady dealers sell units for which they don't even own the title, a pretty sure sign of a fly-by-night dealer, or at least one in financial trouble. They can't produce the title, but offer some complicated explanation, assuring you that everything will be all right. Go somewhere else.

Offers Absurd Figure on Your Trade-in.   They're insulting your intelligence, because you *know* what your trade is worth. You've done your homework. It's obvious that they're getting you on the purchase price. But it's also obvious they're not trustworthy. What other games are they playing?

Sells Brands You Never Heard of.   If the dealers don't represent any well-known national brands, it's quite possible that those manufacturers won't do business with them. You already know to investigate the reputation of RV brands. If the dealers don't carry reputable brands, they're probably not reputable themselves.

Asks You to Fill Out a "Credit Form" as You Walk In.   Some dealerships ask you to fill out an information form when you arrive. They may want to know the size of your family, how you intend to use the RV, etc. That's fine. But if they also ask for your Social Security number or any credit information, refuse to give it, and consider walking out. Your finances are your private business until you actually apply for a loan. If you're arranging financing elsewhere, it's not the dealer's business at all.

Is Underattentive.   This is as inexcusable as high-pressuring. A salesperson who just gestures in the direction of the rigs you want to see isn't interested in you. Someone should accompany you to answer your questions.

Displays No Manufacturers' Stickers.   Although manufacturers' stickers aren't required by law on RVs, posting them is good business practice. Be wary of a dealer who doesn't display them.

> Unscrupulous dealers sometimes spread bad information about their competitors.

> Some shady dealers sell units for which they don't even own the title.

SAVING MONEY ON A TOW OR TOWED VEHICLE

Virtually all of the preceding principles to save you money on your RV purchase apply to the purchase of of a trailer-towing vehicle, or even a towed vehicle to pull behind a motorhome.

As mentioned earlier, you should obtain trailer-towing brochures for every model you're considering. Don't assume that the average car or truck salesperson knows anything about towing.

Although you should purchase your tow vehicle before you purchase your trailer, have a good idea (better yet, know exactly) of the weight and length of trailer you intend to buy so you can purchase a tow vehicle rated adequately to tow that trailer. Pushing the towing limits of a tow vehicle could cost you major repair money.

Before you negotiate the purchase of a tow vehicle, get a copy of *Edmund's Car Prices Buyer's Guide* (available at many newsstands) or order a printout for the vehicle from Consumer Reports Auto Price Service. (Write Consumer Reports, P.O. Box 8005, Novi, Michigan 48050 for information on this service.) *Edmund's* is the cheaper alternative. These allow you to compare dealer cost with list price— a privilege you cannot have in purchasing an RV— and they cover both the vehicle and the options.

Dollar-saving Tip

Knowing the dealer's cost is a valuable negotiating tool.

Top Ten Tips from RV Dealers

I asked a number of dealers what advice they would give to a valued friend or relative who is shopping for an RV. The following are the most common responses I received:

1. *Don't shop for price alone.* In other words, consider the other factors that go into a good deal—service and parts department, attitude, and the like.
2. *Buy locally.*
3. *Choose manufacturers who stand behind their products.*
4. *Beware the over-the-phone lowballer.* Calling a distant 800 number may not get you a fair price for comparing with local dealers. Some of these large dealerships snag customers by "lowballing," that is, quoting a very low price they won't honor when you arrive in person.
5. *Be upfront about your trade-in.* Dealers feel that hiding a trade-in is dirty pool, especially if you're a tough bargainer on the price of the new RV. If you grind down the dealer, then spring a trade on him, you certainly won't be a favored customer. This shouldn't concern a savvy buyer; you've already learned how to negotiate and how to get a good price for your trade-in.
6. *Compare apples with apples.* Dealers are frequently plagued by customers quoting low figures that aren't fair comparisons. For example, "The dealer down the street will sell me the same unit for $50,000," when $50,000 is actually for the same unit without some of the expensive options.
7. *Read everything carefully.* For your sake and to alleviate future aggravation, read every clause in every contract carefully. Know exactly what kind of deal you're getting and what you're paying for.
8. *Allow the dealer fair profit.* Dealers naturally want to remind customers they have to make a living. This shouldn't obligate any customer to become philanthropic, just aware.
9. *Get more than one quote.* Dealers respect this kind of bargaining.
10. *Beware of shows.* Even dealers who do big business at RV shows caution about show-buying, where customers often grab a "deal" on the wrong RV.

Add-ons . . . are big-profit items for the dealer.

With these services, you can calculate the dealer's profit. (He actually has an additional 2 or 3 percent of profit built into the base sticker price.) This figure is fair game for negotiation. Allowing first for the destination charge (on the window sticker of the vehicle), tell the salesperson you know the dealer cost of the vehicle. He may try to tell you that your figure doesn't include dealer preparation. Don't fall for that; dealer preparation is included in the base price.

Ask the salesperson to add the lowest markup his dealership will accept to the dealer-cost figure you have. Insist on a firm price quote. Don't accept any "if you buy today" pressure. Tell him you're price shopping. If he contends that your figures are wrong, call his bluff. Ask him to show you the dealer invoice. If he won't show it to you, stand by your figures. Then get prices from at least two other dealers.

Some add-ons, or "packs" (because they pack the dealer's profit), may already be slapped onto the vehicle, such as paint sealant, rust protection, and fabric protection. These are big-profit items for the dealer. If you can't find the vehicle you want without these add-ons, *order* exactly the model you want. You may have to wait, but you won't have to pad the dealer's profit.

THE "BACK END"

"Front-end" profit is the profit the dealer makes on the actual sale price of the RV. "Back-end" profit refers to other profit avenues the dealer has: financing, insurance, service contracts (extended warranties), and add-ons. Often the back end is as lucrative as the front end. Some dealerships rely entirely on the back end for their profit; they sell at the slimmest of profit margins to attract buyers, then make their money on the back-end items. Let's examine each back-end department.

Financing

Financing and financing sources will be covered in depth in Chapter Six. Most dealerships offer financing, if only in the form of a referral to a nearby bank. It's in the dealer's interest to make financing available to you; after all, he wants you to be able to buy the RV. For a few dealerships, that's the only reason they offer financing—as a service.

But the majority of dealerships make something on financing through their arrangement with the lending institution. Remember, it's never the dealers themselves lending you the money; they're only middlepersons. How much they make is probably in proportion to how strongly they push financing on you.

Still, accepting financing from dealers is not necessarily bad. They may indeed have a good relationship with a couple of banks and can get you a competitive interest rate.

The important thing is for you to have already shopped for financing so you can recognize whether the dealer's financing arrangement is a competitive one (see Chapter Six).

It's also very important that you take your time in the bank's finance and insurance office. Don't sign anything until you thoroughly understand it.

Credit Life and Disability Insurance

Whenever you borrow money, the lender will offer you credit life and credit disability insurance. This insurance pays off the balance of your loan should you die or become disabled and unable to keep up payment. This may *sound* like prudent insurance to buy, but the truth is, it's grossly overpriced and probably unnecessary. No matter what the lender or dealer may imply, *you cannot be required to buy this insurance.*

Another note: You can cancel credit life and disability coverage at any time, no matter what the dealer or lender may say at first when you make such a request.

You'll pay six to eight times *more* for this coverage than for equivalent level term life insurance or income disability insurance. The dealership or bank gets a generous commission on the policy—anywhere from 30 to 60 percent. No wonder they push it! And, because the insurance is usually financed into the loan, you pay interest on the insurance throughout the life of the loan. Insurance is expensive enough; why pay interest on it? Finally, if the insurance cost is added to the loan cost and you insure the total, you're paying for insurance on your insurance!

Not only is credit life and disability overpriced, it's usually not good insurance. A typical policy only takes effect after you've been disabled for thirty days, which is called the "elimination period." Insurance companies know that the vast majority of disabilities last fewer than thirty days. If the company drags its feet after that, you may wait a long time to get your first insurance payment—but all the while, you're expected to make your loan payment.

Also, credit disability may not require a physical examination, but it usually requires a "statement of health" and will not cover pre-existing conditions. They want to cover only healthy folks—the folks who are most unlikely to become disabled.

Credit life insurance is a form of decreasing term insurance. It pays off only the balance of the loan. If you finance a $30,000 RV and die the next week, it pays off the full $30,000. But if you die during the last month of the loan, it only pays off that last payment—for example, $500.

The wise alternative to credit life insurance is level term life insurance, which is much less expensive and offers far better coverage. (If you buy a $30,000 level term policy and die during the last month of your loan, your heirs receive $30,000.) If you don't

N ot only is credit life and disability overpriced, it's usually not good insurance.

Dollar-saving Tip

Consider adding to your term life insurance coverage rather than buying credit life insurance.

have enough term insurance at present, talk to your agent about adding insurance to cover your new loan.

By the way, if you're single, you should certainly not purchase credit life insurance. Buying it would only protect your lender. He can take care of himself.

As for credit disability, remember that most periods of disability are brief. Can you make a payment or two from your spouse's income, or from savings? If you're employed, you probably have disability insurance anyway. You may be eligible for disability funds from your state, or from Social Security. If you're really concerned, speak to your insurance agent about purchasing a disability policy.

Credit life and disability insurance may make sense for a rare few people. If you cannot get the coverage through ordinary insurance—for instance, you're a race-car driver or an avid skydiver—you should buy it. If you're elderly, it may make sense, but talk to your insurance agent first.

D on't sign anything until you thoroughly understand it.

Service Contracts

A service contract, sometimes called an extended warranty, pays for repairs or maintenance on your RV and its systems after the manufacturer's warranty expires. Nearly every dealership will offer you a service contract. The contracts range in cost from a few hundred dollars for a basic contract covering appliances to $3,000 or so for full motorhome coverage. For many dealers, selling these contracts is a major source of profit.

About the only reason to buy a service contract is for peace of mind. RVers are a prudent lot, and many like knowing that their expensive systems are covered against mechanical breakdown. A good service contract will buy you that peace of mind. But you will pay for it, and you will almost never come out ahead.

A bout the only reason to buy a service contract is for peace of mind. . . . But you will . . . almost never come out ahead.

Profit Center for the Dealer

Why are service contracts such a source of dealer profit? First of all, the markup is very high—as high as 70 percent. But remember: *You can negotiate the price of the service contract.* The dealer has a lot of profit to play with. Don't just assume the figure he gives you is engraved in granite. If you really want the service contract, make him bring the price down before you buy it.

Second, you think about *your* costs of repairs when you think about the protection of a service contract. But the $60 an hour in labor the dealer charges you may cost him $20. The parts you pay retail for cost the dealer much less. If you go in for a repair that takes three hours and $200 in parts, you're charged $380. You have a $200 deductible and feel as if you've saved $180. The repair probably cost

How to Scrutinize Service Contracts

Follow these steps to determine the validity of a service contract:

1. *Read every word.* Reading (and understanding) the contract is essential. If you don't understand something, be sure you get it clarified. You may be weary from negotiating, but don't succumb to pressure at this point. Take it home to read it if you wish. That's your right. You can finish up the deal tomorrow. And you can buy a service contract at any time, not just at the time of purchase.

2. *Who is behind it?* Although the service contract is between you and the dealer, every service contract is administered by a third party and underwritten by an insurance company. Many RVers (and dealers) have been burned in recent years by fly-by-night service-contract companies. Even some major service-contract administrators and insurance underwriters have gone bankrupt. You have little recourse in such a case. *Know who is behind the service contract.* Be sure it's a reputable company. If it's not a company you're familiar with, ask your state insurance commission or Better Business Bureau about complaints against the company.

    It's difficult for the average consumer to investigate the solvency of a service-contract company. The Recreation Vehicle Dealers Association recently undertook a major study of such companies. The company RVDA recommends to its membership is United States Warranty Corporation, whose service contracts are underwritten by Continental Heritage Insurance Company.

    Ganis Corporation, which administers Good Sam's RV financing program, sells a service contract underwritten by ITT Commercial Finance. There are other reputable service-contract companies as well.

3. *What is covered?* The contract should be very specific in listing the parts and services covered. It is important to read this section carefully and to consider also what is *not* covered. For example, don't expect a service contract to cover your batteries or tires. The following are a couple of exclusions from *good* service contracts.

    [This contract does not cover] any covered part which is not broken down but which a repair facility recommends or requires be repaired or replaced.

    This service contract does not cover repairs required as a result of normal wear and gradual reduction of operating performance, excessive oil consumption, detonation, loss of compression due to burned or leaking valves or worn piston rings. Failures resulting from overheating or from the improper level of lubricants or other fluids as prescribed by the manufacturer are excluded, regardless of cause.

    In other words, even good service contracts have important limitations. They do not cover plain old worn-out parts that should be replaced. They do not cover preventive maintenance. Essentially, you have to be inconvenienced with a breakdown before the contract kicks in.

4. *Where can you get service?* Some contracts require you to have your RV serviced only at the dealer from which you purchase it. Obviously, such a contract is worthless to anyone who travels. A good contract covers service at any factory-authorized repair center *or* any properly licensed repair facility. A good contract provides you with a toll-free number to call at any time to receive authorization for repairs.

5. *What are your maintenance obligations?* Service contracts require you to comply with certain routine maintenance requirements. In order to make a claim, you must have written records to prove you have complied with the maintenance schedule. You will have to pay for that maintenance, and the contract may require the maintenance to be performed by your dealer or another factory-authorized dealer. If it allows you to perform some maintenance yourself, such as oil changing, be sure to keep receipts for all your purchases.

    The maintenance schedule required is generally reasonable. The company wants to insure that you won't have a major claim. What does that tell you? Of course, *preventive maintenance is your best insurance against expensive repairs.* (See Chapter Nine, "Saving on Service," page 99.) Why pay for an expensive service contract when you already are paying for the best insurance money can buy?

the dealer about $145. He made a profit on the deductible, and he's still free and clear on the money you paid for the service contract.

Finally, most service contracts are included in the financing arrangement, which is already a source of profit for the dealer. You pay interest on the service contract, which may increase its cost up to 40 percent. In the process, you're padding the dealer's (or the bank's) profit. And the dealer benefits immediately, because you begin paying immediately. But you cannot take advantage of a service contract until the manufacturer's warranty expires, usually after one year.

Mechanical-Breakdown Insurance

One way to purchase peace of mind without paying the high price of a service contract is to buy mechanical-breakdown insurance. It may be a better value, and, given the fact that many service contract companies have gone out of business in recent years, less risky. See page 82 for more on mechanical-breakdown insurance.

Who Needs a Service Contract?

Motorhomes obviously have more mechanical systems than trailers or truck campers, and repair bills can be quite high if you need engine or drivetrain work. Motorhome owners may be more inclined to purchase the peace of mind of a good service contract. One way to save would be to buy a contract for the chassis only. As with any form of insurance, a service contract is a gamble. Financially, the odds favor the dealer and underwriter.

Trailer owners should really think hard about purchasing a service contract. Most of the things that go wrong with a trailer's systems occur during the first year and are covered by the manufacturer.

I asked a number of trailer dealers whether they themselves would buy a service contract for a trailer; they all said no.

Other Back-End Deals

Some RV dealers have learned from their counterparts in the automobile business. They push add-ons like rustproofing and fabric protection. These are very high-profit items for the dealer, with little value to you. If you're truly concerned about rustproofing, take your RV to a specialist. If you're truly concerned about fabric protection, buy a can of Scotchgard.

These back-end deals point out the importance of vigilance on the part of the RV buyer. Just when you think the deal's done, they're asking for your money again. Be alert and aware every step of the purchasing process; you'll not only save money, you'll undoubtedly be more satisfied with your purchase.

O ne way to purchase peace of mind without paying the high price of a service contract is to buy mechanical-breakdown insurance.

I asked a number of trailer dealers whether they themselves would buy a service contract for a trailer; they all said no.

CHAPTER FOUR

Buying a Used RV

■ ■ ■ ■ ■ ■ ■ ■ ■ ■

Shopping for a used RV isn't too different from shopping for a new one; it's just a lot cheaper. You must still ask yourself all the questions discussed on pages 16–18. You must know how you will use the RV, what you can afford, and how you will finance it (see also pages 65–74). It's a fact of life that anything motorized depreciates quickly, a sad fact if you just bought a new RV. It began to depreciate when you drove it off the lot and can drop as much as 30 percent in value by the end of the first year of ownership.

Depreciation is not such a sad fact if you use it to your advantage, that is, by buying used. The risks of buying used are obvious, but if you learn to minimize those risks, you can save thousands on the purchase of a good quality, previously owned RV. For the careful, patient buyer, it's one of the smartest of all RV-money moves.

The examples in the boxed copy on page 46 give you an idea of the dramatic dropoff in prices from the dealer's list price to the price the dealer would pay if you drove back onto the lot a year or two later and asked him to buy back the same RV. The dropoff is even greater when you compute mileage penalties for motorhomes. For example, the one-year-old motorhome with a wholesale price of $34,000 drops to $31,475 if it has 15,000 miles.

Travel trailers hold their values better than motorhomes precisely because these mileage penalties do not apply. Additionally, the drop-off in price for each RV is compared to its cost when new, in the original year of purchase. The price tag would be even higher for the same rig if purchased new today—hence, the saving for buying used is even greater.

And if a new-RV buyer purchases dubious back-end deals such as rustproofing, credit life insurance, and fabric protection, he pays even more for the RV. Yet none of these increase the value of a used RV; they cannot be passed along to the next buyer. (The fact that

In This Chapter:

- *How much money can I save by buying used?*
- *What are the risks?*
- *What can I do about them?*
- *What are the best sources for used RVs?*
- *How should I evaluate a used RV?*
- *What if the RV is no longer manufactured?*

How Much You Save

How much can you save by buying used? Let's look at some examples of RV depreciation. These examples are taken from the *Kelley Blue Book* and *N.A.D.A. RV Appraisal Guide* for travel trailers and motorhomes. The prices assume "a clean RV, fully reconditioned and ready for resale," and, in the case of the motorhomes, with "acceptable mileage." Mileage charts in both books indicate dollar figures to subtract from the price for high mileage, as well as figures to add for low mileage. An example of acceptable mileage is 8,000 for a one-year-old motorhome.

In these examples, you'll see the new price (the buyer should have paid less, of course, but this is our index for comparison), wholesale price (what a dealer is likely to pay for the used RV), and the retail price (at which a dealer may sell the used RV).

15-foot folding trailer, 1 year old
New: $6,195   Wholesale: $3,850   Retail: $5,055
Drop in value from new retail to used wholesale:
$2,345 or 38%

33-foot luxury travel trailer, 1 year old
New: $38,846   Wholesale: $24,350   Retail: $30,740
Drop in value from new retail to used wholesale:
$14,496 or 37%

33-foot luxury travel trailer, 2 years old
New: $36,663   Wholesale: $21,100   Retail: $26,675
Drop in value from new retail to used wholesale:
$15,563 or 42.5%

34-foot luxury motorhome, 3 years old
New: $209,090 Wholesale: $107,240 Retail: $153,370
Drop in value from new retail to used wholesale:
$101,850 or 48.7%

32½-foot Class A motorhome, 1 year old
New: $56,130   Wholesale: $34,000   Retail: $43,750
Drop in value from new retail to used wholesale:
$22,130 or 39.5%

24½-foot mini motorhome, 1 year old
New: $42,000   Wholesale: $27,700   Retail: $36,370
Drop in value from new retail to used wholesale:
$14,300 or 35%

24½-foot mini motorhome, 2 years old
New: $39,900   Wholesale: $22,800   Retail: $30,250
Drop in value from new retail to used wholesale:
$17,100 or 43%

24½-foot mini motorhome, 4 years old
New: $37,867   Wholesale: $20,036   Retail: $25,690
Drop in value from new retail to used wholesale:
$17,831 or 47%

Dollar-saving Tip

Knowing the wholesale price is a strong negotiating tool on a used RV.

these are not reflected in the value of the coach indicates just how much they're worth in the first place.) Once more, the saving for buying used becomes greater.

THE RISKS, AND HOW TO OFFSET THEM

Isn't buying a used RV risky? It's a reasonable question. The answer is yes, but not as much as you might think. And for every possible risk in buying used, there's a strategy (or several strategies) for offsetting or minimizing the risk:

The risk: Used RVs may be in bad mechanical condition and fraught with hidden mechanical problems. You're just buying someone else's problem.

The counter: Inspect the rig thoroughly. The section beginning on page 50 details how to inspect a used trailer or motorhome. You should learn to conduct your own preliminary inspection, so you can assess obvious problems and narrow your choice.

When you have decided on a used RV you'd like to buy, take it to an experienced RV mechanic.

Do not buy a motorhome without first having it inspected by a qualified mechanic. If the seller objects, go somewhere else! Most RV-service centers are happy to conduct mechanical inspections. Go to one you trust or to whom you have been referred. A thorough inspection should take two to six hours, and you will be billed at standard labor rates, so it's not cheap. You can, however, bring the cost down by making your own inspection as thorough as possible. Obviously, you want to save the mechanic's inspection for the RV you're serious about. But the investment in an inspection pays off. Not only do you learn about hidden or potential problems, you most likely will come away with bargaining chips as well.

The risk: There's no guarantee or warranty when you buy a used RV.

The counter: If a guarantee is important to you, buy from a dealer. You'll pay more, but if the dealership is reputable, they'll stand behind the product—to a degree. Few dealers will give a written guarantee on a used RV, although you should always ask for one. It can be a good bargaining chip for either party. Some will offer a short-term guarantee, especially if it's a late model. But any good dealer will inspect the rig carefully and put it in good working order. And a reputable dealer will put right anything that escaped the initial inspection.

You can, by the way, purchase a service contract or mechanical-breakdown insurance for a used RV—expensive, but possibly worth the peace of mind.

Your best counter to the lack of a guarantee, though, is the mechanical inspection.

Finally, keep in mind that you are saving a great deal of money by buying a used RV. If a portion of that money saved goes toward some mechanical repairs, you're still ahead.

The risk: A good used RV is harder to find.

The counter: That's true. The best counter to that are these questions: Is it worth thousands of dollars to you to work a little harder? Are you willing to compromise a bit in floorplan or other features?

Actually, used RVs are not that hard to find. You won't have the same supermarket-style convenience you enjoy when shopping for a new one, but if you're alert, you can find what you want. Scan the classifieds in your newspaper and your local free-classified weekly shoppers. Consumer magazines like *Trailer Life, MotorHome,* and

Do not buy a motorhome without first having it inspected by a qualified mechanic. If the seller objects, go somewhere else!

Any good dealer will inspect the rig carefully and put it in good working order.

Highways have classified sections. Clubs are a great source for used RVs. If you don't know of clubs in your area, contact the national offices of a club or clubs and ask to be referred to a local chapter. If you're interested in a particular brand, see if that brand sponsors a club; contact the club and ask for their newsletter (see Appendix, page 247).

Buying from a rental agency is another option. Rental agencies frequently sell used motorhomes at well below blue-book prices. Rentals get a lot of hard use, but the agencies maintain the rigs carefully. Big agencies buy in quantity, so they get good prices in the first place. They make up for first-year depreciation by renting the unit out—the income offsets the loss. In other words, rental agencies can afford to offer attractive prices, but you should be prepared to negotiate, and you should have their motorhomes checked out just as you would any used vehicle.

You'll often find RVs for sale in RV storage lots. You won't be able to enter the lot, but you can probably see "For Sale" signs through the fence and jot down phone numbers. The sellers may be tired of paying storage charges on rigs they want to sell and should be willing to bargain. Campgrounds are an obvious source of RVs for sale, but beware of so-called gypsies (see page 25).

A drive through residential areas—especially in suburbia— usually turns up several RVs posted for sale. Look for notices on bulletin boards—possibly in campgrounds or laundromats, or at your place of work. Schools, police stations, and engineering firms often have good bulletin boards; perhaps you have a friend who works at such a place. Swap meets, especially in popular RVing destinations, are another source.

You can also try placing an ad in any of the classified sections mentioned previously describing the size and price of RV you want to buy. If a seller contacts *you,* you probably have the upper hand in negotiations.

The risk: Used RVs have low resale value.

The counter: The value has already dropped. It works to your advantage.

Look at the examples in the boxed copy on page 46. Notice the 33-foot luxury travel trailer. It depreciated 37 percent during the first year, but only an additional 5½ percent the second year. Or the 24½ foot mini motorhome, which depreciated 35 percent the first year, but only 43 percent after two years, and only 47 percent after four years. Of course, motorhome values drop further if the mileage is high, but the point is, RVs depreciate a lot the first year, and much less thereafter. Depreciation is the original owner's problem, not yours. Once you buy it, it will continue to depreciate, but at a much lower rate.

The risk: Used RVs are difficult to compare.

Rental agencies frequently sell used motorhomes at well below blue-book prices.

Dollar-saving Tip

Listing services are another source for used RVs; check the classified ads in RV magazines.

The counter: It's true that you won't be able to deal as you would for a new RV, when you can comparison shop and buy from the dealer who offers the best price (see pages 34–37). But the already-low price of a used RV easily offsets that advantage.

USED RV SOURCES

Friends

Some financial pundits caution against doing business with friends, but if a friend or relative has a used RV for sale, he or she might be your best source. Why?

First, because a true friend won't try to hide anything from you. However, be aware that he or she may not know of a particular problem that only manifests itself after you've made the deal. For this reason, you should have the used RV checked out by a mechanic. Also, get everything in writing. Even good friends sometime misunderstand each other, and its better to get all points nailed down than to lose a valued friend over a petty disagreement later on.

Second, dickering should be minimal. Why? Because you can visit several dealers with your friend, getting appraisals that will, of course, be at rock-bottom wholesale prices. Offer your friend a profit above the wholesale quotes the dealers give, and you're both happy. Your friend won't have to go through the hassle of advertising and showing it to get a better price, and you won't have to shop around.

> I t's better to get all points nailed down than to lose a valued friend over a petty disagreement later on.

Other Private Parties

You should be able to get a better deal from an individual than from a dealer. Individuals don't have overhead to maintain, nor professional salespeople looking out for the dealer's overhead and their own pocketbooks. Armed with the strategies we'll discuss shortly, you should be able to strike a fair deal for both parties. Find individuals with RVs for sale by investigating the sources mentioned on pages 47–48.

Another advantage to dealing with a private party is that you're more likely to learn straight information about the RV's history—how it has been used and what its problems are.

Some of those classified ads you'll respond to may actually be individuals fronting for a dealership. When you respond to an ad, ask the party if the vehicle is titled under his or her name. If you get a vague response, ask to see the title.

Be careful about buying an RV that is advertised for a low down payment and "TOP" (Take Over Payments). Undoubtedly, the seller is in the hole—that is, owes quite a bit more than the rig is worth. You just take over his problem. He can't sell to a dealer, because he would have to *pay* the dealer to take his RV. Also, he may not have received a good financing deal, which you'll inherit.

Dealers

As mentioned earlier, the advantage of buying a used RV from a dealer is the possibility of some guarantee on service. Many dealers won't offer a short-term guarantee but will still stand behind the vehicle and take care of minor problems after the sale. Press the dealer for a written guarantee, even if it's very short term.

Because some sort of guarantee is an advantage of dealing with a dealer, you should obviously seek out a dealer with an RV-service department. Be very careful about buying a used RV from a used-car dealer who has no service department.

Auctions and Repossessions

An auction is not a good place to buy a used RV. You won't be able to arrange a full mechanical inspection, and most RVs being auctioned are in poor condition. The same goes for bank repossessions. RVers who fail to make their RV payments generally leave their RVs in such bad condition that they're not a good deal at any price.

HOW TO INSPECT A USED RV

Before you begin a thorough inspection of a used RV, ask the seller the following questions:

- *How have you used the RV?* You want to know if it's been put to heavy use (frequent family vacations) or light use—(adults taking it for occasional weekend outings). You also want to know, in the case of a motorhome, if it has has been used for towing. If it has, ask what the sellers have towed. If they have stretched the towing suitability rating of the motorhome, it could have strained the transmission. Ask if an auxiliary transmission cooler has been installed. Towing also adds wear to the brakes, making a mechanical inspection all the more important.
- *Why are you selling it?* This is an important question. The sellers are unlikely to reveal that there are so many problems with it they're trying to dump it on you. But they may tip off something important that you can keep in mind if or when you negotiate. They may be leaving town, giving up RVing or anx-

An auction is not a good place to buy a used RV.

■ **$** ■

Dollar-saving Tip

"TOP" often stands for "Take Over Problems," rather than "Take Over Payments."

ious to buy a new RV. They may have already purchased a new RV, in which case they may be very anxious to sell.

■ *What have you liked most about the RV?* This is a rather innocuous question, although you might learn something. It's really a polite lead-up to the next question:

■ *What have you liked least about the RV?* If you've been politely engaging the sellers in conversation, they very likely will give you a straight answer. Wording the question this way asks them to be specific. If you ask, "Have you had any problems with it?" they can simply answer, "No." This way they'll cite *something*.

■ *How has it been maintained?* Proud, scrupulous owners will produce maintenance records for you. If they don't have records, ask who has performed service on it, and if it has been serviced regularly.

■ *Do you have a service contract?* If the seller has a service contract, that's good for you. The contract for a motorhome has specific maintenance requirements. Among other things, this means that the oil has been changed regularly—the most important routine-maintenance procedure.

■ *Who was the previous owner?* If you're buying from a dealer, ask for the name of the previous owner, which should be on the title. You can then contact the previous owner yourself to ask the preceding questions.

The Exterior

Check the body carefully for the following:

■ *Signs of an accident.* New panels or pieces of aluminum siding that don't quite match are an obvious tipoff.

■ *Hairline cracks.* These are especially common in the cabover sections of truck campers and mini motorhomes, and the truck-over sections of fifth-wheel trailers. Such cracks may indicate poor construction, badly placed jacks or supports, or owner abuse.

■ *False vents.* This is a trick to hide body defects and accident damage: either a full-louvered vent is attached to cover a damaged section, or a small piece of damaged siding is cut out and a vent inserted in the hole.

■ *Pock holes on the siding.* These could indicate water leaks and dry rot.

■ *Loose moldings.* This may mean wood rot lurking under the siding.

■ *Damaged siding.* Inspect the corresponding area inside the coach; it may be more than superficial.

■ *Chassis dings and pits.* Chassis dings and pitted wheel wells may indicate rough, off-road use.

Look for signs of repainting or fresh undercoating that might be covering up rust damage.

- *New caulking compounds.* Check around seams, juncture points, windows, and vent holes. This could be a sign of past leakage. Any conscientious RV owner applies new caulking from time to time, so it's not necessarily a bad thing. But a rig with numerous leaks probably was not constructed well. Check carefully for leak damage inside areas newly caulked, discolored interior paneling, or ceiling. Bulges indicate past saturation. Also be suspicious of caulking in disrepair, which may have invited leaks.
- *Rust.* Inspect the wheel wells, underbelly, frame, and cross-members. Look for signs of repainting or fresh undercoating that might be covering up rust damage.
- *Cracked glass or plastic.* This includes all windows and light covers.
- *Inoperable lights.* This includes taillights, turn signals, hazard lights, parking lights, low- and high-beam headlights. If a light is out, replace the bulb. If it is still out, there could be an electrical problem.
- *Damaged or leaking holding tanks and dump valves.* Fill the holding tanks with water, and let them stand full for fifteen or twenty minutes to inspect for leaks. See also how the water and holding tanks are suspended and supported. Are they and the pipes and conduits supported with enough brackets and welded points to be secure?
- *Propane-tank supports.* Check fasteners for tightness and the tank for rust and deterioration.
- *Tires.* Inspect for wear, damage, and deep sidewall cracking. Tread wear should be even. Look for large repair plugs, bubbles, or other irregularities. You may need an expert to assess tire wear and sidewall checking.

The Roof

Check the roof for the following:

- *Gouges and dents.* Check the roof, as well as the contour of the roof. A slightly concave roof will collect water that can seep through seams.
- *Dings.* Check around the edges. These could indicate close encounters with tree limbs or roof overhangs.
- *Loose moldings.* Also check punctures, rips, or repairs to the roof skin.
- *Television antenna damage.* Does it move as it should?
- *Refrigerator vent.* Is it covered?
- *Roof vents.* Look for cracks or damage.
- *Air conditioner.* Check for proper alignment. Is the exterior shell in good condition?

The Interior

A quick look usually indicates the level of care the coach has received, but be sure to inspect every aspect carefully:

- *Flooring.* As you walk through the coach, listen for signs of strain in the flooring, or feel the flooring for sponginess. It's a good idea to lift the carpeting to inspect the floorboards for rot.
- *Carpeting.* Inspect the carpet for excessive wear or signs of water leakage from the exterior.
- *Upholstery, curtains and paneling.* Inspect for abnormal wear and obvious damage.
- *Cabinets and drawers.* Do the latches work smoothly and securely? Slide drawers all the way out and inspect their structure and sliding mechanisms. Are countertops level? Do cabinet doors line up with cabinet frames?
- *Gas-burning appliances.* Inspect and operate the burners and pilot flames. Flames should burn cleanly and steadily, with a violet or blue color above a lighter blue base—no yellow in the pilot, very little in the burner flame. Otherwise, the burner could be out of adjustment, or something could be wrong in the LP-gas-feed system.
- *Oven.* Check the oven with your own thermometer to make sure the thermostat is accurate. Check to make sure the doors close properly.
- *Refrigerator.* Check the refrigerator for proper operation on each power source. (This can take some time.) Inspect the back of the refrigerator for signs of discoloration, which may indicate it has leaked some of its charge.
- *Heating.* Operate furnaces and check each duct for heat output. Check the wall thermostat; measure the temperature in the room, move the thermostat control higher to see if the furnace cycles on, and then lower it to see if it goes off.
- *Water.* Inspect the water system for proper operation. Flush the toilet and operate the faucets. Inspect the water lines for leaks. Have a professional conduct a high-pressure test.
- *Propane.* Trace the entire LP-gas system, making sure fittings and connections are sound and tight. Sniff for a telltale "rotten egg" odor. If the RV has an electronic LP-leak detector, make sure it is operable. Use it, and/or inspect for leaks with soapy water. However, a thorough LP-system check is best left to a professional.
- *Electrical.* Turn on every light and electrical appliance. You can check for obvious problems, but a complete examination of the electrical system is best left to a professional.
- *Auxiliary generator.* The generator should start readily and run smoothly. A professional can assess the output of the generator/converter.

It's a good idea to lift the carpeting to inspect the floorboards for rot.

Dollar-saving Tip

Make notes during your inspection and pass them on to your mechanic.

Driver Compartment

In the driver compartment, check the following:

- *Brakes.* Depress the brake pedal and hold it. If the pedal continues to give, there may be a leak in the brake system.
- *Leakage.* Look under mats and carpet for rust and signs of leakage. Check along windows and the headliner for stains and signs of leakage.
- *Upholstery.* Look under seat covers to inspect the condition of the upholstery.
- *Windows.* Check the operation of the windows. Also, check for windshield cracks and pits.
- *Electrical.* Operate the radio, wipers, horns, and interior lights.

Under the Hood

Although you'll leave the nitty-gritty under-hood inspection to a mechanic, do have a look under the hood of a motorhome. You might spot some obvious problems:

While the Engine Is Cold

Perform the following procedures:

1. Remove the radiator cap and look for rust.
2. Remove the transmission-oil dipstick, and check the color of the oil. It should look something like new oil, not dark brown and dirty, which might indicate overheating.
3. Inspect the insides of the belts for cracks.
4. Inspect hoses for wear and cracks.
5. Check the battery for corroded terminals. Look at the battery-water levels. If a cell is dry, the battery has not been maintained properly.

Knocking could indicate a valve problem.

While the Engine Is Running

Have someone start the engine and check the following:

1. Check for ease of cold start. Start several more times during course of test.
2. Listen for knocks. Knocking could indicate a valve problem.
3. Look for signs of leakage on and around the engine block.
4. Listen for grinding or clicking noises. Make a note of them for the mechanic.

5. After the engine has run several minutes, look underneath for drops of liquid. Inspect them. If they are red or brown or clear and slippery, suspect problems with the transmission, engine seals, or engine block.

The Test Drive (Motorhome or Tow Vehicle)

If you're interested in purchasing the motorhome after the preceding checks, ask to take it for a test drive. Offer to put several dollars worth of gas in the tank, and drive it for a half-hour or so. The seller should come along. Drive it in a variety of conditions; be sure to climb some hills and take it up to freeway speed. Carry out the following tests:

- *Pep.* Check for engine responsiveness.
- *Transmission noise.* Listen for grinding or humming sounds in the transmission. If the motorhome has an automatic transmission, note how the gears shift. If the shifts are jerky, there could be a problem with the gear mechanisms. When accelerating firmly, the gears should shift quickly. The transmission should downshift automatically when the accelerator is pressed to the floor. With a standard transmission, listen for grinding sounds. Make sure each gear is easy to enter, including reverse.
- *Brakes.* Check the brakes for fade, pulling, or grinding sounds.
- *Steering.* Check the steering. Is it loose? There could be a linkage problem. Is it jerky, or does it resist turning? There could be a problem in the power-steering system.
- *Bounce and sway.* Pay attention to any excessive bouncing or sway. The shocks may need replacing, or there could be a more serious problem with the suspension system. Make notes for your mechanic.
- *Air conditioning.* Check the air conditioner, even if it's the dead of winter.

Check the air conditioner, even if it's the dead of winter.

The Test Drive (Trailer)

You should already have a suitable tow vehicle before you purchase a used trailer. (See page 33 and read Chapter 8, "How to Choose a Tow Vehicle," in *The RV Handbook* by Bill Estes.) If you are buying a tow rig and trailer combination, ask to see the literature in the tow-vehicle owner's manual. And no matter what, check the dry weight and the gross vehicle weight rating of the trailer to be sure it's suitable for the tow vehicle's tow rating. Better yet, as Estes strongly recommends, *weigh* the trailer yourself. Hitch up and drive the tow vehicle/trailer. Check the following:

- *General stability.* Disconnect the sway-control device if there is one so it does not camouflage inherent trailer instability.

- *Trailer brakes.* They must function in tandem with the vehicle brakes, as well independently, via the manual control lever.
- *Sway control.* At about 20 MPH, turn hard to the left, as if avoiding an object in the road. Do it again at faster speeds, controlling the trailer brakes manually; the sway oscillations should diminish.
- *Positive control.* Take the trailer out on a busy freeway. A properly balanced trailer should remain stable, even when passed by a speeding 18-wheeler. You will undoubtedly have to make a steering correction, but you should be able to control the rig easily.
- *Stability.* Check stability on downgrades at freeway speed.
- *Hitch weight and balance.* You should seek the assistance of a good hitch shop if you're not familiar with these procedures.

If you're purchasing a trailer somewhat different from the type you've towed before, you might need to make some adjustments with your hitch and sway control. Again, a good hitch shop or RV service center can assist you.

Visit Your Mechanic

You should note for your mechanic anything you observed in your inspection that you suspect might indicate mechanical difficulty. Also ask the mechanic to inspect anything in the coach that is beyond your expertise, such as the condition of the generator, electrical (battery condition, voltage drop, adequate reserve capacity), water, LP-gas systems, and the frame. If you want to be really certain, ask him to reinspect everything you've already checked yourself.

Parts for Orphan RVs

RV manufacturers come and go. Although it's smart to buy a used RV that is still manufactured by a reputable company, it's also possible to get a good deal on an "orphan" RV—one that is no longer made. You can even use that fact in negotiating the price down.

It's easy to tell if the RV is an orphan. The N.A.D.A. or Kelley appraisal guides will not carry current listings for that brand. (They will carry listings for past years, though.) If you're in doubt, contact the RVIA (see Appendix, page 249).

In some cases, it's not just the RV that's an orphan; it's certain components that are no longer made.

In any event, sources do exist for parts for orphan RVs. Take your rig to an RV dealer or service center; they should be aware of wholesale distributors of orphan parts such as D.T.I. and LaPorte's:

D.T.I. Appliance Parts
P.O. Box 286
304½ North Main
Middlebury, Indiana 46540
(800) 289-0919

LaPorte's Parts Distributors
4500 US-15 North
Hartsville, South Carolina 29550
(803) 332-0191

Mechanic's Checklist

On a motorhome (or tow vehicle if you're buying a combination), ask the mechanic to inspect all the systems you've inspected (pages 50–55), with the following additions:

Engine:
■ Cylinder compression
■ Spark plug condition. Check for oil consumption and ignition wire
■ Cylinder leakdown test, to indicate condition of piston rings and valves
■ Timing chain for stretch and wear

Cooling system:
■ Adequate radiator size
■ Radiator condition
■ Heater
■ Radiator tubes for blockage

Transmission:
■ Performance evaluation
■ Hoses for damage
■ Fluid condition

Brakes:
■ Condition of pads and shoes
■ Check for leakage and deterioration of hoses, cylinders, and seals
■ Rotors and drums

Battery:
■ Check condition

Tires:
■ Correct rating for weight of RV
■ Irregular wear, excessive sidewall checking

Suspension:
■ Check all components, including shock absorbers, ball joints, struts

Exhaust system:
■ Check for damage and leaks

Ask the mechanic to give you a repair estimate on everything that needs attention. You might also ask for estimates for cosmetic problems, such as upholstery repair or paneling replacement. It doesn't matter if the seller says he is selling the RV "as is"; you can still use these estimates as negotiating tools.

MAKING THE DEAL

First, be sure to read Chapter Three, "Dealing with Dealers," for background before you deal for a used RV. But negotiating for a used RV is somewhat different. As noted earlier, you can't comparison-shop; you can't pit one dealer's price against another's for an identical rig. Used RVs are never identical.

Nor do you have a suggested list price to deal with. You have something better: You have a wholesale price.

As mentioned earlier in the section on depreciation, you can look up the average wholesale price of the RV you're interested in. Look at the Kelley and National Automobile Dealers Association appraisal guides, available at some banks and libraries. Obtain the wholesale price on the year, make, and model of the RV, making sure you adjust for the mileage on a motorhome or tow vehicle.

Be prepared to dicker. It's part of the game of buying and selling.

Dollar-saving Tip

Don't hesitate to offer less than blue-book value when the condition is less than immaculate.

Your goal is to get the price down right around the wholesale figure (assuming the rig is in good condition), or less. If you're dealing with a private party who has offered his rig to dealers, he has almost certainly been presented with less-than-wholesale prices. The appraisers have pointed out the rig's faults to him and dropped the price. So should you.

Sellers often have an inflated notion of their rig's worth. Some might even ask the blue-book retail price or more, unaware of the rate RVs depreciate. If similar rigs are being advertised at less money, point that out. Blue-book prices are meaningless if the local market will not support them.

Blue-book prices are also meant for RVs in good, clean condition. Dealers who fully recondition a rig and offer a warranty can understandably ask a higher price. Individuals can't offer a guarantee.

Point this out when you tell the sellers their asking price is off. Point out the problems you've observed: carpet unacceptably worn, dings and scrapes on the exterior, whatever. Offer them an amount based on the wholesale figure or lower.

Be prepared to split the difference once they've come down close to your asking price. That's only fair in the bargaining process.

When you agree upon a price, write up a simple agreement and leave a deposit. Stipulate on the deposit receipt that the price is contingent on a clean bill of health from your mechanic. It will be lowered depending on the extent of repairs needed. If those repairs exceed a certain figure, for example, $500, state that you have the right to recoup your deposit.

When you return from the mechanical inspection, show the sellers your mechanic's estimate of needed repairs. Tell them they either can have the repairs made at their expense, or you'll take care of the repairs if they'll drop the price.

Be prepared to bargain again, and be happy if you negotiate a new price that covers most of the repair estimate.

FINANCING

Shop for your financing in advance, just as you would for a new RV (see Chapter Six). Find the best rate possible; it may vary depending on the age of the vehicle you plan to purchase. Learn approximately how much a lender will lend you. The actual figure will depend on the age and condition of the RV. Lenders will typically finance 75 to 85 percent of the low blue-book figure—that is, the wholesale figure, adjusted for the mileage and equipment on the RV. If you have followed the steps above, you're paying well below wholesale, and you should only have a minimal down payment to make.

With careful shopping and maintenance, you should be able to take advantage of the good deals available on used RVs and enjoy many money-saving years on the road.

CHAPTER FIVE

Selling an RV

■ ■ ■ ■ ■ ■ ■ ■ ■ ■

S ell your RV yourself. No dealer will pay you anything close to what *you* can get for your RV. They will pay you less than wholesale for your rig, then turn around and sell it at a retail price. The difference is profit, and that profit can be yours. To understand the buying and selling game, you should read the preceding chapters. Then follow these steps:

Clean It Up

A clean RV has a great psychological impact. Buyers are impressed by a shiny exterior and clean interior. Many will assume that a clean RV is also mechanically sound and will not investigate its true working condition. Consider having your RV detailed by a professional detailer or car wash if the following procedures below are too much for you to do yourself.

■ Wash your RV with a car-wash product available at auto parts or RV-supply stores. Use a finish restorer such as Protect All to remove stubborn grime and oxidation. Use rubbing compound on badly deteriorated paint surfaces. Use tar and bug remover on the front of a motorhome. Wax the entire vehicle and use black-tire dressing to spiff up tire sidewalls.

■ Use caulking compound if chunks of caulk around vents, windows, and seams are missing or deteriorated. Remove screens and wash them with a hose and soft brush.

■ Do a complete interior housecleaning. Deodorize the refrigerator by washing it with warm water and baking soda. Use mild sachets or potpourri to keep the entire interior smelling fresh. You might lay inexpensive throw rugs on badly worn carpeting (or inexpensive floor mats in the driver's compartment). The

In This Chapter:

■ *What are the money-saving advantages of selling my RV myself?*
■ *How can I best advertise my rig?*
■ *How do I determine an asking price?*
■ *What should my negotiation strategy be?*

seller will pick them up and notice the wear, of course, but will also notice how meaningless the wear is when covered with an attractive rug.

■ Inspect cabinets and doors; tighten hinge screws and lubricate squeaks.

Don't Make Major Repairs

There's no reason to make major repairs on an RV you're selling. The cost of repairs is grounds for negotiation with the buyer. If repairs are necessary, be prepared to drop your asking price. Chances are, you will reach some middle-ground figure that is less than the actual cost of repairs.

Determine an Asking Price

Look up the value of your RV in the N.A.D.A and Kelley RV appraisal guides, available at some banks and libraries. Read the tables carefully, adjusting for the mileage if you're selling a motorhome or tow vehicle, and for extras like air conditioning. Use the retail and whole-sale prices as guidelines. (Wholesale is what a dealer would pay for the RV.) In reality, the dealer would probably pay less, and of course, retail is what it would sell for.

Check the ads in the classifieds to learn what others are asking for similar RVs. See what dealers are asking. You want your price to be competitive. Naturally, you want to get more than the wholesale price for your RV. The best way to do so is to make it so clean and shiny that you can ask something close to retail—you might get it. Ask at least 15 percent over wholesale.

Advertise

Use as many free advertising sources as possible. Most communities have weekly shoppers and auto traders that carry free classifieds. Start with the free sources before you pay for advertising. Put a sign in several windows of the RV. (Make sure this is legal in your community.) Put notices on bulletin boards. Get the word out at your RV club and among friends. Always state your asking price, so you'll only receive calls from shoppers who are interested. State specific hours for customers to phone, so you won't be bothered at inconvenient times.

If you're not successful with free sources, take out an ad in your local paper, club newsletter, and even national publications such as *Trailer Life, MotorHome, Highways,* or *Family Motor Coaching.* For a fee and a percentage of the sale price, you can list your RV with a listing-service company, which in turn will advertise in these and

---

There's no reason to make major repairs on an RV you're selling.

$

Dollar-saving Tip

An immaculate rig can get top dollar, that is, close to the blue-book retail figure.

other publications. Use only a reputable listing-service company that takes a low up-front fee. (For more about these companies, which also sell used campground memberships, see Chapter Thirteen, pages 140–141.)

Set Aside Specific Times to Show It

Because most people who call never show up to look, you should minimize such inconveniences; set aside certain times to show the RV. Tell callers you're showing it, for example, between noon and 5:00 P.M. on Sunday. Ask callers to make appointments, and take their names and numbers. Ask them to call you if they can't make it.

Go Along on the Test Drive

No matter how honest a customer seems, you should ride along on the test drive. Even if the prospective buyer leaves his or her own mother as "ransom," go along. Too many sellers have watched their units be driven away, never to be seen again.

Know Your State's Selling Procedures

Contact your motor vehicle department to learn exactly what steps you must take to register a sale. If you've lost your title ("pink slip"), arrange for a replacement. Once the deal is complete, you'll sign the title over to the buyer. You'll need a bill of sale, which the motor vehicle department can supply, or you can make your own (see Figure 5.1).

Give one copy to the buyer and keep one for yourself. Buyers who are financing a used RV will need to know the year, make, model, mileage, extra equipment, and vehicle identification number of the RV. Have that information prepared on a slip of paper that can be given to the bank.

Negotiate

Never ask your rock-bottom price up front. That's not playing the game. You're always expected to negotiate. Be willing to come down, especially if the buyer pays for a mechanical inspection and determines that repairs are needed.

But here are some points to stress in the negotiation:

■ The buyers can't come close to your price at a dealership. Show them the retail figure in the appraisal guide (you can photocopy the page). Tell them they can expect to pay at least that to a dealer.

> Ask callers to make appointments, and take their names and numbers. Ask them to call you if they can't make it.

Dollar-saving Tip

Knowing how to drive a bargain when you buy can help you do the same when you sell.

Bill of Sale

Sold to: _____

_____

_____

_____

By: _____

_____

_____

_____

One: _____
(Year, make, and model of the RV)

VIN: _____
(Vehicle identification number)

Date: _____

**Your
signature:** _____

Figure 5.1: Typical Bill of Sale

- If they counter with a low figure, remind them that your unit is exceptionally clean and well cared for. Tell them that those numbers are just guidelines, national averages, not dogma. Your price is a fair market price, and that's what counts. Remind them what they would pay for such a rig new.
- Tell them what a joy the RV has been for you and your family. Be upbeat, even sentimental. Smart dealers "sell the sizzle." So should you.
- Produce maintenance records, if you have them, that show the RV has been well cared for.
- If you have a service contract, show it, as well as the maintenance requirements that you have complied with to keep the contract valid. Point out the transfer clause in the service contract; it can usually be transferred for a small fee. The buyers may feel as if they're getting a guarantee, and it costs you nothing.
- Have a rock-bottom price in mind. Don't go below it—at least not until you've offered the unit for sale for a while. Once the buyers have negotiated down to that price, tell them you won't go any lower. Tell them to shop around if they wish, but that they won't find a better RV for the price.

If you end up about halfway between appraisal-guide retail and wholesale, you've probably done well, and both parties should be satisfied.

Accept Only Cash or a Cashier's Check

It's too risky to accept a personal check, and it would be wise to call the bank to verify even a cashier's check.

Selling an RV yourself requires a little extra effort, but keep in mind that the extra profit you'll derive can go toward the new RV you're coveting.

S mart dealers "sell the sizzle." So should you.

Dollar-saving Tip

S ome buyers think you should drop your price if they offer cash. In fact, *insist* on cash or a valid cashier's check.

CHAPTER SIX

Financing

■■■■■■■■■

Because it costs money to borrow money, shopping carefully for financing is just as important as shopping carefully for an RV. You might save more in the long run by making a good deal on your financing than by making a good deal on your RV. By considering every possible source of financing and by knowing how to compare loan terms, you can greatly reduce the cost of borrowing money.

CASH VERSUS FINANCING

If you consider yourself a cash buyer, shopping for financing may not seem to be a concern. But don't be smug about it; you *do* pay extra costs when you pay cash—that is, the loss of the earning power of the money you pay, or "opportunity cost." Ask yourself how much money you will *not* earn from your savings account, real estate, stocks, or bonds because you liquified the cash to buy an RV. The answer, of course, is usually conjecture, because dividends and interest rates fluctuate, but you can estimate opportunity cost well enough to know that paying cash does cost you.

You should also keep in mind that any income derived from liquidating an asset may incur a capital-gains tax. Also, if your money is in a bank certificate of deposit (CD) that has not matured, you'll incur that proverbial "penalty for early withdrawal." The penalty is the cost of paying cash. You also miss out on a tax deduction; interest on most RVs is tax deductible (see page 66).

In general, of course, the money you would earn from your investments will be less than the interest you will pay a lender. But cash buyers should investigate the loan market. If you have a high-yield investment, or you're concerned about your financial "cushion," you might consider financing at least a portion of your RV purchase.

In This Chapter:

- *Should I pay cash or finance my RV purchase?*
- *Why is selecting the best financing source so important?*
- *What are my sources of financing?*
- *How and why should I compare financing terms?*
- *Can I refinance my RV?*
- *What are my credit rights?*

IT PAYS TO SHOP

Why is it important to shop carefully for a loan? The following example illustrates the comparative costs of two loans that differ by just *one-half of one percent* (see Table 6.1).

You're purchasing a motorhome for $62,500. You put 20 percent down, so you're financing $50,000. You want a fifteen-year loan to keep your monthly payments as low as possible. You find a lender willing to loan you the money at 11-percent interest. Your monthly payment will be $568.50. Here's what the loan will cost you:

Total loan amount ($568.50 × 180 months) = $102,330
Total interest = $52,330

The monthly payment for a loan of 10½ percent interest will be $553. If that doesn't seem like much difference, look at the total cost:

Total loan amount ($553 × 180 months) = $99,540
Total interest = $49,540

The difference between the two loans, one at 11 percent and the other at 10½ percent, is $2,790!

If you found the motorhome you want selling for nearly $3,000 less at one dealership down the street from another, you'd surely go down the street. So, too, should you go elsewhere for financing.

Pay Off Your Loan as Quickly as You Can

Within the numbers of Table 6.1 is sage advice: Pay off your simple-interest loan as quickly as you can. Make the highest monthly payment you can handle. This means paying less in the long run, because interest on extended loans really adds up.

As you already know, if you buy a motorhome for $62,500 and finance $50,000 over 180 months (15 years) at 11-percent interest, you will pay $52,330 in interest.

Using Table 6.1, let's see what the same loan paid back over 60 months (five years) would cost.

Dollar-saving Tip

If you extend your loan too long, you may never have equity in your RV.

Tax-Deductible Interest

In an era when interest deductions are dwindling away, interest payments on recreational vehicles are still tax deductible. An RV that has cooking, sleeping, and toilet facilities on board qualifies for the federal income tax second-home deduction. (Tax laws change, of course; be sure to check with the IRS or an accountant before taking this deduction.) Of course, you cannot take advantage of this deduction if you already own a second home or another RV. If this is the case, you should consider a home-equity loan to finance the purchase of your RV (see page 72).

Table 6.1
How to Determine Monthly Payment and Interest Payment on RV Loans

Interest	Monthly payment per $1,000					
Rate	48	60	84	120	144	180
10.0	$25.36	$21.25	$16.60	$13.21	$11.95	$10.75
10.5	25.60	21.49	16.86	13.49	12.24	11.06
11.0	25.84	21.74	17.12	13.77	12.54	11.37
11.5	26.09	22.00	17.38	14.06	12.83	11.69
12.0	26.33	22.24	17.65	14.35	13.13	12.01
12.5	26.58	22.50	17.92	14.64	13.44	12.33
13.0	26.82	22.75	18.19	14.93	13.75	12.66
13.5	27.07	23.01	18.46	15.23	14.06	12.99
14.0	27.32	23.27	18.74	15.53	14.37	13.32
14.5	27.57	23.53	19.02	15.83	14.69	13.66
15.0	27.83	23.79	19.29	16.13	15.01	14.00

Look under the "60" column (the term of the loan), where it intersects the interest rate line of 11 percent. The figure is $21.74. That's the monthly cost *per thousand dollars* you are borrowing. Multiply that by 50 for the monthly payment.

> 50 × $21.74 = $1,087 (monthly payment)
> $1,087 × 60 = $65,220 (total payment)
> $65,220 − $50,000 = $15,220 (total interest)

Using this example, you would save $37,110 in interest by paying the loan off in 60 months, rather than 180. If you pay it off in 144 months (12 years), you would save $12,042.

Paying back a loan as quickly as possible also increases the equity in your RV at any given time. If you extend your payments too far, you may owe more than your RV is worth. You're "upside-down," or "in the hole," and you'll have to come up with that difference should you decide to sell or trade in the RV.

The time to shop for financing is *before* you purchase your RV.

SHOP IN ADVANCE

The time to shop for financing is *before* you purchase your RV. Why? Because you should never automatically accept a dealer's financing. You might do better elsewhere. And you should never allow financing to become a factor in your price negotiation. An astute salesperson can juggle the interest rate to fit the monthly payment you desire—an interest rate that could be far higher than you need pay. Keep financing separate from the negotiation of purchase price. Also, shopping for financing in advance allows you to know exactly what you can spend for an RV. (See also pages 30–32.)

Check with several different loan sources, including the dealer from whom you intend to buy. Compare the factors outlined in the

Thankfully, most
RV loans today are
calculated on a simple-
interest basis.

section that follows. When you find the best source, ask if you can be pre-approved for a loan. Do this a week or so before you intend to make the purchase.

Make an appointment with the loan officer and ask what materials you need to bring: most likely, your Social Security number, credit cards, your checking and savings account numbers, plus information on any installment loans you are currently paying or have recently paid off. If you are self-employed, you will need your tax returns from the past few years. Tell the loan officer the specific RV you intend to buy or the approximate price range if you're not certain.

HOW TO COMPARE LOANS

The following are the factors you should consider before deciding on a particular loan source:

Is It a Simple-Interest Loan?

Thankfully, most RV loans today are calculated on a simple-interest basis. This is the most straightforward way to repay a loan. You pay interest monthly on the unpaid balance of your loan. You do not pay a penalty if you prepay a portion or the entire balance of the loan.

This is in contrast to "add-on" interest, a method used less and less these days. This was a confusing way of disguising true interest rates, and it involved a considerable penalty for early payoff. Using the complex "rule of 78s," you had to pay more interest in the early payments than in later payments. Be certain your loan is calculated on a simple-interest basis.

Annualized Percentage Rate (APR)

The government requires every lender to reveal the annualized percentage rate (APR) of every loan. APR tells you the true interest cost of any loan, no matter how it's calculated. It also factors in points and finance charges. APR is the key index you should use to compare loans.

Other Fees

Certain fees may not be included in the APR, but they add to the cost of a loan: title-recording fee (set by the state), credit-report fees, application, and documentation fees. The latter may be a subtle way for a lender to pad the cost of a loan. If this fee is in the hundreds of dollars, raise your eyebrows. Better yet, raise an objection. Fifty to

$100 is a typical application fee; if the fee is a few hundred dollars, question it. Some institutions hungry for business will waive the application fee altogether.

Prepayment Penalty

Simple-interest loans involve no prepayment penalty per se, but the institution might still assess a fee for early payoff of a loan. It may be a minor factor, but still one to ask about.

Credit Life and Disability Insurance

You can't be required to carry this insurance. In fact, in most cases, you should *not* carry it. This is discussed in detail on page 41.

The Permission-to-Travel Clause

Some contracts specify that you can't move your vehicle or take it out of state without permission from the lender. This is to prevent unscrupulous buyers from skipping town to avoid paying off a loan. You obviously don't want to seek permission from the lender every time you want to take a vacation, so be sure the lender is willing to delete this clause if it's part of the contract.

Coupon Book or Monthly Statement

If you travel a lot or full time, monthly statements have a hard time catching up with you. A payment book makes it easier for you to keep up with your payments on time. Also, most lenders will arrange to have an automatic payment deducted from your checking or savings account, which simplifies matters more for RVers on the road. They may offer a break on the interest rate for automatic payment. (Of course, you must be certain that you have money in the account to cover the payment on the day it's deducted.)

LOAN SOURCES

Lenders have discovered the RV market in recent years. They know that RV owners have an excellent payment record, that is, a low delinquency rate (around 2 percent), better than many other categories of borrowers. Hence the market for RV loans can be competitive—find out just how competitive by comparing at least three sources.

$

Dollar-saving Tip

Be sure to compare application fees when comparing loans.

Lenders . . . know that RV owners have an excellent payment record.

Having a relationship with a lender can be a great advantage in obtaining a loan, especially during periods of tight credit.

Dealership Loans

Most RV dealers offer financing. For some, it's a major profit center. For others, it's mainly a service to their customers, with an understandable ulterior motive—that is, offering convenient and reasonable financing is one way to attract and keep potential buyers. But it's still profitable.

Dealers usually have working relationships with one or more banks; it is the bank that actually does the lending, which is why this type of loan is called an "indirect loan." Good dealers have already done the loan-shopping you should do. They have sources that favor RV loans and offer competitive rates.

Some dealers offer manufacturer financing. In many areas, Fleetwood offers competitive financing through its own Fleetwood Credit Corporation. Other manufacturers have arrangements with banks to offer customers attractive financing. The manufacturer sometimes "buys down" the bank interest rate to offer customers an attractive financing deal, often during a special promotion or on a certain line of RV.

The obvious attraction of financing through your dealer is convenience. But that in itself is not a compelling enough reason to finance through a dealer. How inconvenient is it to drive down the street and learn what terms a nearby bank will offer? Remember what a difference just one-half of one percent makes!

Bank Loans

Having a relationship with a lender can be a great advantage in obtaining a loan, especially during periods of tight credit. Your bank should certainly be one of the loan sources to look into. Some banks offer their own customers a ¼-percent to ½-percent break on loans, and/or a similar break if you agree to have the loan payment automatically deducted from your checking or savings account each month.

Until recently, banks generally didn't offer extended financing on RV loans. Today, though, many banks are offering ten- and twelve-year loans. On most RV loans, the RV itself will be collateral, plus you'll be expected to make a down payment: typically 20 percent for a new RV, 25 percent for a used one.

Other Collateral Loans

You can also negotiate a bank loan using your savings account or certificate of deposit as collateral. You'll certainly pay more in interest on your RV loan than the savings account is earning, but the interest rate on the CD-secured loan is usually lower than on other types of loans. Since the loan is secured by your savings, you'll be unable to withdraw that money until the loan is paid. Essentially, you're borrowing from yourself and paying to do it.

Credit Union Loans

If you belong to a credit union, you should investigate its terms for RV loans. At one time, credit unions were almost always the logical choice; they offered simple-interest loans at lower rates than banks. Competition for the RV market has changed that somewhat. Nearly everyone offers simple-interest loans, and many lenders match the interest rates of credit unions. Still, as with a bank, having a history with a credit union can smooth the process of obtaining a loan.

Whole Life Insurance Policy Loans

If you have a whole life insurance policy that has accumulated some cash-surrender value, you can borrow on that money at a very low rate. If you purchased your policy before 1980, you can borrow at 6 percent; you can still borrow against later policies for as little as 8 to 10 percent. You are essentially borrowing from yourself by borrowing from the equity in your life insurance policy.

Insurance-policy loans not only offer low interest rates, you can also pay them back at your own pace (in some cases you can elect not to pay back at all), although it's wise to put yourself on a monthly pay-back schedule.

Another advantage: You won't have to fill out credit forms, nor disclose the reason you're borrowing.

Check your policy's table of cash values to determine how much you can borrow, or ask your insurance agent.

Broker Loans

If you own stocks, bonds, or securities, you can use them as collateral for a broker's loan. This option is also known as a "margin loan." You can typically borrow up to half the value of the securities in your

Dollar-saving Tip

Lenders are competing for RV loans; remember that as you shop.

Variable Rates

Some loans, particularly home equity loans, offer variable rates. The rates fluctuate with a particular index (treasury bills and the current prime rate are examples), and therefore respond to the ups and downs of the economy. If you are considering a variable-rate loan, shop for one whose rates can rise no more than two percentage points annually and with a rate cap of no more than five to six points over the life of the loan.

portfolio. Because brokers borrow at wholesale from banks, the rate is usually very competitive—one or two points above the prime interest rate (the rate banks charge their best corporate customers).

However, be aware that if the value of your shares drops sharply, you're subject to a "margin call"—that is, your broker will ask you to come up with the difference between the amount you borrowed and one-half the current value of your stocks or bonds.

Home Equity Loans

If you own a home and have equity in it (equity is the difference between the amount you owe on the home and its current market value), you can borrow against that equity at a low interest rate—usually about two percentage points above the prime interest rate. Interest on a home equity loan is tax deductible. This can be attractive if for some reason you don't qualify for the second-home tax deduction on your RV (if, for example, you already own a second home, or your RV doesn't meet second-home requirements, i.e., having sleeping, cooking, and toilet facilities.)

Closing costs on a home equity loan can be considerable, although banks are competing for this market and may offer competitive deals. Also, interest rates can vary. It may be an advantage to borrow from the holder of your home mortgage, but not necessarily. Check with that institution and two others.

Good Sam

Members of the Good Sam Club can apply for SamFinance RV loans through the Ganis Corporation of Newport Beach, California. SamFinance loans are available for terms up to fifteen years, which is longer than most banks will finance an RV. Interest rates and fees are very competitive. Ganis expects a down payment of 15 percent on most RVs, 20 percent on those over $100,000.

> **I**f you own a home and have equity in it, you can borrow . . . against that equity at a low interest rate.

Refinancing

If you bought your RV at a time of high interest rates, or you didn't bother to shop for a competitive rate, you can refinance your RV loan. You may also consider refinancing if you're being strapped by high monthly payments. You can extend the term of your loan and bring the payments down. Just remember, however, you'll be paying out more in interest in the long run, and you'll pay fees for the new loan.

If your existing loan is an add-on interest loan, the payoff cost may be too high to make refinancing worthwhile. A loan officer can run all the figures for you and determine whether or not refinancing is feasible.

SamFinance loans are available for cars and trucks as well, also with longer-than-usual terms—up to seventy-two months. Sam-Finance/Ganis is also very active in refinancing. For more information on refinancing, see the box on page 72.

YOUR CREDIT RIGHTS

In most cases, applying for a loan entails a check of your credit history. As you surely know, credit bureaus, also known as credit reporting agencies (CRAs), maintain files on your credit history. Potential creditors will check these files to find out how you conduct your financial affairs and also to verify the accuracy of your credit application.

Thanks to the Fair Credit Reporting Act of 1970, you have a number of credit rights you should exercise:

- The right to know what is in your credit file. To locate the CRA that has your file, look in the Yellow Pages under "Credit" or "Credit Rating and Reporting." Call each one listed until you locate all the agencies that maintain your file. Upon your written request (be sure to include your Social Security number), the CRA is required to reveal to you *every* piece of information in the report.
  (**Note:** One major credit reporting agency, TRW, offers this service on an ongoing basis for an annual fee. Because you have the right to examine your credit record, it's not necessary to pay TRW every year for the information.)
- This information must be provided to you free of charge if your credit application is denied because of information furnished by the CRA. You have thirty days to make this request. Otherwise, the CRA will charge a small fee for your check.
- You have the right to know why a creditor has denied your application.
- You have the right to dispute any information in the file, or to add to it if the information is incomplete. The CRA is required to reinvestigate the items you question. A credit dispute form is available at any credit reporting agency.
- Even if you don't resolve your dispute with the CRA, you can demand the CRA include *your* version of the disputed information in your credit file and that it be sent to anyone who recently received a copy of the old report.
- Creditors cannot discriminate against you on the basis of sex, marital status, race, national origin, religion, age, or because you receive public-assistance income.
- If you are a woman who has shared accounts with your husband or former husband, you have the right to have a credit file in your own name that lists these accounts. If the credit infor-

Dollar-saving Tip

If a lender turns you down, find out why. There may be a mistake in your record.

You have the right to know why a creditor has denied your [loan] application.

Arm yourself with foreknowledge, shop around, know your rights, never be intimidated, and don't rush into a decision.

mation was reported only in your husband's name, the credit bureau may be willing to add those references to your file—ask. There may be a small fee charged for each item added. From now on, notify your creditors that you want the accounts you share with your husband reported in both names.

By now the formula should be familiar because it applies to so many aspects of your RVing finances: Arm yourself with foreknowledge, shop around, know your rights, never be intimidated, and don't rush into a decision. Apply these strategies to the financing of your purchase, and you're certain to save a lot of money.

CHAPTER SEVEN

RV Insurance

■ ■ ■ ■ ■ ■ ■ ■ ■ ■

I f you're new to RVing, you might be in for a surprise: RV insurance is quite affordable. If you already own an RV, you might also be in for a surprise: You might be paying more than you need for insurance. In either case, there's one key to saving on insurance, and that's to shop for it. We'll discuss many other important ways to save as well. But shopping for the right insurance company is the best way to be pleasantly surprised.

HIGH COST, LOW RISK

Why is RV insurance so reasonable? Statistics show that RV drivers are good drivers. A large percentage are over fifty-five years of age, a category of conservative drivers. Many automobile policies offer a discount to drivers over fifty or fifty-five. Most companies that write RV insurance do not offer an age discount per se, but rather, factor it into their rates. This means that everyone who qualifies for RV insurance from these companies—even those under fifty-five—gets to take advantage of this low rate structure.

Secondly, RV insurance specialists understand that RVs rest idle much of the year, unlike automobiles that are usually used daily. This too is often factored into RV insurance rates.

Trailer owners save in another way: Liability insurance for a trailer is almost always covered by the owner's tow-vehicle policy. Trailer owners pay nothing at all for liability on the road.

The high cost of some RVs, particularly motorhomes, certainly affects insurance rates. You will pay more for insuring a $75,000 motorhome than a $25,000 van conversion. But these rates are not as high as you might expect because RV drivers with good records are recognized as safe drivers and are able to enjoy with other safe drivers the relatively low cost of insuring their rigs.

Of course, not every company treats RVs the same. You simply must shop around.

In This Chapter:

- *Is RV insurance expensive?*
- *What advantages do RV insurance specialists offer?*
- *What coverage do I need?*
- *Should I purchase mechanical-breakdown insurance?*
- *How can I save on insurance?*
- *What about travel in Mexico?*

SOURCES OF RV INSURANCE

If you currently have an automobile insurance policy with a good company and a good agent, you naturally should consider that company for RV insurance. The company might offer a discount for multiple policies.

However, not every automobile insurance company addresses the specific needs of RVs and RVers. For example, many will not cover fulltimers, that is, anyone who claims an RV as primary residence. Others do not offer adequate coverage for personal effects inside the RV. Some do not offer liability insurance when the RV is parked.

Also, some automobile insurance companies charge far more than others for RV insurance. For these companies, RV insurance is essentially a sideline; they set their rates strictly by the cost of the RV, and not the good record of RV drivers.

It's a good idea when shopping for insurance to investigate the rates of the companies that specialize in RV insurance: National General (Good Sam Club), Alexander & Alexander (FMCA), Caravanner, Foremost, and AARP (see Appendix, page 249, for addresses and phone numbers).

While you shop, you should naturally be concerned about service as well as price. Your early impressions can be telling: Are you treated courteously? If you deal directly with the company (insurance companies such as National General and Alexander & Alexander have no agents), is there a toll-free number for your questions and claims?

Most importantly, you need to know how efficiently the company processes claims. Ask the company about its claims-processing policy. Does it guarantee speedy resolution? Even more importantly, ask other RVers to describe their experiences in filing claims with their companies.

Consumer Reports magazine periodically rates insurance-company service; such information, available at your local library, can assist you in shopping for insurance.

The financial solvency of the company is also very important. A. M. Best Company is the most respected rater of insurance companies. Be sure to buy only from companies rated A or A+ by Best.

TYPES OF COVERAGE AND HOW MUCH TO CARRY

The following types of coverage are available for your vehicle. Included in each group are guidelines on how much to carry.

Liability

Liability insurance protects you against the cost of being sued should you or another driver of your vehicle cause injury through negligent driving. Four aspects of liability may be covered:

Bodily Injury

Bodily-injury coverage pays medical bills, lost wages, and "pain and suffering" to those whom you cause injury. Most policies have "split-limit" bodily-injury liability, and it will show on your policy, for example, as $100,000/$300,000. This means the limit of the coverage is $100,000 maximum to any one individual and $300,000 for the entire accident. Single-limit coverage will apply as much as needed to the most severely injured party, within the limit of the policy.

As you undoubtedly know, bodily injury liability insurance is an absolute necessity and required by law in many states.

How much to carry? You must protect, at minimum, your net worth, which is what an injured party is likely to sue for should you be negligent in an accident. However, in this era of expensive lawsuits, you should carry *double* your net worth to cover attorneys' fees. If you have split-limit coverage, the first figure, the per-person figure, should be double your net worth.

Most liability cases are settled out of court for no more than the limit of the insured's policy. However, if you have net worth considerably beyond those limits, the other party may go after it. Obviously, you should be protected.

Property Damage

The property damage portion of your auto or RV insurance covers you for damage to property (other than your own) caused by negligent driving. The property in question is typically another vehicle. But if you negligently bash the gate or kiosk in an RV park, it would cover such an instance.

Interestingly, over 50 percent of all insurance payouts are made for property damage. It too is a critical aspect of your policy.

How much to carry. Many states specify a minimum of $10,000 property-damage insurance. With the cost of vehicles today, that won't go far. It's wise to carry at least $25,000, but no more than $50,000, which would cover 99 percent of all potential claims. If you pull a trailer, your tow-vehicle insurance covers the trailer for property damage liability while you are under way.

Vacation Liability

Also known as "camper's personal liability," vacation liability covers you should someone be injured in or around your RV while it is parked. This type of coverage is usually handled by your homeowner's or renter's policy. But if you're a fulltimer, you should check into this special coverage.

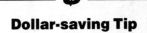

Dollar-saving Tip

Review your liability coverage limits. Most likely, some are too high, others too low.

Over 50 percent of all insurance payouts are made for property damage.

How much to carry. Again, the rule of thumb is to carry twice your net worth.

Umbrella Coverage

If you have considerable net worth, consider supplementing your coverage with an umbrella policy. This may be written as a rider to your vehicle or homeowner's policy or purchased separately. A $1-million umbrella policy, which is surprisingly inexpensive, gives you added liability coverage; it kicks in should a lawsuit exceed your bodily-injury liability coverage. It could also substitute for vacation-liability coverage.

How much to carry. Umbrella coverage typically begins at $1 million and is sold in further $1-million increments. Again, you should figure double your net worth in coverage.

Medical Payments

Medical-payment insurance is important if you have little or no health insurance.

Medical-payment insurance pays for medical expenses for yourself and passengers in your RV, regardless of who is at fault in an accident. The limit of the coverage is per person, not per accident. In other words, if you have $10,000 in medical-payment coverage, and three people are injured in your vehicle, your insurance company will pay up to $10,000 to each of them.

How much to carry. Medical-payment insurance is important if you have little or no health insurance. Most RVers do have health insurance for themselves and their families, and should seriously question the need for medical-payment coverage at all. If you're concerned about nonfamily members riding in your vehicle, remember that they're covered under your bodily-injury liability insurance. If you have no health insurance, by all means buy as much medical-payment insurance as you can afford.

Collision

Collision insurance covers the cost of repairing your RV due to damage caused by collision with another vehicle, or an object, or should your RV roll over. The coverage is not dependent on fault. Nor is collision coverage mandatory; many people with older vehicles drop collision coverage altogether. Collision also covers you if you are driving a vehicle you do not own, such as a rental or a friend's vehicle.

How much to carry. How much is not really a consideration; your insurance will cover the value of your vehicle. The question is whether to carry collision at all. If collision-repair costs exceed the value of the vehicle, the company will "total" the vehicle and pay you approximately its current blue-book value. If you have a fifteen-year-old RV or an eight-year-old tow vehicle, chances are it has depreciated so much that it is not worthwhile to carry collision insurance. Discuss this with your insurance agent or representative.

You should also examine your collision deductible. Although insurance rates vary widely, you always save by raising the deductible. In some cases, the savings are dramatic. In a sense, you self-insure for the first $500 or $1,000 of collision damage. You could go so far as to invest the money you save every year in a special "casualty account." Better you collect interest on that money than your insurance company.

If you can afford a $1,000 payout in the unfortunate event of a collision that is your fault, consider raising your deductible to $1,000.

Comprehensive

Loss caused by nearly anything other than collision is covered by comprehensive insurance. This might include theft, fire, vandalism, flying objects, or even an angry animal. This, too, is optional coverage that is subject to a deductible. Ask your agent if such things as antennas, awnings, and satellite dishes are covered. Companies that don't specialize in RVs may not include these accessories.

How much to carry. Your strategy should be the same as with collision insurance. If you have an older RV, consider dropping the coverage. Take the highest deductible you can afford.

Replacement-Cost Insurance

While collision and comprehensive insurance will reimburse you only to the actual cash value (ACV)—approximately the blue-book value—of your RV, replacement-cost insurance covers you for the amount needed to *replace* the RV with an equivalent one.

Only one company, Alexander & Alexander, currently offers this endorsement, which is available only for manufactured motorhomes (that is, no bus conversions). The company has the option to pay the lesser of:

1. The cost of a new RV of the same model year, make, length, and equipment; or
2. The sum of the actual cash value of the motorhome plus $25,000. The insurance is available initially only for RVs four years old or less, although it may be continued once it is added to the policy. Cost is an additional 15 percent of the sum of collision plus comprehensive.

> **A**lthough insurance rates vary widely, you always save by raising the deductible.

How much to carry. This is not applicable to this category, which gives you replacement value and therefore has the actual cost of the vehicle built into the endorsement.

Personal Effects

If you have homeowner's or renter's insurance on your house, your personal effects are covered up to a certain limit when you are traveling—usually up to 10 percent of your total coverage. Be sure to determine whether this is adequate coverage for the things you carry in your RV.

If you have no homeowner's policy, look into special personal-effects coverage. A minimal amount may be included in your basic coverage, and additional coverage is generally available for about $15 per $1,000 worth of coverage.

How much to carry. You must total up the personal effects you carry and calculate their replacement cost. Remember that certain valuables, such as jewelry and silver, may not be covered, so they should not be included in your calculation.

Uninsured and Underinsured Motorist

Despite laws and common sense, many drivers carry inadequate insurance or no insurance at all. Up to 30 percent of drivers in some states are uninsured, and they cause a disproportionate number of accidents. If one of them causes harm to you or your passengers, your uninsured- and underinsured-motorist insurance (UIM) will cover you.

The accident must be the fault of the other driver for you to collect, and it covers *only bodily injury.* UIM basically pays you what you would be entitled to if the other driver were insured. It will cover bills that exceed your medical-payment insurance, and also covers lost wages and pain and suffering. Many states require a minimum amount of UIM.

How much to carry. If you have good health insurance and disability insurance (worker's compensation, Social Security), you will be covered for medical bills and lost wages. You can probably carry a minimum amount of uninsured-motorist insurance or eliminate it. There's no sense paying for duplicate coverage. Otherwise, buy whatever amount you're comfortable with.

You needn't consider exorbitant attorney's fees in deciding how much UIM to carry. Although this type of insurance puts you in the position of having to collect from your insurance company for an accident caused by someone else, any dispute that arises will be settled by arbitration, not in court.

> Despite laws and common sense, many drivers carry inadequate insurance or no insurance at all.

Personal-Injury Protection (No-Fault States)

Personal-injury protection (PIP) is an option in some states, a requirement in others that have no-fault insurance regulations. This insurance covers such things as medical payments and lost wages.

How much to carry. If you have good health and disability insurance you can probably drop PIP if you have the option, or carry the minimum required by your state.

Another option is to coordinate these no-fault benefits with your health-insurance policy. Agree with your vehicle-insurance company that the first benefits to be paid will be by your health insurance. You can save up to 40 percent on PIP this way.

Towing

Many agents include towing insurance in your policy as a matter of course. Check your policy; you may have substantial or unlimited towing benefits and not even know it. This covers towing in the event of a breakdown, usually on a reimbursement basis. You pay the tow company directly, submit the receipt, and the insurance company pays you back. It usually amounts to just a few dollars a year, but it may be wasted money if you belong to an automobile club that covers towing (this would be for a tow vehicle, not a motorhome), or if you have RV breakdown coverage such as the Good Sam Club's Emergency Road Service (see the section below) or a service contract that covers towing.

Rental-Car Reimbursement

Rental-car reimbursement pays a certain amount per day toward a rental car should your vehicle be disabled for a period of time. Question carefully whether you really need this coverage. If you have a second vehicle, you don't need it. If car rental is covered in your service contract, you don't need it. The odds are against ever using it. And since it usually only pays $15 or so per day, chances are you don't need it, period.

Emergency-Breakdown Insurance

RVers are frequently on the road in remote places or driving at night and appreciate the peace of mind that emergency-breakdown insurance gives. Even if you belong to an automobile club, it may not cover RVs—a least not RV towing. Although you may think you're covered, you may not be. Be sure to ask your automobile club; you may have to pay substantially more for RV coverage.

Question carefully whether you really need [rental-car] coverage.

Dollar-saving Tip

Avoid redundant towing coverage.

Two national RV clubs offer special RV-emergency-breakdown insurance: The Good Sam Club's Emergency Road Service and FMCA's Road America RV Assist. These policies allow you to make a toll-free call and receive mechanical assistance and/or towing. They issue a card, so you will not need to pay cash, as you generally must for roadside assistance. Also, these policies have no limit on roadside repairs and towing; they will cover whatever it costs to get you going if it can be reasonably accomplished at the roadside. If roadside repairs (jumpstart, gasoline, etc.) aren't possible, they provide unlimited towing. Most ordinary towing provisions have a $50 limit, which does not go far. It may not go anywhere at all with an RV. **Note:** Emergency-breakdown coverage does not extend to in-shop repairs.

This insurance is expensive, although certainly worthwhile should you ever need a large RV towed some distance. Be sure to compare it to what your automobile club offers. In each case, include also the membership fee for the RV club or auto club. Finally, if you have a service contract, check its provisions; emergency breakdowns are probably covered.

Mechanical-Breakdown Insurance

Because extended warranties, or service contracts, are not technically insurance, they are discussed in Chapter Three. An alternative to service contracts that *is* actually insurance offers many attractive alternatives to the various disadvantages of service contracts.

Under mechanical-breakdown insurance (MBI), there is no third or fourth party. Where service contracts may be sold as a profit center by dealers who deal with a service contract company that is underwritten by an insurance company, MBI is an arrangement made between you and an insurance company.

At present, only one company, Prudential, offers MBI for RVs (see Appendix, page 249). Because it is true insurance, Prudential MBI is registered with the insurance commissions of each state, and the rates are subject to regulation. Where dealers can sell service contracts for as much or as little as they wish, agents have prescribed rates for MBI. These rates are generally about 30 percent less than service contracts with similar coverage.

MBI's coverage is quite comprehensive, although, like service contracts, it does not cover such things as reduced performance due to gradual wear. MBI covers towing and roadside repairs up to $100 (this cost is reimbursed, unlike Alexander & Alexander or Good Sam Club's emergency-breakdown insurance, which requires only presentation of a card). It covers a rental car up to $30 a day and lodging reimbursement up to $50 a day.

As with service contracts, repairs require authorization from the insurance company, via a toll-free number, and owners must keep up the manufacturer's routine maintenance recommendations.

HOW TO SAVE ON INSURANCE

Many ways to save on insurance have been discussed on the preceding pages, but let's review them and consider some others:

Shop for Rates

Rates vary widely from company to company and from area to area. No single company is consistently less expensive nationwide, so it's impossible to offer a general recommendation.

To illustrate how rates vary in one particular area, we created a fifty-five-year-old couple who reside in Agoura Hills, California, home of TL Enterprises. Neither of our pair has had accidents or tickets in the last three years. The coverage on their mythical mini motorhome includes liability limits of $100,000/$300,000 and $500 deductible for collision and comprehensive. We contacted both RV specialists and automobile insurance companies that write RV insurance. Quotes for our couple ranged from $409 to $935 per year.

Buy Only As Much Liability Insurance As You Need

As previously discussed, you should carry liability insurance equal to twice your net worth. If you don't have a lot of assets, you might be overinsuring yourself.

Raise Your Deductible

Insurance that covers routine repairs, nicks, and dings is very expensive. Consider self-insuring for the first $1,000 of damage under your collision and comprehensive. Our mythical motorhoming couple compared rates for $250 deductible versus $1,000 deductible; they would save between $75 and $120 a year by raising their deductible to $1,000. Similarly, if you buy a service contract, ask for a high deductible.

Drop Duplicate or Unnecessary Coverage

If you have good medical and disability insurance, you can reduce or eliminate medical-payment insurance, uninsured motorist, and PIP. If you have an older RV, consider dropping collision and reducing or dropping comprehensive. Remember, the insurance company will only pay a claim up to the value of the RV. That's not the value of the RV *to you*. That's the actual cash value, as determined by the appraisal guides.

If you're carrying death, dismemberment, and loss of sight coverage, you're paying for extremely overpriced insurance that should be covered by life and health policies. Drop such coverage.

> No single company is consistently less expensive nationwide, so it's impossible to offer a general recommendation [on rates].

Dollar-saving Tip

Insure against catastrophe not against expenses you could reasonably bear.

If you have good medical and disability insurance, you can reduce or eliminate medical-payment insurance, uninsured motorist, and PIP.

Investigate Discounts

Some companies that specialize in RV insurance do not offer much in the way of additional discounts because their rates already factor in age and a good driving record. That is, they incorporate discounts in their rates to begin with. But it's always worthwhile to ask about discounts that might be available to you, such as:

- Multi-car discount, if you insure more than one vehicle with the company.
- Multi-policy discount, if the company also writes your home-owner's or other policies.
- Driver's education discount, if you take an approved defensive driving course.
- Senior's discount, if you're over the age of what the company's determination of "senior" might be.
- Nonsmoker's discount. Nonsmokers can save on auto insurance as well as health insurance.
- Good-driver discount. This usually means no accidents or tickets within a certain period. Companies with very competitive rates may require you to be a good driver prior to insuring you, so they will not offer any additional discount.
- Anti-theft devices. Some companies in some states offer a discount on comprehensive insurance if you have installed anti-theft devices.

Review Your Declarations

Check with your insurance company about the information you gave them when you purchased the insurance: who drives the vehicles, how much you drive per year, whether or not you commute to work, where the vehicle is stored, and so forth. If these factors have changed, you might save money.

You may be jeopardizing your good-driver rating by filing a claim for . . . a small amount.

Change Your Place of Residence

Obviously this is only practical for fulltimers, and RV insurance is only one factor in deciding where to set up home base (see page 235). But vehicle insurance is priced territorily. Rural areas, for example, may be far cheaper than urban areas. It's something to keep in mind.

Don't File Claims for Small Amounts

If you have a collision claim for $550 and you carry $500 deductible, you may be jeopardizing your good-driver rating by filing a claim for such a small amount.

Pay Your Premiums Annually

You save money on most policies by making one annual payment rather than semi-annual, quarterly, or monthly payments.

Ask about Suspended Coverage or Seasonal Insurance

If your RV will be idle for thirty days or longer, some companies will suspend your coverage during that period (you might want to retain comprehensive coverage), saving you money. Or, if you're away on an extended RV trip, you should ask about suspending coverage on other vehicles being left at home. Companies with already low rates may discourage suspended coverage requests on the RV because their rates already assume it will be idle much of the time.

INSURANCE WHILE DRIVING IN MEXICO

Because Mexican authorities recognize only Mexican insurance, you must purchase such insurance before you go to Mexico, or at the border just before you enter. Without Mexican insurance, you could be detained—even jailed—after an accident, until fault is determined. And you must prove your ability to pay for damage and injuries you might have caused; insurance is the best proof and the best way to avoid experiencing a Mexican jail.

Mexican insurance is available by the day, week, month, or year. No American insurance company sells Mexican insurance, but Mexican insurance is available in advance through the American Automobile Association (to members) or Sanborn's (see Appendix, pages 244 and 249, for addresses). Offices of Sanborn's and various Mexican insurance companies are at border crossings. Rates are controlled by the Mexican government, so they should not vary much. But ask about claims procedures and the availability of English-speaking claims adjusters; these factors may determine your choice of an insurer.

Some RV insurance policies include a Mexico endorsement that extends U.S. physical damage coverage for twenty-five miles into Mexico for a maximum of ten days. If that is the case, you may not need to buy Mexican collision and comprehensive, which is expensive. No matter what, you must have Mexican liability insurance if you travel in Mexico.

Note: If you have an accident in Mexico, you must file the claim before you leave the country. Be certain the issuing agent thoroughly explains the procedures for filing a claim before you proceed into Mexico.

Without Mexican insurance, you could be detained—even jailed—after an accident, until fault is determined.

CHAPTER EIGHT

Warranties, Disputes, and Lemon Laws

■ ■ ■ ■ ■ ■ ■ ■ ■ ■ ■

In this era of consumerism, RV buyers have more protection than ever. RV and tow-car warranties are getting better and longer. Laws are protecting buyers from suffering the sour taste of costly lemons. Public and private agencies are offering lots of consumer assistance and legislative advocacy. Despite all this, warranty disputes are still commonplace. One difficulty for motorhome buyers is the dual nature of the motorhome, which is the product of both a chassis and a coach manufacturer. And then there are all the on-board accessories, each with its own warranty. Who is responsible for what? Another perennial problem is the chronic condition that isn't cured by the end of the warranty period. When is a manufacturer no longer responsible for repairs?

Knowing your warranty rights and knowing how to insist upon them can save you a lot of money. But you must be willing to educate yourself and follow certain procedures, which are outlined in this chapter.

In This Chapter:

- *What are my warranty rights when I buy an RV?*
- *How do I resolve a dispute with my dealer?*
- *The manufacturer?*
- *When and how should I sue?*
- *What organizations offer legal assistance to vehicle buyers?*
- *How can I still obtain free service after my warranty has expired?*
- *What if I've bought a lemon?*

YOUR WARRANTY RIGHTS

The modern era of warranty rights began with the passage in congress of the Magnuson-Moss Warranty Act, which has been amended in succeeding years. Under the act, you have the following warranty rights:

When a seller advises you that a product is suitable for a particular use, it must perform as promised.

- Your RV dealer, automobile dealer, and RV-accessory dealer are required to make written copies of all warranties available for you to read before purchasing a product. This means you can add warranty comparison to your shopping list before buying any product.
- Warranties must be easy to read and understand—no legal jargon, no fine print. All terms and conditions must be spelled out.
- Although written warranties are not required by law, *implied warranties* cover virtually every product you purchase. Nearly every state has an implied warranty law. This means the seller implicitly promises that the product will do what it is supposed to do: A motorhome will run, a refrigerator will cool, a furnace will heat. This is also called a "warranty of merchantability."
- Another type of implied warranty is called a "warranty of fitness for a particular purpose." When a seller advises you that a product is suitable for a particular use, it must perform as promised. If you have a 4,000-pound trailer and a tow-car manufacturer rates the car to tow 4,000 pounds, the car must be suitable for towing the trailer. A sleeping bag rated for freezing weather must keep you warm in freezing weather.
- Implied warranties apply even when no written warranty is given—*unless* the product is marked "as is," or the seller indicates in writing that no warranty is given. Several states, including Kansas, Maine, Maryland, Massachusetts, Mississippi, Vermont, West Virginia, and the District of Columbia, do not permit "as is" sales.
- Spoken warranties—promises delivered orally—may not be binding. Any promises a salesperson makes that are not in a written warranty must be put in writing.
- If you reported a defect to the company during the warranty period and the product was not fixed properly, the company must correct the problem, even if your warranty has expired.

YOUR WARRANTY RESPONSIBILITIES

Read the warranty on every product you are considering buying before you buy the product. Be certain you understand the terms of the warranty. Following are some particulars to look for:

- The length of the warranty
- Exactly what parts and problems are covered
- Whether labor charges are covered
- Whether "consequential damages" are covered. For example, most warranties will not reimburse you for your time and expenses in getting the product repaired. Or, if your refrigerator breaks down, the maker will generally not reimburse you for spoiled food.

■ Whether special procedures are required to get a repair, such as shipping the item to the factory. A good warranty will allow service at factory-authorized outlets and provide a complete list of those outlets.

Follow these recommendations to insure you do not invalidate your warranty.

■ You must use the product according to the manufacturer's instructions. Overloading a motorhome or exceeding a car's tow rating are examples of misuse. Misuse or abuse of a product almost always cancels a warranty.

■ You must perform specified maintenance and regular inspections as required by the warranty. In the case of cars and motorhomes, this means following the prescribed intervals for oil changing, lubrication, and so forth, and showing proof that you did.

■ Keep in mind that a warranty is only as good as the company that offers it. An excellent warranty offered by a fly-by-night trailer company is a fly-by-night warranty. Even with the law on your side, it can be very difficult to get warranty satisfaction from a disreputable or financially shaky company.

■ Understand that the company has a right to fix its warranted product, and you don't have an automatic right to a refund or replacement.

> Keep in mind that a warranty is only as good as the company that offers it.

RESOLVING WARRANTY DISPUTES

Warranty disputes can take many forms. A dealer might seem to be dragging his feet in making a repair. He might not complete the repair to your satisfaction. You might have to return again and again to have the same repair made. The dealer might claim you have misused the rig—failing to make regular oil changes, for example. Your rig might be out of warranty, but you feel the manufacturer should cover a certain repair anyway, usually because the condition wasn't corrected when it was covered by the warranty.

The following are the steps you can take to resolve a warranty dispute. Remember one cardinal rule: Document everything, every step of the way. Keep copies of all bills, invoices, and correspondence. Make notes after every relevant conversation.

Extended Warranties

Extended warranties, or service contracts, are not warranties; they are insurance. A true warranty is a guarantee offered by the manufacturer. An extended warranty is an agreement between the consumer and a third party. Service contracts are covered in detail on pages 42–44.

Dealers occasionally drag their feet or even refuse to perform warranty work.

Work It Out

Always try to work out the situation with the dealer. If you don't receive satisfaction from the mechanic or service writer, move up the chain of command to the service manager or owner. Even at this level, put your complaints in writing. Make it clear that you intend to report the situation to the manufacturer if the situation is not fairly resolved. Warranty work is important to most dealerships. Although there is a time lag in payment, the dealer is generally fairly reimbursed by the manufacturer for warranty work. The shop does not want to lose its "authorized service center" status.

Nonetheless, dealers occasionally drag their feet or even refuse to perform warranty work. It may be for a repair that they feel the manufacturer does not reimburse sufficiently. Or, perhaps you bought your rig out of town and took it in to a local dealer for warranty work. The dealer would probably give your repair low priority. In either case, you still have a right to have the work done.

In the case of a vehicle or motorhome, if it has to be serviced three or four times for an identical problem, or has been out of service for thirty days within the first year or 12,000 miles after purchase, it might be considered a "lemon." Your complaint procedure would then be different. (See "Lemon Laws," page 94.)

Contact the Manufacturer

You will find that customer-relations people try very hard to resolve disputes.

If you can't resolve the situation at the local level, it's time to contact the manufacturer (see Figure 8.1.) Read your warranty and owner's manual. They should detail the procedure for filing a complaint to the manufacturer. Many owner's manuals list toll-free telephone numbers as well as addresses. If you are dealing with an automobile or chassis manufacturer, the problem usually goes to the zone level. If the dispute concerns a trailer or motorhome coach, you will probably deal with the customer-service office of the manufacturer at the national level.

The nature of motorhomes can complicate matters, although the correct channel is usually obvious: if the problem is with the coach, contact the motorhome manufacturer; if it's with the chassis (for example, engine, drivetrain, fuel system), contact the chassis manufacturer. If it's not clear who is responsible (for example, the fuel system has been modified by the coach maker), contact them both.

If you have misplaced your warranty or owner's manual, the dealer should be able to refer you to the appropriate customer-relations office.

When you contact the manufacturer, be sure you have important information at hand, such as vehicle identification number, date of purchase, and current mileage. A phone call just opens your file. The customer-relations person will ask you to mail in copies of all the relevant documents: bills, invoices, and correspondence.

How to Complain to Your Dealer or Manufacturer

The following is a suggested format to follow when writing a letter of complaint to your dealer or manufacturer:

Date

John Doe, president
Acme RV, Incorporated
Address

Dear Mr. Doe:

I am writing concerning a problem I have with my new (year, make, model), which was purchased on (date). The vehicle identification number is (_____).

   I experienced my first breakdown with my (vehicle) on (date) and have had repeated problems with it since then. The major problem at this point is (description). As a result of this problem we have been unable to use our (vehicle) since (date), and have spent (amount) thus far trying to get it repaired and back on the road. I attempted to get help through (service manager, dealership) on several occasions, but the (vehicle) remains unrepaired and is not roadworthy. The following is a list of the repair attempts:

   (date) (problem #1)
   (date) (problem #2)

   Attached are copies of work orders and receipts, plus additional receipts for incidental expenses, towing, etc. A reply at your earliest convenience would be appreciated.

Sincerely,

Your name and address

Figure 8.1: Letter of Complaint

Allow Enough Time

Dealing with the manufacturer may take some time. You should allow at least a week for the customer-relations people to look into your case.

Tip: You might ask to meet personally with the factory's district service manager. If you don't get a progress report after a week or ten days, call again. The resolution itself may take longer.

If your complaint has safety implications—for example, your brakes fail or you stall in freeway traffic—be sure to make this clear. You'll undoubtedly get prompt action.

Remember, a manufacturer cannot stall a resolution of your problem until the warranty runs out. If the complaint is filed before the warranty expires, the manufacturer is obligated to fulfill the terms of the warranty.

Tip: Although you should be businesslike at this stage, don't be belligerent. Tell the factory representative that you're a loyal customer, you *like* your vehicle, and you intend to be a customer in the future. You are much more likely to get attention this way rather than by flatly stating you'd not buy their brand again in a million years.

Nor should you be sending copies to consumer groups, attorneys, or the media at this point. You lose valuable leverage in doing so; the manufacturer wants to *avoid* publicity. Take advantage of that fact. Mention that you *will* take such action, but that you trust you'll reach a resolution before such dire steps are necessary.

You will find that customer-relations people try very hard to resolve disputes. The manufacturer wants you as a repeat customer and will do all it can to insure that possibility.

Go to the Top

If you receive no satisfaction at the zone level, contact the customer-relations office at the company's headquarters. Again, supply copies of all documents, including correspondence with the zone level.

Warranty Protection on the Road

RVers occasionally run into warranty difficulties while on the road. Your first step, of course, is to find a factory-authorized dealer to work on your rig. Your owner's manual should list addresses and phone numbers. Some warranties cover towing to authorized dealers. Most dealers are very cooperative about helping vacationers in distress. (Politeness in pleading your case helps a lot.)

However, if the dealer brushes you off, tells you to come back in a week, or claims the repair is not covered, a call to the manufacturer, or the zone office in the case of a motorhome chassis or tow vehicle, will almost always pave the way. The manufacturer will call the dealer and give the extra little nudge that will get the job done.

At this stage, it can be helpful to inquire about factory service bulletins that relate to your problem. Some automobile and chassis manufacturers make these available to the public. Or, you can obtain them from the federal government. Write to:

National Highway Traffic Safety Administration
Technical Reference Library, Room 5108
400 Seventh Street, S.W.
Washington, D.C. 20590
(202) 366-0123

Describe the make, model, and year of the vehicle and describe the part that seems to be the culprit.

Other Alternatives

If you receive no satisfaction, you still have some choice of action:

Write: *Trailer Life's* "RV Action Line," *MotorHome's* "Hot Line" or "Action Line" in *Highways* (the Good Sam Club magazine) for assistance (see Appendix, pages 249–250). These columns specialize in handling RV-related problems at no charge to readers. Contacting one of them may save you time and/or legal costs.

Arbitrate: Ask if the manufacturer deals with a dispute-resolution organization, and if it is willing to submit the case to arbitration. This is a way for both parties to avoid legal action. Almost all the vehicle manufacturers subscribe to an arbitration program. In fact, you may be required to go through arbitration before you can take legal action. But the arbitration is almost never binding on the consumer; if you don't like the result, you can go to court or seek other options.

Many states have their own arbitration programs; contact the state attorney general's office in your capital city.

Contact: Contact the Federal Trade Commission. The FTC cannot represent you in a dispute, but wants to know about companies in violation of the federal Warranty Act. You might also contact one or more consumer-assistance organizations (see box, page 94).

Sue: Your final recourse is to sue the manufacturer. If the amount in question is within or near the limit of small claims court in your state (as high as $5,000 in some states), by all means go to small claims. Because attorneys are excluded from small claims court, you'll save considerably in legal fees.

However, the Magnuson-Moss Warranty Act allows you to sue for damages and for any other type of relief the court awards, including

> **A**rbitration is almost never binding on the consumer; if you don't like the result, you can go to court or seek other options.

$
Dollar-saving Tip

If you must sue, small claims court is the reasonable recourse, unless the amount in question is very high.

legal fees. If your case involves a substantial amount of money, hire an attorney and go to court. The Center for Auto Safety (see below) can refer you to a lawyer in your area who specializes in automobile or RV problems.

LEMON LAWS

Sometimes it happens: That sweet baby you bought with such high expectations has a very sour taste. It goes back to the dealer again and again for the same repairs. It may be a lemon.

The definition of a lemon varies from state to state, but the general definition is a motorized vehicle (not a trailer) that has to be

Consumer-Assistance Organizations

In most cases, the most effective consumer-assistance organizations are those on the state and local level. Look in the White Pages of your telephone book under "Consumer Complaint and Protection Coordinators" for the proper bureau in your area. Separately listed, the Better Business Bureau can often provide some assistance. Be sure to notify the BBB if you have a serious complaint against a shop or dealership; the information can help others.

The office of your state's attorney general can provide information on lemon laws and possible state-provided arbitration. In addition, the following private and federal agencies might be helpful:

The Center for Auto Safety
2001 S Street, N.W., Suite 410
Washington, D.C. 20009
(202) 328-7700

This group, originally established by Ralph Nader and the Consumers' Union, represents automotive consumers in Washington. They analyze consumer complaints that often lead to recalls and government investigations. They have played a major role in creating state lemon laws and in exposing secret warranties. The center publishes *The Lemon Book,* which can be useful for lemon owners. Send them a self-addressed, stamped envelope for a list of attorneys in your area who specialize in automotive or RV problems.

Motor Voters
1350 Beverly Road, Suite 115-240
McLean, Virginia 22101
(703) 448-0002

This group focuses on auto safety and air bags.

National Highway Traffic Safety Administration
400 7th Street, S.W., #5319
Washington, D.C. 20590
(202) 366-9550
(800) 424-9393 (Auto Safety Hotline)

Responsible for safety and fuel-economy standards. Write NHTSA's Technical Reference Library, Room 5108, for service bulletins pertaining to your vehicle. Call the hotline number to learn if your vehicle has been recalled for safety repairs.

Federal Trade Commission
6th and Pennsylvania Avenue, N.W.
Washington, D.C. 20580
(202) 326-2222

The FTC regulates advertising practices and administers provisions of the Magnuson-Moss Warranty Act. They cannot represent you in a dispute, but you should report possible violations of the Warranty Act to the FTC.

serviced three or four times for the same problem, or has been out of service for thirty total days, within whichever comes first—a year or 12,000 miles. The period is stretched to two years in some states. Some states give extra weight to safety-related defects.

You can obtain the specifics about lemon laws in your state by writing or phoning the state attorney general's office in your state capital.

Most lemon laws originally pertained only to cars and trucks, but more and more are including motorhomes—although they exclude the coach portion of the motorhome.

If You Have a Lemon

If your vehicle fits your state's definition of a lemon, the steps to follow are similar to those previously outlined for warranty disputes. They should be discussed in your owner's manual.

You should first contact the manufacturer in writing. Most states allow the manufacturer an opportunity to repair the defect. If this isn't successful, and the manufacturer refuses to buy back the alleged lemon, you can resort to arbitration. Manufacturers make every effort to avoid arbitration.

All the vehicle manufacturers belong to an arbitration organization such as Autosolve, Autocap, or BBB Auto Line, or, in the case of Ford and Chrysler, have their own arbitration program. Once again, meticulous documentation is necessary when you present your case to a third-party arbitrator. You should have all repair records, including receipts for such routine maintenance as oil changes, to show the vehicle was well cared for.

An alternative to the arbitration organizations is state arbitration; check with your state attorney general's office to learn if your state offers arbitration.

If you win a lemon-law arbitration, the most likely outcome will be a buyback of the defective vehicle. If you lose, you can still go to court. Remember, though, the wheels of justice turn slowly. Make every effort to resolve the case before going to court. Even if you win in court, the award can be held in escrow if the manufacturer appeals the decision. You may wait a long time for your money.

Lemon Motorhomes

The foregoing certainly applies to tow vehicles, but what of motorhomes? If a motorhome is determined to be a lemon, who is responsible for the buyback?

Under a voluntary program initiated by the RV Industry Association, the RV manufacturer would be required to buy back the motorhome. The manufacturer would then deal with the chassis

M ost states allow the manufacturer an opportunity to repair the defect.

Dollar-saving Tip

D on't suffer with a lemon; state lemon laws protect you.

maker to work out a settlement, rather than the consumer being bounced back and forth between the two parties.

At present, General Motors has agreed with RVIA to abide by the new program. The other chassis makers may soon follow suit.

FREE SERVICE AFTER THE WARRANTY HAS EXPIRED

Every year, thousands of vehicle and RV owners receive free service even after their warranties have expired. Following are some of the circumstances under which you might receive free service.

Secret Warranties

Also called "hidden warranties," secret warranties apply when a manufacturer authorizes dealers to correct a factory defect—even after the warranty expires. Instead of issuing a recall notice, the manufacturer relies on the dealer to correct the problem at the next service interval. The consumer is not notified directly. If the problem is not corrected during the warranty period, the manufacturer will authorize the repair later—but only if the customer notices the problem or hears about the "secret warranty."

Manufacturers claim it is difficult to notify every owner, especially if the defect is discovered a few years after production. They call these repairs "goodwill service." In the past, this practice was kept quiet and only customers who complained loudly got the free service.

Today, manufacturers will usually issue a press release and assume consumers will hear about the defect through the media. However, new legislation at the state and federal level may soon do away with secret warranties and require direct notification of defects.

Consumers can also learn of secret warranties through service bulletins issued by the manufacturers, also available from the Na-

---

$

Dollar-saving Tip

Much warranty work is done after the warranty supposedly expires.

Hot Tip: Get a Pre-Expiration Warranty Inspection

Although some dealers advise their customers when their warranties are about to expire, many don't. You should be aware of the time or mileage that will signal the end of your warranty protection. Shortly before that point, arrange for a pre-expiration inspection. It might be worthwhile to have this performed by an independent mechanic.

Ask the mechanic to assess all of your important systems—include the coach, too, if you suspect problems. Be sure he inspects for signs of oil and fluid leaks—a good mechanic will know exactly what to check. Take a copy of his report to your dealer and have him tend to all needed repairs while you're still under warranty. This is especially important if you do not have a service contract (extended warranty).

tional Highway Traffic Safety Administration (see page 94). Ask for service bulletins related to your year, make, and model. The Center for Auto Safety also acts as a clearinghouse for secret-warranty information.

Goodwill Service

Free service is often performed for customers even when a secret warranty is not in effect. This is true goodwill service and often results from a friendly relationship with a dealer. Dealers have a lot of flexibility (manufacturers might call this "trickery") with expired warranties. If you feel a part has expired prematurely, though out of warranty, discuss it with the service manager (not the service writer). If you have no luck, contact the zone office of the manufacturer; they might authorize the repair to maintain your goodwill.

Problems Discovered before Warranty Expiration

Generally, if you have proof you complained about a problem before the warranty expired, you will have no problem getting the repair made after expiration.

You might run into excuses, though. Be persistent. For example, your claim may be denied if you had work done at an independent repair shop. If, however, it was impractical to get the vehicle to an authorized dealer, and the manufacturer is seeing a high incidence of similar problems, your persistence may pay off.

Another common excuse: You abused the vehicle. Certainly, if you did severely abuse the vehicle, you do not have a valid claim. But remember, implied warranties mean that a vehicle is supposed to perform as intended. It is supposed to provide safe, reliable transportation under normally encountered conditions. "Normal" includes reasonable abuse—occasional hard braking, climbing long grades, and operating in cold weather, for example. Again, stick to your guns and go through the proper channels.

Problems Not Complained about during Warranty Period

Don't assume you're not entitled to service out of warranty just because you didn't complain about it during the warranty period. For example, your transmission fails a few thousand miles after the warranty expires. You didn't notice the problem, but can the factory claim absolutely that it was not the result of a pre-existing condition? You should definitely pursue such a claim. This is another situation when you should explore service bulletins related to similar prob-

> G enerally, if you have proof you complained about a problem before the warranty expired, you will have no problem getting the repair made after expiration.

lems. These can give you extra leverage. Persistence has paid off for thousands of consumers who have challenged manufacturers in such out-of-warranty situations.

Persistence, indeed, is the key to any warranty dispute. With to-day's consumer-protection laws and public-relations sensitivity on the part of manufacturers, you have an excellent chance of getting satisfaction when you doggedly pursue your complaints.

CHAPTER NINE

Saving on Service

■ ■ ■ ■ ■ ■ ■ ■ ■ ■ ■

Recreational vehicles are complex machines. Although technology has greatly improved their working systems in recent years, there's still a lot to maintain. The cost of servicing these systems over the years can be significant. But these costs can be significantly reduced, too. Most RVers know the importance of preventive maintenance, but many still neglect it. And no matter how carefully an RV is maintained, things still go wrong. How do you maintain a proper preventive maintenance schedule and save substantially on those inevitable repairs as well?

PREVENTIVE MAINTENANCE: THE KEY

This most obvious of RV truisms bears repeating: *The key to saving money on service is preventive maintenance.* It bears repeating because so many RV owners neglect this basic rule. Some just run their rigs hard until they need repair. They either have excessive faith in technology or are so intimidated by it they challenge it, in effect telling their RV mechanisms, "work or else." The "else" is usually an expensive repair bill that could have been avoided.

Others understand the importance of preventive maintenance and inspections, but abdicate the responsibility. They count on mechanics to perform even simple preventive maintenance. They may avoid unnecessary major repairs, but they pay a lot for routine procedures they easily could have done themselves (see boxed copy, page 101).

HOW TO GET GOOD SERVICE

Sooner or later, even with the most scrupulous preventive maintenance, you will need service on your motorhome or tow vehicle.

In This Chapter:

- *How can I avoid big RV repair bills?*
- *What preventative maintenance should I perform?*
- *How do I find good RV service?*
- *What about service on the road?*
- *How can I save on the cost of routine service?*
- *How do I dispute a bad repair?*
- *What repair scams should I watch out for?*

Saving money is always the priority in this book, but saving money on service does not always save you money in the long run. That caveat underlies the following suggestions:

Do It Yourself

The do-it-yourselfer (DIY) obviously saves a great deal of money on labor costs. On the other hand, repair shops are full of rigs that DIYers unsuccessfully attempted to fix. It's risky to embark on a project that you're not confident you can accomplish successfully; you may end up wasting your time, paying for a tow to a repair shop, creating more damage than you were trying to fix, and possibly paying for the same parts twice.

On the other hand, you may be a better do-it-yourselfer than you think. Just learning to change your own oil can save you a tidy sum. The workings of an RV are only mysterious to those who have never attempted to understand them. Working with a competent friend and doing your "Required Reading" (see below) may demystify things and help you effect repairs you never dreamed of making.

Required Reading

It's unfortunate that most RV owners do not read their owners' manuals except when something goes wrong. Owners' manuals have specific preventive maintenance recommendations for every working system. You should adhere to the manufacturer's recommendations, not only because they make sense and will prolong the life of your rig, but also because they keep the warranty or service contract valid. Most owners' manuals also have maintenance logs you can fill in to remind yourself when certain repairs were made or fluids replaced and when the next service is needed.

Two other books that should be on your RV bookshelf are Bob Livingston's *RV Repair & Maintenance Manual* and Bill Estes's *The RV Handbook*. These two books combine to cover all the basics of preventive maintenance, troubleshooting, and operating procedures for RV coaches, chassis, and tow vehicles. These books can be ordered from:

Trailer Life Books
29901 Agoura Road
Agoura, California 91301
(800) 234-3450

The libraries and bookstores are full of basic vehicle-care guides that explain the working systems of engines and transmissions. Although not RV specific, they can be very useful in helping you to understand the workings of your vehicle.

Finally, every RVer should invest in the specific shop manual for every vehicle he or she owns. If your dealer does not stock the shop manual you need, it can be ordered from the manufacturer. It doesn't matter if you're not mechanically inclined. You may never perform any of the repairs outlined in the manual, but it's critical to your understanding of your motorhome or tow vehicle. You can learn some basic mechanical vocabulary. You can troubleshoot. You might find that some repairs are far easier than you thought, and you'll certainly be more prepared to deal with the service department should it become necessary.

Remember, you are the only person whose priority it is to save money on repairs to your rig. Having a shop manual is an excellent way to take on more responsibility for your investment.

Find a Good Shop

When your rig is under warranty, your choices of who will work on it may be limited to your dealer or another factory-authorized dealer. Not all RV dealerships offer full service, especially on motorhome engines and transmissions. Your RV dealer should be able to recommend a nearby automotive dealer who works on your brand chassis. But even under warranty, you want to get the best possible service. How to find it? How do you assess the quality of a shop you're considering?

First of all, talk to other RVers. Word of mouth is the best way to determine shops that will give you good service, as well as those that you should avoid.

Preventive Maintenance: A Basic Checklist

The following items should be checked on a regular basis. Remember that lubrication and fluid levels are the most important preventive maintenance items of which you should be aware. Consider them the lifeblood of your motorhome or tow vehicle: Change them according to the manufacturer's recommendations. It's ironic that these, the simplest of all preventive maintenance procedures, are also the procedures that can save you the most expensive repairs. This is not a complete list, but a reminder to consult your owner's manual and maintenance books and perform recommended maintenance regularly.

CHASSIS OR TOW VEHICLE
Check regularly and replace or service as necessary:

- Engine oil
- Transmission oil
- Transmission fluid
- Power-steering fluid
- Brake fluid
- Fuel filter
- Air cleaner
- Water-separator filter (diesel)
- Battery-water level
- Windshield-washer fluid
- Coolant level (recovery unit)
- Tire pressure
- Lug nuts
- Air-bag pressure
- Differential fluid (by qualified mechanic)
- Rubber parts (protect with silicone preservative)

COACH
Check regularly and service as recommended:

- Check for propane leaks
- Air-conditioner filters
- Furnace inlet and outlet for debris
- Refrigerator vent for debris
- Interior and exterior lights
- Mirror mounts
- Exterior—keep clean and waxed
- Remove oxidized paint
- Winter—hose down exterior and underside to remove road salts; park in shade or inside whenever possible
- Rubber parts—protect with silicone preservative

If any of these procedures are mysterious to you, you'll find other RVers happy to assist. Also, see page 100, "Required Reading."

Secondly, look for certification. For RV coach service, ask if the shop's mechanics have received manufacturer training, and ask to see the certificates.

For tow-vehicle or chassis service, look for a sign in the shop waiting room indicating that its mechanics are certified by the National Institute for Automotive Service Excellence. NIASE certifications are given only to experienced technicians who have completed accredited courses in at least one of several specialties and have passed an extensive exam in each category. Technicians who are certified in all eight areas wear the gold patch of a "Master Automobile Technician."

Look also for a sign of approval from the American Automobile Association (AAA). AAA inspects a prospective shop for a number of factors, many of which you can inspect for yourself at any shop:

- Courteous staff
- Clean, uncluttered, well-organized garage
- NIASE-certified mechanic in each area of service offered
- Qualified supervisor overseeing shop
- Sufficient legal liability insurance
- Employees receiving updated training in new systems and technology
- Service reception staff qualified to advise customers on repairs and service

Third, check with local consumer groups or the Better Business Bureau. They won't recommend a particular facility, but can advise if there are an unusual number of complaints against a shop.

Fourth, does the shop guarantee its repairs for a certain period of time? This should be stated on the repair order.

A Special Note about Oil Changing

Changing the oil may be one exception to following the manufacturer's recommendations for fluid changes. You should probably do it more often than the 7,500-mile interval between oil changes typically recommended. RV experts suggest changing engine oil at least every 5,000 miles—every 3,000 miles if you drive in dusty or mountainous conditions. The oil filter, of course, must be changed at the same time. Use only name-brand filters; some discount filters are inferior.

Additives in engine oil dissipate over time. For this reason, even if you're not driving much, you should change the oil every six months.

Don't assume that because the oil looks dirty on the dipstick that it needs changing. Oil gets dirty almost immediately upon circulating through the engine.

What kind of oil to use? Bill Estes's *The RV Handbook* goes into some detail on this subject. Basically, Estes recommends heavier multi-grade oils such as 20W-50 for hot-weather driving and lighter multi-grades such as 10W-30 for winter use. SAE 30 is excellent for summertime use, but should not be used if the air temperature will fall below 40 degrees. Be sure the oil is SG-rated by the Society of Automotive Engineers (SAE).

Finally, a good shop will also give detailed, written estimates and save any replaced parts for your inspection.

HOW TO GET THE RIGHT PRICE FOR SERVICE AND REPAIRS

It's difficult for the average consumer to know offhand a fair price for routine service or out-of-warranty repairs. But this doesn't mean you should accept without question whatever price the shop quotes. Following are some ways you can ascertain the fair price for the job. You should keep in mind that the right time to do this is *before* you agree to the repair.

Shop Around

Assuming you know or have been told what needs to be done, call a few shops to find out their prices for the repair. The variance shouldn't be great; shops consult manuals that give pricing guidelines and prescribe the hours of labor a job should require. If one shop quotes a price considerably lower than the others, double-check to be sure they understand exactly the repair you want, and be certain to get the estimate in writing before you agree to the repair.

For some repairs, a specialist might provide the best price and service: mufflers, brakes, and transmissions, for example. (This is assuming the repair is out of warranty.) If you have a motorhome, be sure the specialist can accommodate it.

While shopping around, watch for advertised specials on service such as wheel alignment and oil changes. These shops may not work on motorhomes, but will certainly work on tow vehicles. Many will match the advertised special price of a competing shop.

Ask for an Explanation of Service Estimate

Always ask the service writer to explain in detail why the job will cost what it will cost. Ask him to break the estimate down into parts and labor charges.

Negotiate the Price

You might be able to negotiate the price for some repairs, especially major ones. If you received a better estimate from another shop, mention that. Don't "play hardball" with the shop over the estimate. That will just backfire on you. You don't want a disgruntled mechanic to take a resentful wrench to your rig's precious viscera. Your approach might be something like, "Hmmm, $650, eh? Bill's Garage

---

For some repairs, a specialist might provide the best price and service: mufflers, brakes, and transmissions, for example.

Dollar-saving Tip

Don't hesitate to secure more than one estimate for a repair.

> Many rebuilt parts are as good as new and carry at least a one-year warranty.

said they'd do it for $550. I'd really rather give you the business. Do you think you can get that down a little?''

If you're satisfied that the shop is honest and does good repairs, it's silly to save a few bucks by going somewhere else. Seeking out bargain-basement service for high-tech repairs could cost you money in the long run.

Ask about Rebuilt Parts

On certain repairs, you can save money by having the shop use rebuilt parts. Many rebuilt parts are as good as new and carry at least a one-year warranty. However, if it's a job that requires major labor to get to the part, it's probably worth the extra money to use new parts. An exception would be a transmission, where an overhaul almost always utilizes rebuilt components. A transmission overhaul should come with a substantial warranty, though.

Consult Your Repair Manual

Look up the job in your shop manual. If it's a straightforward job that should take less than an hour, and the estimate calls for four hours' labor, you should question the price.

Consult Flat-Rate Manuals

Shops use manuals published by either manufacturers (for warranty repairs) or by firms such as Chilton to determine flat-rate charges for repairs. *Chilton's Flat-Rate Manual* (Chilton Book Co., Chilton Way, Radnor, Pennsylvania 19089) tells you the maximum you should be charged for any repair. The shop's price should not exceed this price—or if it does, ask for an explanation.

HOW TO DEAL WITH A MECHANIC OR SERVICE WRITER

One old hand in the RV service business put it this way: "The customer who comes into a shop with a good attitude never gets jerked around." No one should ever get "jerked around" by a service center, but this is the real world. Service managers readily admit they give the best service to customers they like. They're likely to perform little extras, road-test thoroughly, and get the job done promptly for a preferred customer. This doesn't mean you have to be an old customer—just one who treats the service writer like a human being, worthy of respect.

Before the Repair

Be Polite.   Of course you don't relish the fact that you're about to spend money for repairs. But if you talk tough, come on hard-headed, and imply that you're on the lookout for rip-offs, you're cooking your own goose. Be nice, friendly, engaging. You want the service writer to be concerned about you and your rig, to nurse it through the repair process, to tell the mechanic, "Hey, this baby belongs to some really nice folks who are leaving on vacation in a couple of days. Let's do right by them."

Be Specific.   Write down all the symptoms you've noticed—does the problem happen when the engine is cold or hot? At certain speeds? Only when braking or turning? The more specific you are, the quicker and more accurate the diagnosis will be. Hand over a copy of your written list to the service writer, and have him attach it to the repair order, but be sure you discuss each item.

Don't Tell the Mechanic What to Do.   The cocky customer who tells a mechanic exactly what to do often ends up paying for unnecessary repairs. You can tell him what you suspect, but let him check it out. The part you thought needed replacing might be working fine—but he'll replace it if you insist.

Know Your Vehicle's History.   It can be very helpful to the mechanic to know if your rig has had the same or similar problems in the past. Always save your service records so you can pass on this information to the mechanic.

Get an Estimate in Writing.   Although this is generally a standard procedure and required by law in most states, some shops are lax about estimates. Insist on one. If the repair is going to cost more than the estimate, you should be notified before the work proceeds. Be sure to give the mechanic a phone number where you can be reached.

Get a Guarantee in Writing.   A good shop stands behind its repairs, but you only have leverage if the guarantee is in writing.

After the Repair

Take a Test Drive.   If the repair is on your motorhome chassis or tow vehicle, be sure you test-drive it before you leave the area. If the problem doesn't seem to have been corrected, take it back immediately. At this point, it's still useless to "play hardball." Just be straightforward, explain that the problem seems to still exist, and ask the service writer to check it out. It could be much more difficult to dispute a repair if you wait several days.

The more specific you are, the quicker and more accurate the diagnosis will be.

If the repair is going to cost more than the estimate, you should be notified before the work proceeds.

If the problem continues after several attempts at repair, or if the shop refuses to cooperate, *then* it's time to complain. If your vehicle is out of warranty, see the section below or Chapter Eight, "Warranties, Disputes, and Lemon Laws."

Don't Expect Too Much. You can't expect most repairs to restore your engine, generator, refrigerator, or whatever to new working condition, especially if the repair was necessitated by abuse.

Go over the Bill. Examine all the charges on the bill and ask the service writer to explain them. You can refuse to pay for repairs or parts that weren't accounted for in the estimate.

Examine the Replaced Parts. Ask the mechanic to show you the worn parts that were replaced. Don't do this as if you're questioning his honesty; explain that you're interested in what went wrong and how you can prevent it in the future.

Disputing an Out-of-Warranty Repair

If your rig is repaired and breaks down again within a short period of time, your first step is, of course, to take it back to the shop. If you followed the preceding steps, you have the original bill and the written warranty on the repair. Ask the service manager to ride with you so you can point out the problem. The shop should stand behind its work, and there should be no problem.

But problems do arise. The number one rule to remember is *document everything. Keep all your bills, invoices, and letters.* Your strategy will be slightly different depending on whether you live near or are camped near the shop, or if you've broken down hundreds of miles away.

What to Do If:

The Shop Fails to Make Good on a Repair. If the shop fails to make good on a repair after you return, go up the chain of command to the service manager or the owner. Inform them of the problem and your intention to file a complaint against them if they refuse to resolve it.

You Still Receive No Satisfaction. If you still receive no satisfaction, contact the local Better Business Bureau. They can advise you on the local procedure for filing a complaint. The BBB may operate an arbitration panel. Or, they may refer you to another agency: either a local consumer-protection agency or the state board of automobile repair.

> The number one rule to remember is *document everything.*

The Shop Was Certified by AAA.   If the shop was certified by AAA, contact the local automobile club office and ask them how to file a complaint.

You Paid by Bank Charge Card.   If you paid for the repair with a bank charge card, put your complaint in writing to the issuing bank and ask them to reverse payment on the charge until the dispute is resolved.

The Repair Was Made at a Chain.   If the repair was made at a chain, such as Sears or AAMCO, take it to an affiliated shop if possible. That shop will honor the other's warranty.

You Receive No Satisfaction When Out of Town.   If you receive no satisfaction and you're out of town, you won't be able to file in small claims court, but by contacting the local Better Business Bureau, you can go through the local and/or state procedures for filing your dispute.

You've Exhausted All Your Alternatives.   If you've gone through ordinary channels with no success, contact the *Trailer Life* "RV Action Line," *MotorHome* magazine's "Hotline," or the "Action Line" column in *Highways,* the Good Sam Club magazine (addresses in Appendix, pages 249–250). Notify local consumer advocates, such as television reporters or newspaper columnists. Send copies of your correspondence to the shop. Outside intervention (and the threat of bad publicity) often helps.

> If all else fails, file suit in small claims court.

All Else Fails.   If all else fails, file suit in small claims court. The filing fee is usually small, and, because you act as your own attorney, you save attorney's fees. If you're out of town when the problem recurs, phone the shop and tell them what happened. Even if you're annoyed, infuriated, or homicidal, keep an even temper and just explain the situation. A reputable shop will tell you to get the problem repaired locally, send them all the paperwork, and they will reimburse you.

Money-saving Repair Miscellany

Take Advantage of Discounts

Good Sam Club members can obtain a 10-percent discount on service and accessories at service centers that display the "Welcome Good Sam" sign indicating commercial membership in the Good Sam Club. You must pay cash and present your membership card in advance.

> If you develop a good relationship with a mechanic, ask him if he does work after hours.

Take Advantage of Lifetime Guarantees

Some items or services at certain shops come with a lifetime guarantee. Some examples are wheel alignments, batteries, mufflers, and shock absorbers.

Find a "Sider"

If you develop a good relationship with a mechanic, ask him if he does work after hours. Many do. He might be willing to work on your rig in the evening or on weekends and will charge you somewhat less for labor.

Don't Pay for Unnecessary "Tuneups"

Many RVers still operate under the old guidelines of annual or even more frequent engine tuneups. Some items that used to be replaced in a tuneup, such as breaker points and condensers, do not exist in modern engines—those made in the 1980s or later. Computers make engine-timing adjustments unnecessary, and many engines do not have carburetors to overhaul.

Engines today require a "maintenance tuneup" only about every 30,000 miles; this involves changing the spark plugs and running checks of the ignition system; check your owner's manual.

How to Avoid Repair Scams

When you deal with reputable, accredited shops, the chances of their ripping you off are extremely remote. However, should you find yourself in need of repair away from home and you can't get to a recommended shop, you must be on guard against repair scams:

■ Be wary of "bonus" diagnoses that are unrelated to the problem. If your radiator is boiling over and the mechanic also notices you need a front-end alignment, be concerned. Tell him to pay attention to the radiator, you'll worry about the alignment later.

■ Be wary of the determined pessimist who insists it is "too dangerous" for you to continue without buying a certain part or repair, especially when you've stopped just to fill your gas tank.

■ Keep an eye on a service station attendant checking your rig. Some common ripoff practices include puncturing a tire while checking tire pressure; dropping a seltzer tablet into a battery cell to cause it to fizz over; squirting oil on a shock absorber and claiming a leaky shock; and "short-dipping" a dipstick to indicate you need a quart of oil.

■ Beware of advertised specials that are a come-on. An amazingly low price for a wheel alignment, for example, may be a ruse to get you to buy shock absorbers or other items you may not need.

■ Pay for repairs at a service station with an oil-company credit card. If a dispute arises over cost, the company might reverse an overcharge.

■ Don't be intimidated into expensive repairs. Even in an urgent situation, it can pay to phone around for a better price if you suspect an inflated charge.

If your rig is not running properly, don't just automatically assume it needs a tuneup. You could be wasting your money. It's better to ask for an engine diagnosis on a sophisticated engine analyzer, which will pinpoint the difficulty.

Don't Get an Unnecessary Wheel Alignment

Many drivers assume that any vibration or shimmy in the steering wheel at speeds over 40 MPH requires a wheel alignment. Most of these problems can be corrected by wheel and/or tire balancing. Warning signs for wheel alignment are a drifting or pulling to one side and uneven tire wear.

Don't Use Unneeded Additives

SG-rated oils come with all the additives they need. Automotive engineers at the motor companies consistently maintain that oil additives serve no useful purpose. An engine on its last legs, though, might benefit from an oil thickener.

The same principles apply to gasoline. Good gasoline already has such additives as detergents, corrosion preventives, and anti-icing compounds. Use the proper octane gas according to the manufacturer's recommendation. Extra additives are almost always a waste of money. There are two exceptions: Use valve-protecting gasoline additives when it's necessary to use unleaded in an engine designed for leaded fuel. Such additives can prolong the life of an engine under these circumstances. The second exception applies to travel in Mexico, where high-octane gasoline is not always available. Low-octane gas can be supplemented with an octane booster.

Don't Idle a Diesel Engine for Long Periods

Although legend has it that it's wise to keep a diesel idling when you've left it for only a half-hour, it's a waste of fuel and detrimental to the life of the engine to do so.

Drive Economically

You can stretch your gasoline dollars by using a manifold vacuum gauge and tachometer to drive as economically as possible. In his book, Bill Estes describes the process in detail.* In brief, don't drive with a lead foot and try to develop a good feel for downshifting so you neither "lug" nor rev your engine excessively.

*Estes, *The RV Handbook* (Agoura, California: Trailer Life Books, 1990), pp. 58–66.

Some items that used to be replaced in a tuneup, such as breaker points and condensers, do not exist in modern engines.

Dollar-saving Tip

Watch for repair discount coupons in the local papers.

Don't Pay for Emissions-Control Work That's under Warranty

Regardless of the warranty on your vehicle, federal law requires manufacturers to replace all defective emissions-related equipment up to five years or 50,000 miles, whichever comes first. This includes catalytic converters, electronic engine controls, fuel injectors, carburetors, PC valves, ignition wires, distributors, and oxygen sensors—in other words, a lot of the components that can go wrong on a late-model vehicle. This work must be performed at an authorized dealership.

If you live in a state that requires exhaust-emissions testing, another federally mandated warranty covers any part or system that causes your car to fail such a test within two years or 24,000 miles.

FINDING EMERGENCY SERVICE

Virtually all of the preceding strategies apply, whether you're at home or on the road. However, if you're away from home and you urgently need a repair, it may not be as easy to locate a service center—especially one that works on RVs.

If you break down on the road and have emergency breakdown insurance such as Good Sam's ERS, AAA, or Road America RV Assist, you can call a toll-free number and the dispatcher will send assistance and/or a tow truck.

If you need a repair but it's not a roadside emergency, Good Sam ERS members can call their toll-free number and be referred to the nearest authorized service center.

If you're parked in a campground, ask the campground attendant for a referral. Campgrounds often have good relationships with nearby service centers.

Otherwise, consult the *Trailer Life Campground & RV Services Directory*. This directory lists and rates service centers throughout North America. The ratings don't necessarily reflect the quality of repairs, but rather the completeness and accessibility of the facility. The directory will also indicate which service centers offer a 10-percent discount to Good Sam Club members.

Whether you're on the road or in your home town, approaching service from an informed viewpoint—even if you have no mechanical skills—is certain to save you money.

$

Dollar-saving Tip

Emissions-control systems are warranted for 50,000 miles.

CHAPTER TEN

Saving on Fuel and Operating Expenses

■ ■ ■ ■ ■ ■ ■ ■ ■ ■

Most RVers are very sensitive to the cost of getting from here to there. They're reminded of that cost every time they pull into a gas station. So, quite logically, most RVers pay attention to the price of gas. If the same fuel is $1.10 a gallon on one side of the street and $1.14 on the other, they will cross the street for the cheaper gas. However, many of the same RVers burn quite a bit more of that precious fuel than they need to. Many even know a number of ways to save fuel, to increase their mileage, but fail to put their knowledge into practice. For many, the information in this chapter is common knowledge. Perhaps it will serve to remind you what you already know, and will prompt you to take action; other information may be new to you. No matter what, adopting the practices in this chapter, in combination with the routine preventive maintenance discussed on page 101, is certain to save you a considerable amount of money on your RV operating expenses.

In This Chapter:

- *What can I do to save on day-to-day operating costs?*
- *How can I increase my gas mileage?*
- *What driving techniques can I practice to save on fuel?*
- *How can a vacuum gauge and tachometer help save fuel?*
- *Do those miracle mileage devices really work?*

TWENTY-FIVE WAYS TO SAVE GAS AND REDUCE OPERATING EXPENSES

The following hints list money-saving strategies at the gas pump and on the road:

1. *Pay cash for gas.* Many brands of gasoline discounts the price about four cents a gallon for cash, for about a 3-percent savings. A few brands allow you to use a bank ATM card or other debit card for the cash price.

No matter what your opinion of the prevailing 55 MPH speed limit, it does save you gasoline.

Dollar-saving Tip

Cut your engine if a delay will otherwise force you to idle for more than a minute.

2. *Avoid bargain-basement gas.* The very cheapest gas may not save you money in the long run. It may lack the additives that good-quality gasoline contains. Poor-quality gas can contribute to decreased mileage, fuel-system deposit buildup, and premature engine wear.

3. *Buy the right octane.* Buy gasoline with the octane rating recommended in your owner's manual. If the octane rating is too low, it can contribute to preignition, or ping, which can wear pistons, rings, and valves prematurely. But don't assume that higher-than-recommended octane is better; in fact, unless you're experiencing ping, it's a waste of money.

4. *Keep a full tank.* Because RVers often spend more time parked than driving, condensation in the fuel tank can cause water buildup. Water can be damaging to the system's metallic parts, and in winter can cause freeze-up of fuel lines. Don't, however, "top-off" your tank by filling it to the brim. Some spillage inevitably results—if not while you're filling up, perhaps later when your fuel expands as its temperature rises.

5. *Obey the speed limits.* No matter what your opinion of the prevailing 55 MPH speed limit, it does save you gasoline. Although ambient conditions such as wind and terrain also affect mileage, driving at 55 MPH rather than at 60 MPH can reduce your fuel consumption by 8 to 9 percent. It's like reducing the cost of gas at least a dime a gallon.

6. *Use cruise control.* Use cruise control in flat terrain, where it can keep a steadier throttle than you can.

7. *Don't use cruise control on grades.* Don't use cruise control in mountainous conditions. Cruise control can't see a grade up ahead; it only senses the grade when you get to it, so it will apply heavy throttle to maintain the set speed. A smart driver will anticipate the grade, switch off the cruise control, pick up a little momentum before, and be willing to slow down a little while ascending.

8. *Pass wisely.* If you have to floor the accelerator to overtake a vehicle, you can offset 100 miles worth of feather-touch driving. If you can't pass by keeping a steady pace, don't pass.

9. *Don't idle excessively.* Whether you have diesel or a gas engine, idling for long periods wastes fuel—a minute of idling uses more fuel than restarting. In a diesel, contrary to conventional wisdom, idling contributes to accelerated engine wear. When starting an engine cold, about twenty seconds of fast-idle (but don't rev) should be sufficient to circulate oil. In fact, it's *better* for your engine to limit warm-up to this brief period.

10. *Minimize use of air conditioning.* You can probably feel the horsepower drop that results when you switch on the air conditioner. This is robbing your gas mileage; use natural ventilation to keep cool whenever possible.

11. *Have your windows tinted.* Tinting windows helps to keep your interior cool. It's another way to minimize use of air conditioning.

12. *Check tire inflation regularly.* Underinflated tires not only wear faster, they can cost you several miles per gallon. Tires that are low can cut fuel economy. Maintain the proper tire pressure for your tires and load, and check it regularly.

13. *Rotate tires regularly.* Rotate tires every 7,000 miles, or sooner if you notice abnormal wear.

14. *Reduce the weight you carry.* Just because you have a certain payload doesn't mean you have to carry it. Although a few pounds matters little, substantial weight reduction saves fuel. Incidentally, extra weight at constant speed makes very little difference. It's during acceleration or climbing hills that extra weight affects your mileage, which leads to another obvious fuel-saving practice.

15. *Avoid stop-and-go driving.* City driving is, on the average, 17 percent less efficient than steady highway cruising; short trips, especially, consume extra fuel because the engine has not had time to reach normal operating temperature. This is the rationale for the next few suggestions.

16. *Get a tow-along.* Motorhomers who tow a small car can save on operating expenses if they do a lot of driving once parked in a campground. Don't expect towing a "dinghy" to save you a lot of money, though, unless you own one already. (If you're in the market for a new tow-along, see page 39 for some money-saving tips.) The cost of purchase, maintenance, and insurance for a second vehicle can offset what it saves you in fuel expenses. For most RVers, towing a dinghy is more for convenience than for money saving. If saving money is your primary concern, either or both of the next two suggestions are more practical.

17. *Get a bicycle or moped.* A bicycle, for a few hundred dollars, provides the most inexpensive (and healthful) way to run those little errands for which you might be considering a tow-along, which is at least twenty times the expense. A bike shop can get you outfitted with racks and panniers (saddlebags) for carrying items. If you're nervous about balance, you can even buy a three-wheel utility bike (Camping World sells a folding model) with a basket.

    If you're not up to pedaling a bike, consider a moped or scooter for those errands and sightseeing. Initial cost is at least three times that of a bicycle, but less than a small car. The cost of operation is very small. However, transporting mopeds requires a special carrier that can cost several hundred dollars.

18. *Plan your trip wisely.* You can save a lot of money by planning your trips with operating expenses in mind. For example, you

---

City driving is, on the average, 17 percent less efficient than steady highway cruising.

Dollar-saving Tip

Bikes and mopeds are inexpensive alternatives to towing a small car.

can eliminate the need for any kind of tow-along by selecting a vacation destination that has everything you want and need in one place: a lakeside resort, for example, with a store and restaurant beside a boat dock. You might choose to avoid mountainous routes that cost you in gas mileage. Or, obviously, shorter trips and staying longer in one place can save you operating expenses. Trip-planning resources are covered in Chapter Fourteen.

19. *Choose the right vehicle.* An under- or over-powered tow vehicle for the weight of your trailer may be costing you more than you need to spend in operating expenses. Read the chapter "How to Choose a Tow Vehicle," beginning on page 169, in Bill Estes's *The RV Handbook* for a detailed discussion of this subject.

Mileage Miracles

Every year sees the introduction of some new miracle products touted as great gas savers. The pitch for many of them is familiar: it's always some product that a backyard engineer claims the Detroit auto makers are quashing because they're in cahoots with the oil companies. He claims to have sent his miracle product to all the major manufacturers, none of whom responded. An obvious conspiracy, he concludes.

Even products that obtain patents seldom meet their advertising claims. Many products require altering an engine illegally. If you do so in a state that requires inspections, you'll end up paying more in a fine than you might have saved in gas costs.

Many consumers sincerely tout the effectiveness of a gas-saving product, but the truth is, the ordinary consumer does not have the ability or the equipment to test for precise changes in gas mileage. Too many variables affect fuel consumption, such as traffic, road and weather conditions, and the condition of the vehicle.

If a product claims to have been approved by the federal government, ask to see the test results. The federal government does not "approve" products, but the Environmental Protection Agency does evaluate products that claim to improve mileage. You can contact the EPA directly for test results:

Even those test results will not indicate any long-term effect on the engine. Air-bleed devices, for example, were once all the rage among miracle-seekers, but these devices, by leaving out the air-fuel mixture, could cause an engine to ping, misfire, and wear prematurely.

Exhaust headers are one product that many RV owners swear by. Again, be careful that modifications to your exhaust system do not affect your emissions-control equipment. Even when properly installed, steel tubing exhaust headers do not generally affect the fuel economy of most V-8 engines. They may produce a slight increase in mileage, but not enough to offset their expense. They do, however, boost engine performance, and should be considered more of a performance product than a mileage saver.

If you bought any product touted as a gas saver and are not satisfied, contact the manufacturer for a refund, even if the guarantee period has expired. You should also contact your local or state consumer-protection agency.

The best ways to experience "mileage miracles" are to be scrupulous about performing preventive and routine maintenance and to follow the steps in this chapter.

Environmental Protection Agency
Retrofit Device Evaluation Program
2526 Plymouth Road
Ann Arbor, Michigan 48105

20. *Get a wind deflector.* More than half your vehicle's horse-power goes into overcoming aerodynamic drag. Newer RVs are being built far more aerodynamically than in the past. If you have an older, boxy trailer, consider a wind deflector. Tests show that wind deflectors do increase gas mileage, although only slightly, and not for everyone. Be sure to buy a model that folds flat so that it does not increase drag when your trailer is unhitched.

21. *Use a tachometer and vacuum gauge.* Getting the most from every gallon of gasoline requires a deft touch on the throttle and a keen sense of gear shifting. The best way to develop these techniques is by having a tachometer and vacuum gauge installed. Ask your dealer to look up the engine power curve of your engine. Use the tachometer to time your down-shifts so that you remain between torque and horsepower peaks, shown on the engine power curve.

    The vacuum gauge, on both fuel-injected and carbureted engines, provides a constant visual reminder of throttle pressure. On carbureted engines there's another benefit: By maintaining a reading above six inches of manifold vacuum, you can keep the carburetor from switching from its cruise fuel-metering system to is power-enrichment system, for a difference in fuel-flow as high as 24 percent.

22. *Inspect your air filter every 10,000 miles.* Replace as necessary. (Air filters are inexpensive and easy to replace.) A dirty one can dramatically affect your mileage.

23. *Keep your engine cool.* Changing your radiator coolant every two years is a basic maintenance "must," as mentioned on page 101. Use a 50-50 mixture of antifreeze and distilled water (not tap water, which is laden with minerals). You might also consider adding an engine-coolant temperature gauge calibrated in degrees Fahrenheit. This is preferable to an "idiot light" or a regular gauge that does not tell you the exact temperature of the coolant.

24. *Have your brakes checked regularly.* This aspect of preventive maintenance may not seem related to mileage, but some improperly adjusted brakes can cause drag on your wheels.

25. *Keep records.* Merely "eyeballing" your mileage is not enough. You should keep accurate records, which can tell you if your mileage is falling off. If so, it's time to investigate the cause.

Dollar-saving Tip

If you're shopping for a new RV, look for gas-saving aerodynamics.

CHAPTER ELEVEN

Rentals

■ ■ ■ ■ ■ ■ ■ ■ ■ ■ ■

The burgeoning availability of recreational vehicle rentals in recent years benefits both RV neophytes and seasoned veterans alike. Newcomers can easily rent an RV to sample the lifestyle before making a purchase commitment. If you already own one, you know well the joys of an RV vacation. You might be looking for a new RV adventure. Renting one in a far corner of the continent or the world might be the ticket. If you live on the East Coast, for example, and have always dreamed of traveling in Alaska, flying directly to Alaska and renting a motorhome saves you the time of a very long cross-continent drive—and time, for many, is money.

In This Chapter:

- *How can I save on RV rentals?*
- *When does it make sense to rent when I already own an RV?*
- *How do I find and evaluate a rental agency?*
- *What about insuring the rental?*

RV RENTAL SOURCES

Two major companies, Cruise America and Go Vacations, several smaller ones, some car-rental firms, and dozens of RV dealers comprise the North American network of RV rental agencies. Rental agencies are listed in the Yellow Pages under "Recreational Vehicles: Renting and Leasing."

The most complete listing of RV rentals in North America is available for $5 from an affiliate of the RV Dealers Association, the RV Rental Association:

RVRA
3251 Old Lee Highway, Suite 500
Fairfax, Virginia 22030
(703) 591-7130

RVRA does not sanction the quality or prices of the RVs its members rent.

The American Automobile Association (AAA) publishes state and regional lists of RV rentals. Members can pick up such a list at any AAA office.

For rentals abroad, contact your travel agent or Good SamTours at (800) 933-9779.

HOW TO SELECT AN RV-RENTAL AGENCY

The quality and service of RV-rental agencies can vary considerably. Although some small dealers may offer perfectly fine RVs for rent, there are several advantages to dealing with larger companies for whom rentals is a major business and not a sideline.

Large RV rental agencies have all the computerized sophistication of car-rental agencies. They know exactly the availability of their units. They have an efficient reservation system. The nationwide companies even offer one-way rentals, and can often quickly replace a broken-down unit.

Not all RVRA members are large nationwide companies, but members do have a tacit agreement to help customers of fellow members get back on the road after a breakdown. In fact, this is generally true of all RV dealers. They will almost always go out of their way to help a vacationer resume his or her trip as quickly as possible.

No matter what the size or affiliation of the agency, here are some criteria by which you can compare RV-rental outlets.

Reputation of the Agency. If the agency you rent from is one of the national agencies or a respected local dealer, you can be reasonably sure you'll receive professional treatment and that the agency will stand behind its units and services. If in doubt, check with the local Better Business Bureau for any complaints against the agency.

Price. Although price should not be your sole determining factor in selecting an RV rental, it's certainly important. If you are comparing prices, be sure you are comparing apples to apples, that is, like units of similar features and age. Also, be sure to clarify all charges: deposits, mileage rate, the number of free miles, cleaning fees, and so forth.

Age and Quality of Units. Rental RVs see a lot of hard use. You should avoid renting one that is more than three years old or with more than 50,000 miles. If you have a chance to inspect the RVs in advance, do so. Some wear is to be expected, but they should be scrupulously clean.

National Brands. Renting a respected, national brand of RV offers two advantages: a quality coach and availability of authorized repair outlets. Although good rental agencies maintain their units care-

> [Rental agencies] will almost always go out of their way to help a vacationer resume his or her trip as quickly as possible.

fully—they certainly don't want to deal with breakdowns any more than you do—rentals do break down. It will be more convenient to find a service center for a well-known national brand.

Size of the Fleet. If the rental firm has a large fleet, you minimize the risk of disappointment. Smaller firms may not be able to offer you the size, floorplan, or even the dates you want.

Documentation. The rental firm should provide a complete contract that spells out all the terms of the rental in understandable language. Don't sign the contract until you understand all the terms. The terminology, especially regarding insurance, can be confusing. Read the entire contract and be sure to ask for clarification of any term that is not perfectly clear.

Trip-Protection Policy. If something happens to your rental coach on the road through no fault of your own, the rental agency should provide food, lodging, and a rental car while your rig is being repaired. There may or may not be a charge for this policy, so the charge, if any, should be among the cost factors to consider when comparing rental firms. If the firm does not offer such a policy, you can ask that the appropriate clause be added to the contract.

Breakdown and Emergency Consultation. The better agencies have a twenty-four-hour number, toll-free in some cases, that you can call in case of a breakdown or malfunction of the coach. This is especially valuable for first-timers, who might become confused about the operation of some RV system. It can be quite disconcerting to be unable to find the sewer hose when the holding-tank gauges read "full"!

Checkout Procedure. The agency should have a standard checkout procedure that includes a thorough explanation of the RV's working systems. Someone should take time—at least a half-hour—and go over a checklist of items and make sure you understand each one. Be sure also that the agency notes any pre-existing damage to the rig, so you will not be held responsible for it when you return.

On-board Manuals. The rental firm should provide a thorough user's manual(s) that you can consult to refresh your memory on the workings of the RV's systems.

Generator Charges. Charges for use of the generator are not generally included in the rental fee. Be sure you understand the charges.

Cleaning. Cleaning is often included in the price of the rental, but some firms charge extra. In any event, you should not be responsible for cleaning the rig before returning it. You will, of course, be responsible for damage—torn upholstery, major stains, and so forth.

Don't sign the [rental] contract until you understand all the terms.

Livability Package. If you arrive from out of town, it can be inconvenient and expensive to outfit a rental with all the items you'll need for a vacation trip: bedding, towels, dishes, kitchen utensils, soap, toilet paper, paper towels, matches, etc. The firm should provide a livability package at a reasonable cost, typically, $35 per person.

Affiliations and Discount Arrangements. Some rental agencies are affiliated with campground chains and offer discounts on camping. Some provide coupons for admission or discounts on tourist-attraction tickets. Be sure to ask about these.

Airport Pickup. If you're flying in from out of town, many rental agencies provide free airport pickup.

How to Save Money on RV Rentals

Follow these hints to save money on renting RVs:

Compare Prices. Check with more than one dealer or rental firm; their prices may vary, although be wary of too low a price. Either the firm is not revealing all the costs, or you may be renting a rig of dubious quality.

Rent from a Friend. If you know someone who owns an RV but doesn't use it a lot, propose renting it at a fair price. That price should be well below the going rate at agencies because your friend does not have the overhead costs of running a business. Be sure to check with your insurance company, and your friends with theirs, regarding insurance coverage. You should also draw up a simple contract specifying that you accept responsibility for any damage, and you will return the rig in a clean state. Be sure to clarify who is responsible in event of a breakdown.

Rent from a Private Party. Newspapers often carry ads for RV rentals from private parties. If the price is right, such an arrangement is worth considering, but be sure you take all the steps mentioned in the paragraph above. Plus, in this case, the other party should assume responsibility for a breakdown and that should be stipulated in your contract. If the other party declines, you can ask to have the rig checked out mechanically, but this can be expensive. The many risks of a private-party arrangement point to the advantages of dealing with a professional RV-rental firm.

Rent in the Off-Season. Most firms offer substantial discounts for off-season rentals. In most areas outside the Sun Belt, the off-season is September 15 to May 15, excluding major holidays.

Avoid Drop-off Charges. If you rent from a large firm that allows one-way rental, you will be charged a hefty fee for that privilege—up to $500. Arrange to return to your point of origin to save that fee.

Plan Your Trip Wisely. Wise planning can save you excess mileage fees. Plan your trip so you stay within mileage limits, and pick up your RV at the nearest convenient rental firm to your destination.

Rent Only What You Need. The price for a van conversion or truck camper may be considerably less than for a motorhome or mini motorhome. If you have a family, remember that bigger is not necessarily better. A mini motorhome with a cabover bed may not only save you money but be more convenient. Some Class A motorhomes sleep only two. The least expensive option is to rent a travel trailer, although they are not as widely available as motorhomes. The dealers who do rent them will install a hitch for a minimal charge.

Ask about Discounts. Cruise America, for example, offers a 10-percent discount to AAA members. Be sure to ask about all available discounts.

Travel in Mexico. Most rental firms flatly prohibit travel in Mexico. Some will permit it at additional cost. You will, of course, have to purchase Mexican insurance (see page 86).

Deposits

Figure on putting down substantial deposits for a motorhome rental. Typical deposits include a $200 to $250 reservation deposit, which is applied toward the rental cost, and a $500 security deposit, which is refunded when you return the rig in good condition. Some firms charge a fuel deposit, in case you fail to gas up the rig before returning it.

Insurance on Your Rental

The best way to be certain you are adequately insured at a reasonable price when you rent an RV is to check with your own insurance agent before you rent. It's possible that your policy fully covers you when you rent an RV. If you're not covered, your most reasonable alternative is to ask that a binder be added to your policy for the period you will be renting. The cost is very reasonable, and you'll have the full coverage of your own policy, both liability and collision, while you travel.

Dollar-saving Tip

Insurance is a profit center for rental agencies, and they may push it. Don't pay for coverage you don't need.

Negotiate. Except at the peak of the travel season, you can usually negotiate with the rental firm for the best possible rate. The firm will not advertise this policy, of course, but they do want to rent their idle units during slow times. The best way to negotiate a low rate is to take a short trip during the off-season. For example, if you are just going from Miami to the Florida Keys, or Los Angeles to Palm Springs, and intend to stay parked most of the time, you will not be putting many miles on the rig. You should be able to negotiate a good daily rate in such a case.

Be Flexible. Demand considerations can affect the price a rental firm will offer you. For example, if small motorhomes are in demand, you might actually be able to rent a larger one at a lower price. Or, if you can wait a week or so when demand is high or go to another outlet, the firm may be able to offer you a better rate.

Fill the Gas Tank before Return. The rental firm will undoubtedly require you to fill the gas tank, usually to the three-quarter mark, or you will be charged a very high price per gallon for the firm to fill it up. You will also be expected to dump the holding tanks yourself before you return, or you'll be charged a fee for that.

Abide by Maintenance Requirements. If you are on the road for a long period of time, you will be responsible, at minimum, for having the oil and oil filter changed—probably at 3,000 miles. Be sure to do this, or you may be assessed a fee for failure to do so and be liable for any engine damage.

Be Attentive during Check-in. It is during check-in that the firm determines whether or not you get all your deposit money back. It's wise to walk through the rig with the person checking it in to make sure you're not assessed for any damage that's not your doing.

Make sure your own
vehicle or health
insurance is adequate
to protect you should
you be injured.

Assuming you have your own insurance, you should not need to accept the insurance the rental firm will offer you, which they call "loss-damage waiver" or "collision-damage waiver." This insurance effectively gives you zero-deductible or low-deductible coverage should you have any collision damage. The cost for this coverage can be as much as $12 to $15 a day—a waste of money if you're already covered.

If you have neglected to investigate your own insurance coverage, ask what insurance is included in the price of the rental. Chances are, some liability and a high collision deductible is included. If you're satisfied with the liability coverage and you're willing to risk the high deductible (usually $2,500), you needn't purchase the collision-damage waiver. If you're an inexperienced RV driver, it might be worth it to you to lower that deductible.

Most rental-firm liability policies do not cover you or your passengers. Again, make sure your own vehicle or health insurance is adequate to protect you should you be injured. If not, such protection is usually available from the rental firm at an extra cost.

Don't be pressured into buying insurance you may not need. Collision-damage waivers bring in a lot of money to rental firms, and many push it on their customers. If you're in doubt, take the time to call your insurance agent for advice—even if you're in the RV-rental office about to leave on vacation.

CHAPTER TWELVE

Saving on Camping Fees

■ ■ ■ ■ ■ ■ ■ ■ ■ ■ ■ ■

RVing at its most luxurious can be an expensive proposition. In some campgrounds, the rates may seem like motel rates—albeit the motel rates of a few years ago. But those rates are generally for parks with an array of amenities, such as recreation halls, miniature golf, saunas, tennis courts, and waterfront sites. RVing has become like any mode of travel: Those who wish to can go first class. It's always possible to spend a lot of money on a night's camping, but it's not necessary in most instances.

Strategies for saving money on overnight camping fall into three groups: Staying in safe, clean, commercial campgrounds but avoiding high fees; finding less expensive alternative campgrounds, usually public parks; and, finally, camping or parking for free.

In This Chapter:

- *How can I save on overnight camping fees?*
- *Where do I find inexpensive campgrounds?*
- *Free campgrounds?*
- *What discounts are available?*
- *How do I set up my rig for "boondocks camping?"*

HOW TO SAVE ON CAMPING FEES

There are many ways to save on camping fees. They include the following suggestions:

Plan Your Overnight Stays. Planning your overnight stays in advance may seem obvious advice, but it's advice many of us consistently ignore. When you plan your overnight stops, you are also planning to save money. When you drive until you are bleary-eyed and saddlesore, you most likely will stop at the first available campground, which is seldom the cheapest.

Shop for Rates. A good campground directory is indispensable for anyone looking to save money on camping fees and allows a comparison of rates among parks under consideration. Directories list the latest available rates at the time of printing, so you can sometimes expect to pay slightly more than the figures listed. Read the descriptions carefully so you know whether there will be extra charges for showers, running an air conditioner, or television-cable hookup, for instance.

Dispense with Frills. If you can do without some of the "extras" that many campgrounds offer, don't spend unnecessary money on them. If you can camp self-contained, you might not be charged for hookups, even when the site offers them. If a park charges for options such as cable TV, don't opt for them unless you really plan on using them. If you can choose a campground that offers fewer or no options, do so. This strategy goes hand in hand with the following suggestion.

Alternate between No-Frills Camping and Full-Facility Parks. Alternating between no-frills camping and full-facility parks is a common practice among many seasoned RVers. They recognize they don't need full hookups and other amenities every night. They find a no-frills site one night and one with full facilities the next. At the full-facility site they can fill water tanks and dump holding tanks in preparation for the next night's self-contained camping.

Take Advantage of Discounts. Good Sam Club members can get a 10-percent discount at Good SamParks, which are listed in the *Trailer Life Campground & RV Services Directory*. You must pay cash to take advantage of the discount. KOA offers a Value Card, currently $6 for two years, which allows a 10-percent discount in KOA campgrounds. Discounts for federal parks are discussed on page 126.

Take Advantage of Long-Term Rates. If you elect to stay in one place for an entire vacation or season, you can save considerably. Long-term rates are not listed in directories, so do some checking to find the best long-stay deals. Typical long-term discounts are 10 percent for a week or two, 20 percent for a month, and up to 50 percent for a complete season.

Stop Early in the Day. If you're "winging it," that is, traveling without a firm itinerary or reservations, it's wise to stop by mid-afternoon. That way you're less likely to be turned away from the campground of your choice, which can mean a driving detour.

Get off the Interstates. Campgrounds conveniently located near interstate highways are generally more expensive than those on secondary roads. It may be worth a bit of a drive to get to a less expensive campground, especially if you plan to stay more than one night.

Alternating between no-frills camping and full-facility parks is a common practice among many seasoned RVers.

Dollar-saving Tip

Save on propane purchases with a Good Sam discount.

Work in a Campground. Many campgrounds hire RVers as seasonal help (see page 216). This usually earns you a free place to park for as long as you're working. You might even arrange a short-term, impromptu situation if you have certain skills. For example, offer to make a repair or provide some entertainment in the recreation hall in exchange for free camping.

Camp during the Off-Season. Many campgrounds offer less expensive rates during their off-season. This doesn't necessarily mean the dead of winter. "Shoulder seasons" such as spring and fall can still be quite pleasant and the rates somewhat lower than during the summer.

Negotiate. This advice may surprise you, but many campgrounds don't offer you their best rate right off the bat. You can often strike a modest compromise, especially when you're arriving fairly late or you want to camp self-contained. Perhaps you might ask, "Is that the best rate you have? I don't need a scenic site, and I don't need hookups. Do you have an overflow area or a barebones site?" You may get the same site for a bit less, or you might get the overflow area. The off-season is also a good time to negotiate, even if the park doesn't offer off-season rates. Be judicious when it comes to negotiating a campsite fee. Running a campground is a tough way to make a living. Still, it's only sensible to ask if a less-desirable site or a lower rate is available.

Camp in the Shade. Because most campgrounds are charging extra for running an air conditioner, a site shaded by trees may preclude the need for cooling. Besides, it's a lot more pleasant to awaken parked beneath an awning of green than parked on a bare, concrete pad.

Purchase a Resort Campground Membership. Overnight fees for resort campground members are generally a dollar or two. An analysis of the economics of membership camping is contained in Chapter Thirteen, page 134.

> Many campgrounds don't offer you their best rate right off the bat.

INEXPENSIVE CAMPGROUNDS

A rule of thumb known to virtually everyone who has camped out is that public parks are generally less expensive than private parks. There are reasons this is so. Public parks are subsidized by tax money, and seldom do they provide facilities as complete as those in private campgrounds. Fees for those that do provide more complete facilities, such as hookups and showers, come close to those of private parks.

Campers who favor public campgrounds generally favor natural attractions over man-made facilities. There may not be a video-game arcade or square dancing with a live caller, but there might be a nature walk or campfire program. There may not be hot showers, but there may be a lake to swim in. There may not be cable TV hookups, but there may be pristine forests, a trout stream nearby, pathways to explore, sunsets to savor, birds to watch—all for less money than the private parks charge.

The number of public agencies that operate campgrounds is surprising. Not too surprising is the fact that the National Forest Service maintains more campsites than any other agency. But guess who is number two? The U.S. Army Corps of Engineers, which provides camping at thousands of recreation areas beside its hundreds of water projects, claims the title. Other agencies, public and private, that operate inexpensive campgrounds include national parks, national wildlife refuges, state parks, county parks, state forests, the Bureau of Land Management, the Tennessee Valley Authority, private lumber companies, Indian reservations, utility companies . . . the list goes on and on.

Dollar-saving Tip

The Navajo Nation, larger than West Virginia, offers a number of inexpensive campgrounds in Arizona.

Federal Park Passports

GOLDEN AGE PASSPORT

If you're sixty-two or older, you're eligible for the federal government's free Golden Age Passport, a lifetime entrance pass to any national park, national monument, recreation area, or wildlife refuge that charges an entrance fee. It also provides a 50-percent discount on charges such as camping fees, parking, and boat-launching at any federal recreational facility, including those administered by the National Park Service, the Bureau of Land Management, U.S. Army Corps of Engineers, and the National Forest Service. The card does not cover fees charged by private concessioners. The Golden Age Passport must be obtained in person with proof of age, and is available at most federally operated facilities where entrance fees are charged, as well as at NPS and USFS regional offices.

GOLDEN ACCESS PASSPORT

Blind or permanently disabled persons of any age are eligible for the Golden Access Passport, which provides the same benefits as the Golden Age Passport. You must obtain it in person, with proof of being medically diagnosed as blind or permanently disabled.

GOLDEN EAGLE PASSPORT

If you're between seventeen and sixty-one, you're eligible for the Golden Eagle Passport, which costs $25 a year and entitles a family or carload free admission to any national park, monument, or recreation area. The card is good for the calendar year. It may be obtained by mail from U.S. Forest Service or Park Service headquarters or regional offices or at Park Service and national wildlife refuge units where entrance fees are charged.

NATIONAL PARK PASS

If you frequent one particular National Park Service unit that charges entrance fees, you might prefer to obtain a Park Pass, available for $10 or $15, which is good for unlimited free admission to the park for the calendar year.

DUCK STAMP

If you frequent units of the National Wildlife Refuge system, you can buy a Duck Stamp for $12.50; it's required of waterfowl hunters, but serves as an entrance permit for nonhunters as well. It's available at most post offices, national wildlife refuges, and many sporting goods stores.

HOW TO FIND INEXPENSIVE CAMPGROUNDS

Most campgrounds maintained by agencies such as those previously mentioned are listed in the major campground directories. If you favor a certain type of inexpensive campground—for example, Bureau of Land Management—it might be worthwhile writing to the particular agency for more information. Addresses are listed on pages 244–245.

A hint: Better information is usually available from the regional offices of the larger agencies; addresses and phone numbers are available from agency headquarters.

Information on state and provincial parks is usually provided in the information packages sent out by the individual states and provinces (see pages 250–253), or you can write directly to the parks department in the state or provincial capital.

FREE CAMPING

Although the amenities and the security of campgrounds are important to most RVers, sometimes circumstances or finances cause a traveler to seek a free place to park. Some RVers are independent types and just plain prefer "boondock" camping, away from what they consider to be the unnecessary trappings of commercial or public campgrounds. Others just need a place to park while in transit.

For legal, safety, and security reasons, RVers should look first to the thousands of private and public campgrounds available. The few dollars saved are simply not worth the bother and potential danger of camping outside a designated camping area. Fortunately, many such areas are free, as discussed below.

Dollar-saving Tip

Many states permit sleeping for a few hours in rest areas. Check signs for restrictions.

Free Campgrounds

Hundreds of free campgrounds exist all over North America for RVers willing to forego the amenities of commercial campgrounds. Many of them are not listed in campground directories because they do not meet the minimum standards for inclusion in these directories. Often it is not just a matter of amenities. Many have poor access roads or sites too small to accommodate even small RVs. Others are virtual meccas for RVers, especially certain sites in the Sun Belt known as "coyote camps."

The National Forest Service, National Park Service, and Bureau of Land Management (BLM) all administer some free campgrounds. Those that are free usually have few facilities—usually, just pit toilets and tables. Drinking water is sometimes, although not always, available. Because the facilities are likely to be minimal, access difficult, and, in some cases, the climate harsh, you should always contact the agency at the local or district level for the best information on free camping in any area. The regional offices are listed on pages 244–246.

On many national forest and BLM lands, free camping is allowed outside of designated camping areas. Because these policies vary from location to location, local offices can often provide the best information.

The National Forest Service and the Bureau of Land Management, as well as some state parks, provide free campsites for campground

---

Free and Inexpensive Camping: Information Sources

The following sources will provide you with information on free and inexpensive camping:

Bureau of Land Management
U.S. Department of the Interior
18th and C Streets, N.W.
Washington, D.C. 20240
(202) 208-5261
   (Ask for *Recreation Guide to BLM Public Lands.*)

National Wildlife Refuges
U.S. Department of the Interior
U.S. Fish and Wildlife Service
1849 C Street, N.W.
Washington, D.C. 20240
   (Ask for *National Wildlife Refuges, A Visitor's Guide.*)

National Park Service
U.S. Department of the Interior
P.O. Box 37127
Washington, D.C. 20013
(202) 208-4747
   (Send $1.50 for *Camping in the National Park System.*)

National Forest Service
U.S. Department of Agriculture
201 14th Street, S.W.
Washington, D.C. 20013
(202) 655-4000

Navajo Nation Parks & Recreation Department
P.O. Box 308
Window Rock, Arizona 86515
   (Ask for the free Visitors Guide and a campground list.)

U.S. Army Corps of Engineers
20 Massachusetts Avenue, N.W.
Washington, D.C. 20314
(202) 272-0660

Retired Military Almanac
P.O. Box 76, Department M
Washington, D.C. 20044
   (A directory of FAMCamps for retired military personnel and their families, available for $4.25.)

Coyote Camp Information

Anza-Borrego Desert State Park
P.O. Box 299
Borrego Springs, California 92004
(619) 767-5311

BLM California Desert District Office
6221 Box Springs Boulevard
Riverside, California 92507
(714) 653-3264

BLM Yuma District Office
3150 Winsor Avenue
Yuma, Arizona 85365
(602) 726-6300

Joshua Tree National Monument
74485 National Monument Drive
Twentynine Palms, California 92277
(619) 367-7511

hosts at selected campgrounds (see page 222). Hosts are expected to hand out maps, answer questions, and maintain supplies in the restrooms. In the BLM's coyote camps (see below), the volunteer hosts virtually manage the campgrounds. Assignments are made at the local level, so write to the district offices.

Other free campgrounds are located on lands owned by utility and timber companies.

Coyote Camps

Most of the coyote camps are on Bureau of Land Management land in Arizona and Southern California. The agency has designated those areas as Long-Term Visitor Areas. Stays shorter than fourteen days are free. For longer stays from September 15 to April 15, a $50 permit is required. Permits are available at BLM offices and from campground hosts.

The most famous of all coyote camps is Slab City, or The Slabs, in the Salton Sea area near Niland, California (see Figure 12.1). It takes its name from concrete slabs left behind by the abandoned Camp Gilmore army base. At this writing, camping is still free at Slab City, which is used by thousands of RVers every winter. Since there is no formal administration of the area (it is not on BLM land), no agency exists for further information. The Christian Center at the entrance to The Slabs provides assistance and information to visitors as they arrive. Niland is on State Highway 111 between Interstates 10 and 8. The camp is three miles east of Niland on Beale's Well Road.

Other favorite, free coyote camps are Anza-Borrego Desert State Park and Joshua Tree National Monument. **Note:** The free campgrounds in these parks do not have water, and length-of-stay restrictions apply. (See addresses on adjacent page.)

Camping is still free at Slab City, which is used by thousands of RVers every winter.

Life Without Hookups

Any RV with self-containment features should serve well in a campground or RV rally where you either can't or don't want to use the amenities, or in the boondocks. Obviously, you need to keep an eye on your battery condition, freshwater supply, and holding tanks.

But taking advantage of self-containment for an extended period of time requires some tricks of the trade and perhaps some modifications to your RV (see also Chapter 14, "Living Without Hookups," in Bill Estes's *The RV Handbook).*

Your first priority is conservation: short showers or sponge baths, switching off lights not in use, quick-flushing the toilet, never letting water run unnecessarily, using public facilities when possible, and wearing sweaters to reduce furnace time. Conservation quickly becomes second nature when you camp without hookups. The real trick is to stretch your capacities.

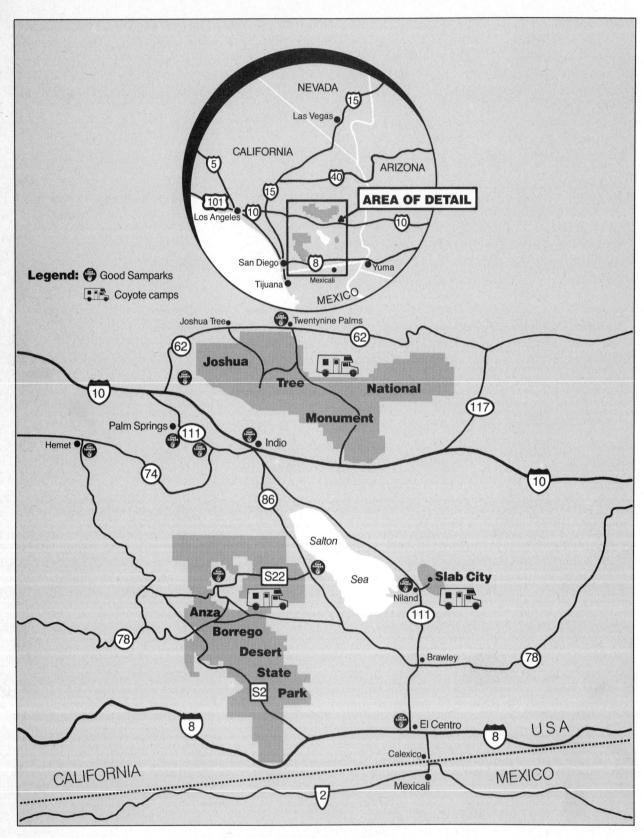

Figure 12.1: A Variety of Campground Facilities in the Southern California Desert

Following are some ways RVers are able to stretch their time without hookups. The products mentioned are all available in RV-supply stores. Installation and maintenance procedures are described in Bob Livingston's *RV Repair & Maintenance Manual.* Another excellent source of information is Joe and Kay Peterson's book, *Survival of the Snowbirds.* (see Bibliography, page 255.)

Electrical Tips

The following tips will aid in preventing electrical problems:

- Keep batteries well maintained.
- Become familiar with your battery capacity and the current draw of the appliances you use.
- Install multiple batteries, such as golf-cart batteries with high-reserve capacity.
- Install an inverter to transform battery power (12 volts DC) to household current (120 volts AC). This will allow you to run accessories such as power tools, televisions sets, computers, and VCRs from your 12-volt system. The higher current-draw accessories such as microwave ovens require a higher-capacity inverter.
- Install fluorescent lights or low-wattage quartz-halogen lamps.
- Use solar power to recharge batteries. This is a very practical alternative to generators for snowbirds who winter in the southwest.
- Use a portable generator if you don't have a built-in generator to recharge your batteries. Buying a portable is considerably less expensive than installing an RV generator.
- Use a propane lamp, such as the Coleman lantern. Be sure to ventilate when using such a lamp inside.
- Use an awning and 12-volt fans to keep cool.

Dollar-saving Tip

Get a hydrometer to check the condition of your RV batteries.

Water Tips

The following tips will aid in preventing water problems:

- If you are on the road but not staying in campgrounds, you can fill your water tank at roadside rests, service stations, city parks, public campgrounds, or at friends' homes. In each case, simply ask permission; you'll seldom be denied. Pick up a "water thief" at an RV-supply store for filling your tank from a non-threaded water outlet.
- If you have a fixed base but can go "into town," use jerry cans and plastic milk cartons to transfer water back to the rig. Collapsible jugs are available to save storage space.

- Install an instant water heater to avoid wasting water during "warm-up."
- Save dishwater in a plastic jug and use for toilet flushing.

Holding-Tank Tips

The following tips will aid in preventing holding-tank problems:

- If you are on the road but not staying in some campgrounds, you can still dump your holding tanks in campgrounds. Private parks may charge a small fee. Public campgrounds often have dump stations just outside the entrance. Others will allow you to dump, but may charge a small fee. Some rest areas have dump facilities, although fewer than in the past. Many other places, such as truck stops, boat ramps, and RV-service centers, provide dump stations.
- Honey wagons are euphemistically named trucks that often circulate in coyote camps, RV rallies, and other places where RVers park without hookups. They charge a small fee for dumping service.
- Use a portable container such as a Tote Tank to transfer waste from the holding tank to a dump station.
- Use a macerator, which grinds up waste in the manner of a garbage disposal and pumps it out through a hose to a toilet, Tote Tank, or clean-out drain.

Propane Tips

The following tips will aid in preventing propane problems:

- If you can minimize use of the furnace, two five-gallon tanks of propane can stretch a very long time. If you park long term, replace standard capacity tanks with 7½-gallon cylinders.
- Use a catalytic heater, which is more energy efficient than a standard furnace; it saves both propane and 12-volt energy. Catalytic heaters consume oxygen, so ventilation is necessary.

You'll undoubtedly learn by experience and from other RVs many other ways to stretch your stints in the boondocks. Doing so is a natural way to make full use of your RV's practical features and to save money in the process.

Dollar-saving Tip

Save on propane purchases with a Good Sam discount.

CHAPTER THIRTEEN

Membership Campgrounds

■ ■ ■ ■ ■ ■ ■ ■ ■ ■ ■ ■ ■ ■

M embership camping has allowed hundreds of thousands of RVers to enjoy free or near-free camping at fine, full-facility RV resorts once they pay a membership fee. Like country-club members, they're entitled to use a home resort with all its amenities, and possibly affiliated resorts as well. Such is the basic concept of membership camping, which at its best is a worthwhile and highly valued development in the world of RVing. However, the membership campground industry has been fraught with confusion and controversy. Bankruptcies, false promises, shoddy marketing tactics, and high-pressure sales pitches have put membership campgrounds in a bad light for years.

Fortunately, that is beginning to change. As the industry matures, poorly financed ventures have fallen by the wayside, and more professionalism has found its way into both the marketing and the operation of membership resorts.

Here's how membership campgrounds are supposed to work: You purchase a membership at a camping resort that entitles you to camp free at that resort as long as you hold the membership. You purchase a right to use the campground; *you do not purchase a lot in the campground.* You own no real estate; you own a membership, as in a country club. In addition to the purchase price, you also pay an annual membership fee.

If the resort at which you purchase a membership is affiliated with a system of resorts, you can become a member of that system (for an additional, reasonable fee) and have the right to stay at those resorts free or for a dollar or two per night.

Membership campgrounds have length-of-stay restrictions, typically seven or fourteen days, and require an interval between staying and returning to a particular resort. Length-of-stay restrictions are more generous at the home resort.

In This Chapter:
- *Can buying a membership in a resort campground save me money?*
- *How do I evaluate a membership campground?*
- *How do I deal with a sales pitch?*
- *How do I resell a membership?*

You also have the right, with some restrictions, to sell your campground membership. These restrictions vary (see "The Resale Market," page 139).

At the time of this printing, membership in a resort with national affiliation sold for about $8,000, although used memberships were available for considerably less. Resort annual dues averaged $300. These figures vary, of course, but are useful in examining the concept from a monetary point of view.

THE COST OF MEMBERSHIP CAMPING

Let's take an $8,000 membership and look at the cost of camping over an upcoming ten-year period. In a simplified example, that cost will be $1,100 per year: $800 payment toward the membership and $300 per year membership fee. In this example, we are not counting interest on the membership, which is usually financed (interest a like amount could earn if invested elsewhere), nor possible escalation in membership fees, nor inflationary rises in camping fees in nonmembership campgrounds. Let's say you camp an average of thirty nights a year and pay an average of $16 per night. That comes to $480 a year in camping fees. The ten-year cost for ordinary camping is $4,800, versus $11,000 for membership camping.

If you camp sixty nights a year at an average of $16, you pay $960 a year for camping. That's getting closer to the $1,100 per year membership camping cost. The ten-year cost is $9,600 versus $11,000.

So even at sixty nights a year, the membership loses in this comparison *until* you calculate some other factors:

1. You can sell the membership. If you sell the membership for $4,000, your ten-year cost is reduced to $7,000.
2. The cost of nonmembership camping is likely to increase, as will membership dues. A 10-percent increase one year in camping fees will cost the thirty-night camper an extra $48 a year; the sixty-night camper, an extra $96. A 10-percent increase in membership fees costs the membership camper only $30. (Membership-fee increases, incidentally, are usually tied to the Consumer Price Index.) In other words, equivalent inflation affects the nonmember camper more than the membership owner.
3. The member camper eventually pays off the membership, then pays only the annual membership fee, while the nonmember is still paying ever-increasing camping fees.

On the other hand, there is no guarantee that the member will be able to sell the membership at $4,000, or at any price. And if he is able to sell it, he usually must pay a transfer fee—5 to 15 percent of the selling price.

Dollar-saving Tip

A campground membership pays off if you use it frequently.

It boils down to this: A campground membership *can* make sense financially—certainly to someone who camps a lot and can visit reciprocal campgrounds. But the quality of the home resort; the quality, number, and location of the reciprocal campgrounds; the value you place on the amenities of resort campgrounds—these are all factors that should enter into your decision of whether or not to purchase a membership.

It's impossible to be certain that you'll get your money's worth in a straight financial comparison with nonmembership camping. But if you're delighted with your home resort and stay there often, that may be enough to justify a membership purchase—*if* it's a well-run resort that delivers what it promises.

It can't be stressed too much: You must be certain to use a membership extensively to make it financially worthwhile.

Membership in a resort campground can pay off only if the campground remains in business and delivers what it promises.

MEMBERSHIP SHOPPING: PRACTICAL CONCERNS

Financial Stability

Membership in a resort campground can pay off only if the campground remains in business and delivers what it promises. Unfortunately, the resort campground business has been plagued by bankruptcies and undelivered promises. You should be concerned about the financial stability of the member resort you are buying into, as well as the network with which it is affiliated.

Although most membership campgrounds in financial trouble are sold and continue operation, some are dissolved in bankruptcy. In such cases, the creditors have no obligation to you. You can lose your money.

Check with the local Better Business Bureau and the state attorney general's office for complaints or legal action against the resort. Talk to other members about their dealings with the resort—has it lived up to its promises? Have the dues been raised unreasonably?

Some resorts are quite open with their finances. They will show you a business plan and discuss their history and projections. To an extent, though, you must utilize your intuition. If the resort seems well managed, the facilities are well maintained, and the members are happy, chances are the resort is reasonably stable and warrants your further interest.

Don't assume that affiliation with a resort network is any guarantee of an individual resort's stability. It isn't.

If the resort is still in the planning stages, be extremely cautious. No matter what promises are made, you cannot really know if the resort is viable. Even though the deal may be very attractive compared to the price of a membership in an already existing resort, it's a risky investment. Your caution may be allayed somewhat if the same company has developed another successful resort.

Right of Recision

The right of recision means you have the right to change your mind after you sign an agreement to purchase a membership. Because many resorts use high-pressure tactics (such as "today-only" pitches), it's important to have the right to change your mind after you return home. Some states require a three-, five-, or seven-day right of recision. If the right of recision is not in a membership campground contract, insist that it be included in writing.

Disclosure Statement

Be sure the resort provides a clear, readable listing of its obligations and your rights. You should read this carefully before signing anything. It should spell out the resort's amenities and the exact terms of

---

Who's Who in Membership Campgrounds

While there are many individual membership resorts and small regional networks, these are the principals today in membership camping:

Camp Coast to Coast. Approximately 500 resorts are affiliated with Camp Coast to Coast. Membership in CCC ($46 at press time) is an extra annual charge on top of home-resort membership. It allows camping privileges at any CCC resort for $1. Reservations are not centralized, but can be made through the individual resorts.

A Coast to Coast Resorts membership is $3 more per year, which entitles members to the same privileges as a CCC membership, plus low-cost use of rental cabins and trailers at resorts with those facilities.

CCC Welcome Coupons are a good way to try out membership camping. Six coupons for $59.95 allow six nights' camping and use of the facilities at Coast to Coast Resorts, without any sales pitches.

Camp Coast to Coast
64 Inverness Drive East
Englewood, Colorado 80112
(800) 368-5721

Thousand Trails/NACO. Thousand Trails, with thirty-nine resorts, and NACO (North American Company), with thirty-two, are separate companies owned by the same parent organization, the Southmark Company. With an ordinary membership, Thousand Trails members enjoy free camping priv-

ileges at other Thousand Trails resorts, and NACO members may camp at other NACO resorts. However, by purchasing a "Gold Card," members of one can also use campgrounds of the other. Gold Card memberships can be sold and resold in perpetuity. For an additional fee, Thousand Trails/NACO Gold Card members can join RPI (see following listing).

Thousand Trails/NACO
12301 N.E. 10th Place
Bellevue, Washington 98005
(800) 562-4000

RPI (Resort Parks International). RPI, also owned by Southmark Company, has about 290 affiliated resorts. Membership in the network is $40, above the individual resort's annual fees. Members have reciprocal camping privileges in NACO resorts as well, but not in Thousand Trails. Camping fees are $2 a night, and reservations are centralized via a toll-free number. Many RPI resorts are also affiliated with Camp Coast to Coast.

Resort Parks International
3711 Long Beach Boulevard
P.O. Box 7738
Long Beach, California 90807
(800) 635-8498

membership. If the resort has different membership options, it should include those options so you can consider the best one for you. It should detail the procedure for transferring and selling the membership, including any transfer or resale fees. It should spell out the annual dues and how increases in the dues are determined.

Also, if certain amenities have been promised that aren't yet in place, the resort should prove to you that they have posted a bond assuring their availability.

Affiliation

Although your satisfaction with the home resort should be your prime consideration in buying a membership, be sure you understand the resort's affiliation with other resorts. With how many campgrounds does it have reciprocal agreements? What standards must those campgrounds meet? How are parks inspected? What does it cost to camp in affiliated campgrounds? Does the chain have a reservation system?

> The larger resort campground networks . . . offer some extra benefits . . .

Campsite Availability

Campsite availability is a real concern among resort-campground members. A campground must sell memberships to make a profit; annual fees alone will not sustain a resort. Also, most campgrounds make spaces available to nonmember overnighters. This can mean a lot of competition for campsites. Ask what kind of guarantee of availability, if any, members have. Ask current members if they have difficulty obtaining sites.

Ancillary Benefits

The larger resort campground networks like Camp Coast-to-Coast and Thousand Trails/NACO offer some extra benefits, such as discounts on cruises, condos, and hotels, and availability of emergency road-service insurance. These should not be primary considerations, but do inquire about them and find out about extra charges for these services.

Beware the Low-Cost Membership

You might encounter a resort selling memberships for an extremely attractive price—even as low as a few hundred dollars. Be very careful, especially if the resort is not yet constructed. Resorts rely on membership sales to finance the construction of amenities. If the cost of membership is absurdly low, the resort may have difficulty

If the resort won't give you a straight answer about dues increases, be careful.

paying for what it promises. Obviously, you're much better off paying for an expensive membership in a legitimate resort than an inexpensive one in a resort that folds.

Ask about Dues and Dues Increases

Naturally, you should inquire about the annual dues at the membership campground, but don't stop there. Ask about the maximum allowable annual increase in dues. Ask how often and how much the dues have been raised in the last five years. Many membership owners have reported increases up to 300 percent in five years. Some of these increases are couched in terms like special assessment fees.

If the resort won't give you a straight answer about dues increases, be careful. Either take your business elsewhere, or talk to current campground members. If fees have been raised substantially and special assessment fees have been suddenly imposed, it could indicate that the resort is in trouble. They might be trying to get as much money from their members as possible before bailing out.

Also, be sure to ask if dues are frozen when members reach the age of sixty-five. Many resorts offer such an inducement to seniors.

Dues are often part of a purchase negotiation. You might be able to negotiate the first year or two free, or perhaps negotiate dues at a frozen rate.

THE SALES PITCH

Although the membership campground industry is cleaning up its act, high-pressure sales and deceptive marketing practices are still all too common.

The Win-a-Valuable-Prize Pitch

Because many membership campgrounds are in remote locations, they resort to luring prospects out with a promise of valuable prizes. A typical direct-mail pitch promises: (1) a new car, (2) a Hawaiian vacation, and (3) a 35mm camera if you come out in person and attend a ninety-minute sales presentation. The pitch must tell you your odds of winning each prize. In the case of the new car, the odds will be extremely remote. The odds will be against the vacation, and it is probably over-valued anyway. In the case of the camera, the odds will probably be 1:1.

You can safely assume that camera will be of inferior quality and that it cost the resort very little. Such a prize is not worth the time and the cost of the gas for the trip out.

Don't attend a sales presentation merely for the sake of an attractive prize. Only attend if you're genuinely interested in a campground membership.

The Today-Only Pitch

The next most common sales device is the "today-only" pitch. The salesperson obviously wants to close the sale before you go home to think about it. He may insist the price he is offering is good *that day only.* Or he may offer you an annual dues rate well below the set rate, but he'll insist you can get this rate only if you sign today.

"Most resorts, regardless of what they say, would take your money if your returned the next day or next week or next year and asked to buy," says Richard LaCroix, a former membership campground salesperson and author of *Exposed: History of the Membership Resort Campground Industry.* An assistant attorney general for the state of Wisconsin explains what should be obvious: First-day inducements are generally "contrived solely as an artificial device to create a false sense of urgency and pressure consumers into making a purchase before they can do any competitive shopping or review the contracts."

The attorney general's implicit advice is to take your time, don't succumb to the first-day pitch, go home and think about it, and to compare other resorts if possible.

Some high-pressure salespeople may resort to outright falsehood to get you to sign up. They may promise future amenities for which there are no real plans; they may misstate your length-of-stay privileges; they may even imply that a membership purchase is an investment, a claim that is probably illegal. It most definitely is not an investment in the sense that you can turn a profit on the sale of your membership.

All this points to the importance of going home, reading the contract and disclosure statement carefully, and comparing them to what the salesperson told you. Don't even take your checkbook with you to the sales presentation. Make your decision in the rational, tranquil environment of home.

Dollar-saving Tip

Don't take your checkbook to the sales presentation. Make your decision later.

THE MEMBERSHIP RESALE MARKET

Campground memberships can be resold, but the typical membership has a three-owner limitation. Some memberships, such as the Thousand Trails/NACO Gold Card, can be traded forever. The resale market presents obvious advantages to both buyers and sellers. Buyers can purchase used memberships for less than the price of a new one. Sellers can recover part of the cost of their original purchase by putting their memberships on the market.

But it's not quite that simple. Generally, sellers may not sell their memberships until two years after purchase. They also may face a competitive market and not be able to charge nearly what they hope to get.

Buyers generally are required to pay a transfer fee to the resort—anywhere from 5 to 15 percent of the sale price. Buyers will also always pay the current rate for dues, not the low or frozen rate that the seller may be enjoying.

Classified advertisements in national and regional RV magazines are a good source of resale listings, as are club newsletters. In these publications, you'll also see ads for companies that specialize in selling used memberships. These listing services can work well for buyer and seller alike, but read the following section before utilizing such a service.

> The concept [of listing services] is valid, but the customer must beware.

LISTING SERVICES

The resale market has spawned the burgeoning business of listing services, many of which have been shady or downright fraudulent. The concept is valid, but the customer must beware.

The listing service works like this: The customer who wishes to sell a campground membership lists the membership with the service. The company takes an up-front fee for the listing, then maintains an up-to-date computer listing of a wide variety of campground memberships that it advertises in various publications. The seller, not the listing service, determines the asking price.

The prospective buyer contacts the company and asks for a list of

---

Listing Services—Sorting the Good from the Bad

Listing services provide valuable services to RVers. They can help you sell a campground membership. But some of the services have proven to be unscrupulous. How can you be certain you are dealing with a legitimate company? Ask the following questions:

- How long has the company been in business?
- Will they refer you to past customers?
- Will they send you detailed literature on their services?
- Has the company been approved by the American Membership Campers Union? (Some listing companies, incidentally, waive the up-front fee for AMCU members.)
- Does the company sell other products, such as timeshares and RVs? You're better off with a company that specializes in campground memberships or one with a special division for membership sales.
- Will the company send you a printout of your ad so you can insure its accuracy?

If you have any doubts, check with the Better Business Bureau in the town where the listing service operates.

memberships for sale in a particular park or area. There may or may not be a fee for the list.

Some listing companies take a low ($100 or less) up-front fee from the seller and charge a commission, usually about 10 percent, upon sale of the membership. The up-front fee is applied to the commission.

Others take a high up-front fee (up to $500) and no commission. Be wary about dealing with such a company. Obviously, these companies make money on selling listings and care little about selling memberships. They may put the listing in their data bank, but they have no incentive to sell the membership.

How can you be certain you are dealing with a legitimate listing service? Ask how long the company has been in business. Ask to be referred to past customers. Ask for printed literature on the company. Ask if the company is affiliated with and has been approved by the American Membership Campers Union (See Appendix, page 248). (Some listing companies, incidentally, waive the up-front fee for AMCU members.) If you have any question about the company, check with the Better Business Bureau in the city where the company does business.

If you utilize a listing service, make sure the company provides you with a printout of your ad so you can insure its accuracy.

Some listing services sell other products, such as timeshares and RVs. You're better off with a company that specializes in campground memberships, or at least has a special division for membership sales.

Dollar-saving Tip

Don't pay a high up-front fee to a listing service. It has no incentive to sell your membership.

American Membership Campers Union

Members of resort campgrounds have a clearinghouse for information on their membership and resale rights in the Florida-based American Membership Campers Union. The group's quarterly newsletter informs members of legislative developments around the country and alerts them to issues of concern.

Mike Parker, executive director of the nonprofit organization, reports that a large number of calls to the group concern resale rights and complaints about listing services that take a large up-front fee and fail to deliver a sale. The union is working toward elimination of up-front money to listing services, contending that the companies should be paid on a commission basis, as are real estate agents. Some listing-service companies already waive any up-front fee to AMCU members.

AMCU also engages in lobbying and educational efforts. Parker points out that many resort-campground members are retired and/or elderly people whose life savings may be at stake if they're taken by an unscrupulous company. He hopes the clout of his organization will protect their rights and eliminate such situations.

Membership is $39 for one year, $65 for two. Contact:

American Membership Campers Union
9753 S. Orange Blossom Trail, Suite 203
Orlando, Florida 32821
(800) 755-5777

THE CO-OP ALTERNATIVE

The Texas-based Escapee Club is quietly pioneering a different type of membership campground that is nonprofit and relies on voluntary labor from its members to build and maintain facilities. Members of SKP (Escapee) Co-Op Parks (address in Appendix, page 247) own a lifetime membership. They can maintain and improve their individual lots as they wish (within the guidelines of the co-op) but do not actually own the lot itself. Because the plan is nonprofit, a member cannot resell a membership; it is instead sold to the co-op, which retains the right to resell it.

Each co-op park must maintain a no-hookup area in which any Escapee Club member may park for a limited period of time. With a great deal of volunteer labor and self-government, Escapee members have managed to hold costs down considerably; the first co-op members paid less than $2,000, later ones as much as $6,500. About a dozen of these co-op parks are now operating, mostly in the west and southwest.

If any type of membership campground interests you, by all means check it out. Be as certain as possible of two things: that you will use the park enough to justify the membership fee, and that the park is financially stable enough so that you can enjoy the benefits of membership for as long as you wish.

CHAPTER FOURTEEN

Trip Planning

■■■■■■■■■■■■■

Mobility is one of the great joys of RV travel. You can go anywhere at any time, always open to whim and discovery. There's just one problem with whim and discovery: They're often quite the opposite of practicality. In other words, they can be expensive. I'll never forget the sight I came upon once in a tiny village in Mexico. The streets of the village were barely wide enough to accommodate a single car in either direction. But an RVer—towing a 30-foot fifth-wheel trailer behind a large pickup—had been so open to whim that he'd ventured right on into the village. He couldn't have known the main street of town dead-ended unpredictably. But he found out soon enough. His rig looked like a beached whale. A crowd had gathered to watch the fun. The driver would have little choice but to back up several hundred feet. He was absent when I came upon the scene. Perhaps he had decided to give up his RV—and RVing.

A little trip planning can help you avoid a lot of dead ends and save time, money, and aggravation. Trip planning needn't eliminate the possibility of whim. It's just that you can make a lot of your discoveries in *advance,* through maps, guidebooks, and other sources. Trip planning doesn't mean dispensing with your mobility. Quite the opposite. Trip planning is the best way to take advantage of your mobility.

When you begin to pay attention to trip planning, it becomes nearly as exciting as the trip itself. There's nothing like spreading maps, guidebooks, and tourist brochures out on the dining-room table, charting possible overnight stops, attractions to see, events to attend, routes to follow. The trip begins to come alive in your mind. You know something of what to expect, what not to miss.

Of course, trip planning has no place in this book unless it's with the intent to save money. If you keep money saving in mind during every phase of the planning, you can select campgrounds with rea-

In This Chapter:
- *How can I best plan my travels to save money?*
- *What planning resources are the most useful?*
- *How can a good campground directory save me money?*
- *What planning services do Good Sam and other clubs offer?*

sonable rates, attractions that cost little or nothing, direct routes that save you gas and time. It becomes fun and a thoughtful challenge, with tangible dividends.

HOW TRIP PLANNING CAN SAVE YOU MONEY

Before we explore the many sources for intelligent trip planning, let's examine some of the many money-saving factors to keep in mind as you organize your RV travels.

Planning for Weather.   By knowing in advance the seasonal climate of any area you're interested in visiting, you can avoid a route or a destination that takes you through extremes of weather. This is not just a matter of personal comfort. Remember that running the air conditioner or furnace costs you money. Extreme cold weather can cause pipes to freeze if you're not prepared. Extreme hot weather can contribute to vapor lock or engine overheating. Strong head-winds can decrease your gas mileage dramatically.

Dollar-saving Tip

Gas prices often drop after the peak vacation season.

Planning for Off-Season Travel.   Tourism is like any business: Supply and demand fix the prices. Demand is highest during peak travel season—in most parts of the country, Memorial Day through Labor Day. And rates are accordingly higher during those months. Gasoline, campground fees, and admission fees to attractions are examples of rates that can vary by season.

Trip planning by season requires some extra attention, though. While some campgrounds and attractions feature lower seasonal rates, others are closed during the off-season. You can avoid disappointment and costly dead ends by knowing in advance the exact seasonal dates of the places you wish to visit.

Geographical Trip Planning.   One obvious example of geographical trip planning that many RVers follow is avoiding mountainous routes. Mountains take a toll on gas mileage, engines, and brakes. Of course, mountainous regions also provide some of the most compelling RV destinations. But if you're simply trying to get from one place to another and can avoid some tough mountain grades, you can save on gasoline and mechanical wear and tear.

Big-city rush hours are another thing to avoid. If you can skirt metropolitan areas during prime drive times, you will avoid gas-robbing stop-and-go situations, not to mention a lot of aggravation.

Good maps can also help you avoid the fate of the hapless RVer in the Mexican village. By utilizing local and regional maps, you can avoid a lot of dead ends and wrong turns.

Traveling among some lakes, rivers, and bays requires ferry-hopping. Planning in advance can get you to the right ferry at the right time.

Planning the Best Route.   Although the most direct route isn't for everyone, it's obvious that saving miles means saving money. Also, as attractive as back roads can be, if they lead you frequently into large towns, you'll end up doing a lot of stop-and-go driving.

But the most direct route is not always the best route, even from a money-saving point of view. If a highway is undergoing extensive construction work, you can be delayed and spend a lot of time idling needlessly. With wise trip planning, you can know up-to-the-minute conditions along the route you wish to follow.

Planning for Special Needs and Interests.   Resource materials are available to assist travelers with almost any special need or interest. Handicapped travelers, for example, can utilize books and brochures that detail facilities available to accommodate them. Certain attractions, for example, aren't yet equipped with wheelchair ramps, and a handicapped traveler might waste a trip to such a place.

Travelers with special interests can avoid a lot of hit-or-miss traveling, such as:

■ Birdwatchers can research the locations of national wildlife refuges and learn the best places and times to visit.

■ History buffs can learn of historical museums that charge little or nothing, yet provide a wealth of interesting information.

■ Craftspeople can plan to visit as many crafts fairs and local festivals as possible, where they can sell their wares and earn extra traveling money.

■ Members of RV clubs, lodges, churches, and fraternal organizations can obtain membership directories and calendars (write to the headquarters office) to learn of free places to park, dinners, socials, and conventions.

■ Hunters and anglers can learn in advance about season opening and closing dates, license requirements, limits, and the best places to pursue their pastimes. There's nothing like a hefty fine to bust a budget and ruin the satisfaction of a great catch.

Planning to Save on Camping Fees.   By planning overnight stops in advance, rather than taking whatever is nearby, you can save on camping fees. Additional ways to save on camping fees are discussed in detail in Chapter Twelve, "Saving on Camping Fees."

Planning by Region or Country.   Although you can find bargains anywhere, most travelers find prices in the Midwest to be generally less than along the coasts or in the Sun Belt. Mexico, of course, is always a great bargain, and the dollar is very strong in Canada. Planning your travels to take advantage of these regional differences can save you money.

Planning Short and Close-to-Home Trips.   Travels in your own backyard are a terrific way to save money and to become closer to

By planning overnight stops in advance, rather than taking whatever is nearby, you can save on camping fees.

your native landscape. All too often we eagerly explore distant, exotic realms and neglect the wonders to be discovered close to home. Visit a bookstore or library and pick up books on your local history, flora, fauna, and historical attractions, then explore them. Make it an adventure. Seek out interesting campgrounds, restaurants, and attractions just as you would anywhere you travel. You might find yourself more indulgent in little luxuries when you're not spending money on gasoline for a long trip.

PLANNING RESOURCES

I heartily suggest you begin your trip planning by utilizing the least expensive of all resources: the library. You'll be astounded at the wealth of information in your public library—or, for that matter, in any library wherever you travel. Libraries have travel books on nearly any state or region that might interest you. They are also stocking more and more travel videos, which are generally better for inspiration than for specific trip-planning information.

Use the *Reader's Guide to Periodical Literature* or *The Magazine Index* to find magazine articles on nearly any place. If you're interested in the local area, wherever you may be, local libraries always stock regional travel materials and historical pamphlets on the area.

Library reference sections have books like *Festivals Sourcebook* that list fairs and festivals throughout the country. Almanacs and encyclopedias can provide useful background material.

If the library doesn't have what you're looking for, ask a librarian; most libraries have lending agreements with other libraries and can usually find almost anything you need.

Dollar-saving Tip

Take advantage of the wealth of free information available.

The States: Free Maps and More

You don't have to belong to an auto club or purchase an expensive road atlas to get good road maps. Maps and all sorts of other information are available from the state and provincial offices of tourism (see pages 250–253). Drop a postcard or call a toll-free number, and you have access to a very inexpensive source of useful material.

It's not just state maps that save you money. Perusing materials I've recently received from a few states, I find such things as a calendar of events, listing dozens of free or inexpensive fairs and festivals; a directory of pick-your-own fruit and vegetable farms; information on hunting and fishing licenses; a listing of antique shops and shows; a listing of factory outlets; a listing of golf courses; weather information; an intrastate mileage chart; and so forth.

All this information has a way of creating clutter in an RV. A good way to manage it is to bring along a portable file-manager—stationery stores sell plastic ones with a carrying handle—in which you can file your materials alphabetically.

If you don't obtain materials in advance, take advantage of the welcome centers many states maintain near their borders. They generally have the same materials, plus additional local material that might include discount coupons for attractions and shops.

Chambers of Commerce and Visitors' Bureaus

Nearly every town in the United States has a chamber of commerce or a visitor's bureau that can provide more localized information than state agencies. This information is always free.

You can almost always reach the right agency by simply requesting information and addressing a postcard (remember, postcards are a dime cheaper to mail) to the chamber of commerce, the name of the town, and the zip code (available in a directory at your local post office or library). The packages the chambers send back often include money-saving discount coupons.

Considering all its useful features, any good campground directory is a bargain.

Campground Directories

Of all the reference materials available for RV trip-planning, none is so indispensable as a good campground directory. See Figure 14.1 for instructions on how to read a campground listing.

Trailer Life Campground & RV Services Directory

Trailer Life's excellent *Campground & RV Services Directory* for example, lists:

- Specific directions to every campground, so you don't waste time and miles looking. Many advertisements add a small map to further assist you.
- The latest available rate information so you can plan to stay in parks that are relatively less expensive.
- The location of Good SamParks, which offer a 10-percent discount to Good Sam members. The TL directory is the only one that lists Good SamParks.
- Opening and closing dates so you don't waste a trip to a campground that closes for the winter.
- A complete description of facilities, plus ratings for the campground, restrooms, laundry facilities, and scenery, so you can compare prices for completeness of facilities and recreational offerings.
- Elevation of the campground, so you know if you'll have to pull a grade to get there.
- RV-service centers and LP-gas centers, so you needn't drive around looking for these places.

The Money-Saving Way to Read a Campground Listing

The smart RV traveler learns how to read a campground listing with saving money in mind. Every listing is full of clues that can help you save money by knowing in advance such information as the exact location of the campground, its rates, and the completeness and quality of its facilities. The following example is from the *Trailer Life Campground & RV Services Directory*, which carries a full explanation of all its symbols and details. Be sure to read the explanations along with these "reading-between-the-line" money-saving hints.

Location on map. Check for the proximity of the campground. Is another one closer?

Elevation. High elevation may mean a long, steep (gas-burning) climb.

Good Sam Club. The Good Sampark symbol means that Good Sam Club members save 10 percent on camping fees if they pay cash.

Season. Avoid an unnecessary drive; be sure the campground is open. Rates may be lower during "shoulder" seasons, in this case, April and October.

Access. Good access roads mean saving wear and tear in getting there.

Directions. Precise directions save you a telephone call and searching time. If the campground is just off an interstate, it might be more expensive than another farther from the highway. If it's a remote campground, save backtracking by picking up supplies in advance.

Regulations. In this case, if you have a dog, you know not to waste a trip to this campground.

Site description. You can save an unnecessary trip if the sites are unsuitable for your needs. The availability of shaded sites may mean less air-conditioning time (note the extra charge for running an air conditioner, indicated by the dollar sign). Note also the availability of hookups. If you don't need them, compare the number of available sites to the number of hookup sites. If some sites do not have hookups, you can probably save by requesting such a site. Note also extra charges for cable TV and running an electric heater.

Facilities. Evaluate your needs of the moment; if you need some simple groceries, or to fill your LP tanks, the availability of such services can save you a side trip.

Recreation. If the campground seems to have enough to interest every member of the family, you'll undoubtedly save on day trips away from the campground. If there's a boat ramp, you'll save the launch fees you'd pay elsewhere.

YORKTOWN — B2

Parks and Campgrounds

SHORELINE RV PARK (priv) wooded hills. Elev 3210 ft. Apr 15 to Nov 1. Fair gravel access rd. From Jct I-80 & Exit 46 (SR-447), N 5 mi on SR-447 to Elm Ave, W 1.5 mi. Good paved interior rds. No pets, no tents. **SITES:** (150 total spaces). Avail: 75 paved, 25 grass, 10 dirt, 18 ft avg site width, no slide-outs, 40 ft max RV length, 14-day max stay, mostly shaded, 75 pull-thrus, 110 W, 75 S, 110 E (20/30 amps), AC $, elect heat $, cable TV $. **FAC** ⬧ Restrooms, showers $, dump, security, pay phone, laundry, ltd groceries, ice, snacks, RV supplies, LP gas, BBQ.**REC** Twin Oaks Lake: trout, fishing, tackle, swimming, boating: ramp, dock, marina, rental. Pool $, spa, adult lounge, shuffleboard, horseshoes, rec hall, game room, planned activities, playground, rec field. Last year's rates $10 to $14.25, MC, Visa, no reservations. (818) 555-4908
✓ **TL: 6/7/5**
See ad this page.

Rate guidelines. Rates listed in the *Trailer Life Directory* are for two adults, exclusive of additional fees. These are always just guidelines, but useful for comparisons with other campgrounds. If you like, enjoy the "float" period that charging allows; note that charge cards are accepted.

Ratings. These are just as important as the rates. They tell you what you're getting for your money: the completeness of facilities, the condition of the restrooms, and the campground's scenic and environmental quality.

Advertising. The presence of an advertisement can be useful; an ad may supply additional information, such as a map that just might determine your choice of campground.

Figure 14.1: The Money-Saving Way to Read a Campground Listing

In addition to these useful listings, this directory has a reference section with a road atlas and other trip-planning resources such as a calendar of events. "Rules of the Road" is particularly important to RVers; it lists size limitations, equipment requirements, restricted tunnels and bridges, and tells you whether overnight parking is permitted in rest areas. A weather chart gives seasonal temperatures, and another chart lists fees for fishing licenses. Some advertisements include money-saving coupons.

Trailer Life's directory is a real bargain if ordered before publication (toward the end of the year), when it's available at a discount of 50 percent to Good Sam Club members, and 45 percent to non-members, not including shipping. Those discounts drop to 45 percent and 38 percent after publication, when the directory is also available in bookstores and RV dealerships, also, usually, at a discounted price.

Other Directories

Considering all their useful features, any good campground directory is a bargain. The major directories are listed in the Appendix, page 246. Also available are less complete bargain directories from campground chains such as KOA and the AAA regional directories, available free to members.

Dollar-saving Tip

If you're paying for an auto-club membership, take advantage of its free services.

Good Sam Club

Good Sam Club members can take advantage of the club's free trip-routing service. The traveler specifies a starting point, a destination, and any cities to be visited in between, and Good Sam provides the recommended route, the mileage and approximate driving time. A deluxe version of the service, for which there is a charge, includes the routes marked out on a map, plus a road atlas.

One way to simplify the trip-planning process is to join an RV caravan; campground reservations, itineraries, and entertainment are all planned and booked in advance, and the RVer need only drive. Good Sam's Caraventures venture all over North America as well as Europe, New Zealand, and Australia.

Good SamTours

Good Sam members also have access to the club's full-service travel agency, which can be especially helpful with cruise bookings and travel abroad. The club uses its volume buying power to pass on discounts of 5 percent on airline tickets and 15 to 20 percent on cruises. Good SamTours can also book foreign motorhome rentals.

Most of these magazines [RV and travel] are indexed in libraries, so you can look up and obtain past copies and particular articles.

AAA and Auto Clubs

All of the major automobile clubs offer free maps and trip-routing services to their members (see Appendix, page 244). Detailed county and city maps can be especially useful to RV travelers. AAA offers an excellent series of state and regional guides called Tour Books. Local AAA offices can provide information on road and weather conditions within each state.

Magazines

Travel stories and calendars of events in RV and travel magazines can be very useful in trip planning. *Trailer Life, MotorHome, Highways,* and *Family Motor Coaching* are the major publications that specialize in RV travel. National travel magazines such as *National Geographic Traveler, Travel Holiday, Condé Nast Traveler,* and *Travel & Leisure* are also excellent sources of information and inspiration. Most of these magazines are indexed in libraries, so you can look up and obtain past copies and particular articles. Savvy RVers clip out articles of interest as they appear (from their own copies, of course—never from the library copies) and keep them in their files.

Finally, you shouldn't overlook the input of friends who can steer you to some of great places you might otherwise overlook. But don't try to duplicate the trip of another; you might sacrifice the satisfaction of making your own plans and discoveries. Which leads to a final word of advice regarding trip planning: Don't overplan. You might become a slave to your itinerary, obsessed with schedules and reservations—the very things you probably want to escape on your RV travels.

CHAPTER FIFTEEN

Shopping: For the Road, on the Road

■ ■ ■ ■ ■ ■ ■ ■ ■ ■ ■ ■

"Shop till you drop." "Born to shop." These well-known slogans are anathema to anyone truly interested in budgeting their money. But they also point to a syndrome that's undeniably real: shopping has become a recreational pastime that can, if wholly indulged, borders on frenzy. That's risky, of course, if you're trying to watch your expenses. The trick is to curb the frenzy and to enjoy shopping, not only for its necessity, but also for its pleasures. Acquiring certain items for your RV and your travels is among the pleasures of RVing. But part of that pleasure is in acquiring these things at a reasonable cost and knowing what is necessary to purchase and what isn't.

RVers also find their travels take them to interesting corners of the world, where certain stores and items—crafts, antiques, art, clothes, whatever—represent the character of the region itself. Shopping becomes part of the experience of traveling, just as important as sightseeing or visiting museums. Of course, this kind of shopping doesn't have to mean *spending*.

In This Chapter:

- *How can I save on my nonfood purchases?*
- *How do I find good prices in unfamiliar territory?*
- *Where can I save on my RV accessories?*
- *How can I find out about flea markets?*
- *Do factory outlets offer real savings?*
- *Where do I find them?*
- *Can I save by mail order?*
- *What are buying services?*

BEFORE YOU SHOP: SOME GENERAL PRINCIPLES

Curbing impulses and imposing judiciousness on your shopping decisions are obvious keys to saving money. But how to do that? The following principles will help.

Avoid Stores. Although this is a principle you're certain to violate frequently, it's still important. You can succumb to temptation only when you are exposed to it. If you walk into a shopping mall, you're

Why add unnecessary trappings of the very kind you're probably trying to escape?

bound to find a bargain, and, no matter how terrific the savings, if you didn't really need it, it's not a bargain. This needn't prevent you from visiting stores that are of particular local interest. Just be judicious.

Keep "Simplicity" as a Motto. There's no end to the gadgetry you can acquire for your RV and for the activities you enjoy on the road. But keep in mind the built-in simplicity of an RV. It is wonderfully and harmoniously designed to provide all the necessary functions of a domicile in a relatively small space. Why add unnecessary trappings of the very kind you're probably trying to escape? Do you really need an electric can opener when a manual one will do? A down comforter when an extra blanket will suffice? A video camera when your still camera will record your memories just fine? Also consider maintenance and ancillary costs, such as dry-cleaning the comforter or purchasing videocassettes for the camera.

Consider the Necessity of Discretionary Items. This requires an honest look at yourself and your lifestyle. And it applies to gifts for your traveling companions as well as things for yourself. Ask yourself: Is this really important? Will it truly add something of value to my life? Will it take up money, space, or time that I can better use another way? If you answer those questions truthfully, even for inexpensive items, you'll eliminate all unnecessary impulse purchases.

Look around a campground at the discretionary items people buy: satellite dishes, lawn ornaments, funny bumper stickers, banners, croquet sets. If having such items brings real pleasure or fills a need, fine. But if the item is a frill with no real importance to *you,* you can live without it.

Maintain a Wish List. You can also call this a reward list. There's no need to constantly deny yourself pleasures. You might want to keep more than one wish list—one for the RV, one for its occupants. The list includes items you would really like, but don't absolutely need— indulgences you can grant yourself, or gift hints that others can heed. When you've been frugal, or if you find your budget isn't quite as tight as you thought, you can pull out the wish list. The wish list serves as a reward system, but it also has a money-saving function: When the money's there, you purchase things off the list that you will truly value, rather than indulging an impulse, which often leads to foolish purchases.

Before Replacing an Item, Try to Repair It. In this disposable world of ours, we often overlook the fact that nearly anything is repairable. Clothing can be mended. How-to books at a bookstore or library can be very useful in assisting with mechanical repairs. This also reminds you to take good care of your possessions—to lubricate, clean, wax, or do whatever is necessary to assure their long life.

Be Resourceful. This is so important for RVers, for whom space, if not money, is always a limitation. It means making items serve more than one purpose: A food processor serving as blender/mixer, using the oven instead of a food dehydrator, or using binoculars instead of a telescope. It may mean using items from home on the road, rather than duplicating them. And it means looking for inexpensive substitutes for expensive items—a slipcover instead of reupholstering, a throw-rug instead of new carpeting.

Don't Be Wasteful. Throwaway items are not only environmentally harmful, they also cost you money. Try using cloth napkins instead of paper, a sponge instead of paper towels, rechargeable batteries instead of disposable ones. Reuse plastic vegetable bags for storage instead of buying expensive containers. Reuse clean aluminum foil. Many more ideas are included on pages 227–232.

NOW YOU'RE SHOPPING

The following items are additional hints to keep in mind when you're out in the shopping arena:

Make Price Comparisons. Obvious advice, but consumers so often neglect to compare prices. If you're truly interested in saving money, you should always make one or two price comparisons before buying anything. Some people keep a large catalog around as an index, such as Sears Roebuck, Best, or Montgomery Ward, and Camping World for RV supplies, a handy way to make a quick price comparison. The Yellow Pages and the 800-number directory published by AT&T (available for $9.95; call [800] 426-8686) can also be useful in making price comparisons.

Research Your Purchases. Consumer-help magazines such as *Consumer Reports* and *Consumer's Digest* carry evaluations of hundreds of products, from stereos to tools to laundry detergents. Current and back issues are available in any library. Particularly useful is *Consumer Reports Annual Buying Guide,* which carries helpful information on dozens of common products.

Question All Discounts. Many items are advertised at a certain percentage off "list price." Such items are almost never sold for list price. What's important to you is the lowest price you can obtain the item for. Even at "50% off list," the item's not a bargain if it's cheaper somewhere else.

Buy in Bulk When Practical. Buying in bulk almost always saves money, whether it's food (see Chapter Sixteen, page 172) or dry goods. Storage can obviously be a limiting factor, especially for

Dollar-saving Tip

Don't compare the offered price to suggested retail; compare it to the price offered by another source.

fulltimers. But most RVers can buy in bulk and divide up the items—some for home, some for the RV, and perhaps some to divide with friends.

Shop at Membership Stores. Membership stores buy items in huge quantities and stock them in no-frills outlets. They can be especially useful for making bulk purchases. If you belong to a membership store at home, ask the store for a directory of its sister stores. Some membership stores offer a one-day membership if you're just passing through.

Don't Buy Dry Goods at Grocery Stores. Nongrocery items such as deodorant, laundry detergent, and razor blades are generally more expensive at grocery stores than in discount or membership stores.

Deal with Reputable Retailers and Manufacturers

Dealing with reputable suppliers applies especially to expensive items such as cameras, tools, and RV awnings. Companies with a solid reputation value that reputation. For example, I once purchased a down sleeping bag from Eddie Bauer. At least two years after I purchased it (it had a one-year guarantee), an interior baffle broke during washing. It was probably my own fault. I called Eddie Bauer to ask if the bag were repairable. Instead, the company replaced the bag free of charge. This is the kind of customer relations that quality stores develop, and why it pays to patronize them.

Negotiate. Consumers are usually reticent about negotiating with retailers, but under certain circumstances, it's perfectly acceptable. For example, if you notice a cosmetic flaw in an item you wish to purchase, point it out; the clerk can usually take a percentage off. Another way to negotiate is to point out an ad on the same item in a competing store. Many stores have a policy of meeting the price of any advertised special. You might notice some merchandise in a corner of a store that's obviously going nowhere, such as odd-sized items or out-of-season goods. If it's an item you want, ask the clerk for a mark-down.

Check Local Papers for Specials and Sales. Whether you're at home or on the road, scan local newspapers for advertisements that offer significant savings. Read the ads with good money sense, though. As mentioned earlier, a percentage off "list price" is meaningless; only price comparisons are meaningful. Many stores have permanent "sales." This is especially true of camera and auto-stereo shops. You must read ads carefully, and always make price comparisons.

By the way, save yourself an occasional quarter by looking for weekly "shoppers" distributed free in bins outside shopping cen-

M any stores have a policy of meeting the price of any advertised special.

ters. Also, local papers are often found in campground laundry rooms and recreation halls.

Save on Sales Tax. If you're traveling cross-country, plan to purchase nonfood items in a state with low (or no) sales tax. Ordering by mail may save you sales tax, but not always (see page 160).

SAVING ON RV SUPPLIES AND ACCESSORIES

Outfitting an RV is a bit like dressing a child. It can be a source of joy, but also a drain on the pocketbook. And it seems like you always need something more. All of the principles already outlined in this chapter apply to shopping for RV accessories. Following are some additional ways to save.

Negotiate for Accessories When You Purchase Your RV. The best time to save on items such as awnings is at the time you purchase your RV. It can be a factor in the purchase negotiation. For example, ask the dealer to sweeten the deal a bit by selling you an awning at a substantial discount.

Shop at the Major Supply Stores. If your local supply store is a mom-and-pop operation, they may have neither the prices nor selection that a larger RV-supply center can offer. If you don't know where such a store is located in your area, check the ads in RV or camping magazines and tabloids.

Take Advantage of Discounts. Good Sam Club members receive a 10-percent discount at 500 "Commercial Member" RV supply and service centers and 1,000 LP-gas centers in the United States and Canada. Participating operations are listed in the *Trailer Life Campground & RV Services Directory.* You must pay cash to take advantage of the Good Sam discount. Camping World's President's Club also offers members a 10-percent discount on supplies purchased at Camping World stores or through the company's mail-order catalog. Membership in the club is $20 for the first year; annual renewals are $15.

Compare Installation Fees. The cost of complicated installations can add significantly to the price of many RV accessories, so be certain to clarify the exact installation charges in advance and compare them with charges at other RV centers.

Install It Yourself. Many installations don't require special skills, genius, or tools to accomplish, such as awnings, for example. Many RVs today are marked with the exact mounting points. All you need is a drill and some basic hand tools, and you can save considerably.

Dollar-saving Tip

RV magazines publish do-it-yourself articles that can save you installation fees.

Some other items require expertise worth paying for, such as installation of a furnace, hydraulic jacks, or a hot-water tank.

Shop in the RV Magazines. Magazines such as *Trailer Life, MotorHome, Highways,* and *Family Motor Coaching* have small ads and shopper sections that offer some good deals on RV accessories. Most of these are specialty items rather than basic supplies, but if you're in need of such an item, check the ads; you can probably order directly from the manufacturer and save money.

Shop by Mail. Camping World is the major source of RV accessories by mail and frequently offers very good prices. Many other catalogs offer items of interest to RVers, such as outdoor wear and fishing equipment. Be careful in buying RV accessories through the mail that require installation. If you can't do it yourself, you'll no doubt pay top dollar for a local dealer to install it—if he'll install it at all. More details on mail order begin on page 159.

Save on Film and Processing

Recording your RV travels on film is a wonderful way to preserve memories, but the cost can really add up. The following are some ways to save:

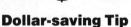

Dollar-saving Tip

Processing slide film is less expensive than print film.

- Buy 36-exposure film, which generally saves you several cents per exposure compared to 24-exposure film.
- Buy slide film instead of print film. Consider having slide shows instead of making scrapbooks; you'll save as much as 20 to 25 percent on the cost of film and processing. You can always make prints of any slide you particularly cherish. Slides are easy to store, too.
- If you are using color print (negative) film, ask for a contact sheet, then have only the pictures you decide are "keepers" printed.
- Buy in bulk. Most shops and mail-order outlets will give you a 10-percent to 25-percent discount on film purchases in bulk, depending on the quantity, usually with a 10-roll minimum.
- Buy and process through the mail. Look in the back of any photographic magazine for labs that offer mail-order film with prepaid processing; it can be up to 50 percent cheaper than film and processing at one-hour labs or camera stores.
- Shop around, and watch for special deals. If you prefer not to order through the mail, there's no precise rule of thumb to determine whether to patronize a one-hour lab, a discount store, or a camera store. Phone one of each to check the prices in your area. Some offer special deals, such as two prints for the price of one, that might make one place a bargain compared to the others.

■ Keep your film in the refrigerator. Hot temperatures can damage your film. Keep it stored in the refrigerator, but take it out to "thaw" an hour or two before you shoot, to avoid the possibility of fogging your shots.

ALTERNATIVES TO RETAIL SHOPPING

Shop at Secondhand Stores.   Thrift shops and secondhand stores are in almost every town and can hold some wonderful bargains. It's easy to outfit an RV with appliances, cookware, and tools purchased secondhand. Such stores are also great for sweaters, knockabout clothing such as sweatshirts and jeans, raincoats, even reading material. Most secondhand shops willingly negotiate prices, especially if you buy several items. If the shop benefits a charity, though, you should keep bargaining to a minimum. When you stop for lunch in a small town, check the Yellow Pages for the local thrift shops. They provide recreational shopping at its cheapest and practical shopping as well.

Shop at Flea Markets.   The concept of the flea market has become highly elevated in recent years. The average flea market is no longer a collection of junk with a few hidden treasures. Most flea markets carry at least as much new merchandise as used, and the prices are usually very reasonable and, often, negotiable. Flea marketeers have little investment in overhead or labor, so they can offer attractive prices. You probably won't find attractive refund and exchange policies, but the prices may well be attractive enough that you won't mind. Socks, tools, luggage, purses, T-shirts, and towels are among the many items of interest to RVers typically found at excellent prices in flea markets.

> Thrift shops and secondhand stores are in almost every town and can hold some wonderful bargains.

Your Warranty Rights

No matter whether you're purchasing a $50,000 motorhome or a $25 flashlight, you have clearly defined rights spelled out in the Magnuson-Moss Warranty Act of 1975. If a product costs more than $15, a copy of the warranty must be available *before* purchase. This includes mail-order items; mail-order companies must supply upon request the written warranties on products they sell. The warranty must state the exact duration of the warranty and procedures for obtaining repair or replacement under warranty.

Products also carry "implied warranties," meaning they must function properly for their intended use. Implied warranty laws in some states may give you protection beyond what is included in a written warranty, so it is always worthwhile to inform your state consumer-protection agency of a warranty dispute.

Warranty rights are covered in more detail in Chapter Eight, pages 87–88.

Clark's Flea Market USA is a quarterly publication that lists flea markets nationwide. It's available for a single-issue price of $7.50 from:

Clark's
419 Garcon Point Road
Milton, Florida 32570

It may also be in the reference section of your local library.

Shop at Surplus Stores. You don't have to be the type who plays weekend survival dressed like General Schwarzkopf to benefit from shopping at surplus stores. Surplus, or army-navy stores, offer good values on outdoor wear, boots, flashlights, tarpaulins, mosquito netting, raincoats, jeans, first-aid kits, and much more.

FACTORY OUTLET SHOPPING

"Factory Outlet: Brand Names at Big Savings!" is another slogan for our era. It's one that RVers are delighted to applaud, as they take advantage of "big savings" at outlet stores, even entire outlet malls, encountered on their travels.

Factory outlets generally do offer real savings. Major designers utilize them to sell excess merchandise since factory orders are placed at least one year in advance of shipping. Quantity miscalculations are inevitable, and these excesses are passed on the you at factory outlets. Outlets exist for many more items than designer clothing, although those are the best known; shoes, towels, and dishes are also often available. Designers and manufacturers have discovered that outlet stores allow them to take more direct profit on their leftovers than they would get by selling to discount stores. Because the stores are factory owned, the middleman is eliminated, and the consumer reaps a real price benefit. The merchandise is generally high quality, and even great bargains can be ferreted out by savvy shoppers.

Most outlet stores and malls are found in small towns and rural areas, often near tourist attractions. The remote locations are to avoid direct competition with ordinary malls and department stores. This, of course, is ideal for RVers who prefer to stay away from urban centers anyway.

Outlet stores offer immediate savings ranging from 25 to 70 percent. The savings can be even greater. Some put merchandise on sale—discounts on top of discounts. The discounts can be even greater on items that are marked down over and again until they are sold. The item has nowhere else to go; it must be marked down until it's sold.

If you've never shopped at outlet stores, or if you haven't checked them out recently, you may be pleasantly surprised. Most sell first-quality goods, not defects and seconds. Many are clustered near one

> If you've never shopped at outlet stores, or if you haven't checked them out recently, you may be pleasantly surprised.

another in towns such as Freeport, Maine, and Flemington, New Jersey, places that have become veritable shoppers' Disneylands. Others are found in huge outlet malls in places like Sawgrass Mills, Florida, and near Niagara Falls, New York, with appropriately huge parking areas, eateries, amusements—several notches above the dingy warehouse-style outlets of yesteryear.

With over 265 outlet malls and thousands of outlet stores in the United States and Canada (and more being built), a directory is useful to outlet shoppers. *The Joy of Outlet Shopping* is available for $5.95, P.O. Box 17129, Clearwater, Florida 34622-0129. *Fabulous Finds Directory* is available for $12.95 from Fabulous Finds, Inc., 9109 San Jose Boulevard, Jacksonville, Florida 32217.

Outlet shopping can be great fun and truly save money, but keep in mind the following caveats:

- Many outlet stores feature very expensive designer lines. Even greatly discounted prices may be more than you would find in a reasonable retail or discount store. A $500 Anne Klein outfit for $250 may still be more than you really want to spend.
- Refund and exchange policies vary, but often are not as generous as those found in retail stores.
- To help hold prices down, outlet stores have few or no sales assistants. You must fit yourself when buying shoes and clothing.
- Outlet stores engender buying frenzy. You must keep in mind the principles outlined earlier in this chapter. Even at 80 percent off, you should still ask, "Do I really need this?"
- Sizes, colors, and quantities may be limited. Fashions are usually a season or several seasons behind retail stores. This latter fact can work to your advantage because outlets often sell clothing for the current season rather than the upcoming season, which is often the case in most department stores.
- Some stores claiming to be "factory outlets" aren't. You can ask in a store if it is owned by the manufacturer, a true factory outlet, and ask for the store's literature. But if the prices are good, it really doesn't matter who owns the store.
- Because so many outlets are located in rural areas, they may require you to go out of your way and spend more for gas than you save on merchandise—unless you're planning some serious shopping.

MAIL-ORDER SHOPPING

Almost anything is available through the mail. Everyone is familiar with such mail-order standbys as Sears Roebuck and Montgomery Ward. What may surprise you is the amazing array of merchandise available through hundreds of specialty catalogs, much of it at discount prices—often 30 percent below retail.

Advantages of Mail-Order Shopping

The advantages of shopping by mail are many. You can do it at leisure at any time; you can save time and gas otherwise spent on shopping trips; you can easily make price comparisons; and you can almost always save money compared to shopping in retail stores.

A mail-order tip: Mail-order companies that compete with one another will often match their competitor's prices. When you're placing a telephone order, inform the clerk the price of the item in the competing catalog, the date of the catalog, and the page number. You can often receive an immediate discount.

In many cases, you can save on sales tax by ordering through the mail. If you're ordering from a firm that has a presence in your state, though, you will have to pay tax. Some states are getting aggressive about collecting taxes from out-of-state mail-order companies, calling them "use taxes." Most mail-order firms are challenging these taxes and will not ask the customer to pay them.

Most mail-order firms have toll-free numbers, many of which operate twenty-four hours, seven days a week. Calling in an order not only saves time, but if you pay with a credit card, the order can be processed immediately. Otherwise, the company waits for your check to clear. Also, ordering by phone saves you from having to calculate shipping and sales tax. The mail-order clerk can make these calculations for you, so you can quickly learn the total cost of your order. Remember, it's the *delivered* cost that you should use in making price comparisons, whether against retail stores or other mail-order catalogs.

This isn't to say you will always receive your order promptly. Delays can be significant sometimes, which can be upsetting when you've already paid for the item. How to deal with delays? See "Your Mail-Order Rights," page 163.

Disadvantages of Mail-Order Shopping

One disadvantage of mail order has almost disappeared, and that's the waiting time for a shipment. Ordering by telephone and using a credit card eliminates the time waiting for your check to clear before shipping. And once payment is confirmed, mail-order firms have become quite efficient, and shipping even by regular post, you will usually have the order in your hands within ten days. The availability of courier services, such as Federal Express or UPS, means that for a reasonable cost you can have your merchandise in one or two days. This is a boon to the RVer on the road, who was formerly unable to take advantage of mail order because of an unsure itinerary.

Other disadvantages of mail order are obvious. With clothing and shoes, you will not be able to try on the merchandise, and you may

Dollar-saving Tip

Be sure you compare taxes, shipping, and handling charges as well as purchase price.

have to return items for proper fit. With delicate electronics or complicated machinery, you will lack the services of a helpful in-store clerk. As you probably know from buying such items as cameras and VCRs, it can be very helpful to consult a clerk while shopping to have features and operations explained and to be able to call the store for assistance after you make the purchase. For these reasons, it is probably better to buy such specialty items from a good retailer and save your mail-order purchases for goods that are either uncomplicated or for merchandise that you understand well.

Items that require complicated installation, such as car stereos or RV air conditioning, are also best purchased from specialists who can install them.

Return policies vary from company to company. Most firms permit returns within a stated period, but be certain you understand the exact return policy before you place any order. Many reputable mail-order firms have "satisfaction guaranteed" policies that permit you to return items "no questions asked." Hats, underwear, custom-made items, and bathing suits may be exceptions. In most cases, you will be responsible for shipping charges on returns.

> One disadvantage of mail order has almost disappeared, and that's the waiting time for a shipment.

Mail-Order Sources

Every RVer has a few favorite mail-order catalogs. Camping World contains hundreds of common RV accessories. L.L. Bean has a dazzling selection of outdoor-oriented items, from its famous boots to canoes to its fishing gear. Campmor has excellent prices on camping supplies such as flashlights and raincoats. Cabela's specializes in fishing and general outdoor gear, and Orvis in fishing gear.

But the availability of catalogs extends far beyond such familiar names. Liquidators buy factory overruns or close-outs of all sorts of

---

Cameras and Electronics by Mail

The mail-order camera and electronics businesses have long been plagued by questionable sales practices. Some companies strip down camera outfits supplied by the manufacturer, replacing lenses, cases and flash units with inferior-quality products, or selling such accessories separately, bringing the total price close to retail. Some cameras and electronics are imported through the "gray market," products intended to be sold in foreign countries. Also known as "parallel imports," these items may feature low prices, but may not have warranties valid in the United States. The product may not be made to the same specifications as the same brand intended for sale in the United States.

As always, you must ask about a product's warranty *before* you order it. Make certain the product is made for sale in the United States and the warranty will be honored by service centers in the United States. If it isn't, ask if the mail order company itself will stand behind the product. Get their warranty in writing. Otherwise, you may be purchasing a very risky bargain.

merchandise and sell them through catalogs. Hobbyists can find almost any art or craft item available by mail. Fabrics, patterns, gourmet food, pet supplies—well, as stated earlier, almost anything is available by mail. The number of interesting catalogs make it impossible to list all of them in this book.

The best way to discover catalogs for whatever may interest you is to refer to one of the following books, available in bookstores, from the publisher, or in the reference section of most libraries:

> ***The Wholesale-by-Mail Catalog***
> The Print Project
> HarperCollins Publishers
> 10 East 53rd Street
> New York, New York 10022
>
> ***Catalog of Catalogs***
> Edward L. Palder
> Woodbine House
> 5615 Fishers Lane
> Rockville, Maryland 20852

For $6 annually, you can subscribe to the *Shop-at-Home Directory*; each issue lists over 300 specialty catalogs.

Another source of catalog companies—those that feature 800 numbers—is *AT&T's Toll-Free 800 Consumer Directory,* available for $9.95 from AT&T ([800] 451-2100).

Some mail-order items are often available directly from the manufacturer, rather than from a mail-order company per se. Examples are the products advertised in the shopper section or classified ads of RV publications. Although the company may not publish a catalog, you should write or phone for literature before purchasing an item from such an ad.

BUYING SERVICES

Telephone buying services are a twist on the mail-order concept. These services don't have catalogs, but maintain computerized listings of thousands of items. A member who is interested in a particular item—for example, a cordless vacuum—calls the buying service and gives the exact brand and model number of the vacuum. The buying service searches its computer files and locates the best price for the vacuum. With some services you can order the vacuum through the service itself; others will refer you to a vendor. Some buying services guarantee their prices; if you find the item elsewhere for less, you're refunded the difference.

Buying services can save you money, but they have disadvantages. They're great at giving price quotes, but seldom can offer any infor-

---

B uying services can save you money, but they have disadvantages.

mation on the products themselves. You must know exactly what you want. They claim to list almost any item (except clothing), but they tend to stick to familiar brands. You might be able to find the same product made by a lesser-known manufacturer cheaper.

The following are two of the larger buying services:

Quota Phone
47 Halstead Avenue, Suite 207
Scarsdale, New York 10528
(914) 835-5300

Shoppers Advantage
40 Oakview Drive
Trumbull, Connecticut 06611
(800) 526-4848

Hobbyists can find almost any art or craft item available by mail.

YOUR MAIL-ORDER RIGHTS

Unsatisfactory Merchandise

An automatic right of return is *not* one of your mail-order rights, although nearly every mail-order company has some sort of return policy. The point is, learn about the company's return policy in advance *and* check the warranty on the product before you buy it. The latter is especially important on expensive purchases and purchases of delicate or complicated items.

No matter what, if an item arrives and it breaks down, is badly made, or is not what the catalog described, seek a refund or replacement. If you're denied a straightforward return, write or phone the president of the company. Explain the problem, provide proof of purchase, and inform the president that you will notify the deputy chief postal inspector for his or her region if you don't get a refund or replacement in seven days. Your own post office will assist you in obtaining a consumer service form, which will allow you to turn the matter over to postal inspectors.

Delays

The Federal Trade Commission's Mail-Order Rule states that you must receive your order within the time promised by the company, or within thirty days after the company receives your completed order and payment. The company must notify you in writing of a delay, and if the new promised date is more than thirty days later than the original date, you can cancel and receive a full refund. The company has ten days to refund your money.

If you're denied a straightforward return, write or phone the president of the company.

Technically, this rule does not apply to telephone orders yet, but the FTC is planning to extend some sort of similar protection to such orders. Telephone orderers *are* protected under their credit-card rights, though. See "Filing Complaints," below.

Some delays can be avoided by making certain you carefully fill out the order form and enclose all the proper taxes and shipping and handling charges. Never send cash for an order; pay by check, money order, or credit card so you have proof of payment. Don't even send cash for a catalog that costs more than $2.

Filing Complaints

If you don't receive satisfaction from a mail-order company regarding a delay, a return, or a refund, contact one or all of the following:

1. *Your local post office.* Even if you placed a telephone order and the shipment was by a private carrier, if you received a catalog through the mail, the post office has jurisdiction to handle your complaint. In some cases, they will withhold mail delivery to the company in question until a dispute is resolved. Your post office can provide the appropriate forms and the address of the inspector's office with which you should deal. Or you may write to Chief Postal Inspector, U.S. Postal Service, Washington, D.C. 20260.
2. *Your credit-card issuer.* An item not delivered as promised constitutes a billing error on your credit-card bill. Notify your credit-card issuer in writing and have the charge removed.
3. *Your bank-card issuer.* If you pay for mail-order merchandise with a credit card and the mail-order company does not meet the FTC's thirty-day rule, it constitutes a billing error; you can request a credit from the issuer of your credit card. You must notify the company in writing and send copies of receipts and correspondence. For more about your credit-card rights, see page 205.
4. *Local consumer agencies.* City, county, and state agencies may mediate your case for you. Look under "Consumer Protection Agencies" in the White Pages of your phone book.

An Invaluable Consumer Resource

A handy book for every consumer is the *Consumer's Resource Handbook*, available free from the Consumer Information Center, Pueblo, Colorado 81002. The book lists addresses of national and regional offices of consumer-protection agencies and details procedures for filing complaints. It also lists Better Business Bureau offices.

5. *Better Business Bureau.* Your local Better Business Bureau office can provide advice and may mediate your dispute.
6. *Mail-Order Action Line.* Contact the Direct Marketing Association, 11 West 42nd Street, New York, New York 10036. The DMA maintains records of complaints against mail-order firms and will assist you with your complaint.
7. *Federal Trade Commission.* Although the FTC does not deal with individual cases, it gathers records and will take action against certain firms for which it receives many complaints. Write: FTC, Correspondence Branch, Washington, D.C. 20580.
8. *Action-line columns.* Sometimes extra clout helps; "RV Action Line" in *Trailer Life,* "Hotline" in *MotorHome,* and "Action Line" in *Highways* can assist with mail-order disputes.

Most mail-order customers experience few or no problems with their orders. The competitive nature of retail-versus-mail order (mail order has taken over 20 percent of the market) has created a strong service orientation among the companies. For the RV customer, it means more choices than ever for good prices and good services, whether you're shopping on the road or for the road.

Most mail-order customers experience few or no problems with their orders.

CHAPTER SIXTEEN

Food: Dining In, Dining Out

■ ■ ■ ■ ■ ■ ■ ■ ■ ■ ■ ■ ■

Whether you dine in or out, meals on the road are among the great and consistent pleasures of RV travel—and among the greatest and most consistent strains on the budget. Temptation constantly rears its alluring head to travelers who like to savor the sampling of regional cuisines. Temptation also allures those who favor convenience over fiscal prudence.

It's possible to strike a balance among all these temptations. Sampling the cuisine of any region is part of the traveling experience not to be missed. Convenience is certainly important to most RV cooks, who naturally prefer to spend more time enjoying their vacations than working in their kitchens. Both convenience and prudence can be balanced by allowing for occasional splurges while still utilizing the inherent ease of taking your kitchen with you wherever you travel.

In This Chapter:

■ *How can I find the best prices on my RV food purchases?*
■ *What alternatives to convenience foods can I find?*
■ *Are coupons really worthwhile?*
■ *Does buying in bulk make sense for RVers?*
■ *What about dining out— where do I find good food on the road without ruining my budget?*

DINING IN

RVers take along their shelter and their kitchens when they travel, and therein lies the main economical advantage of the RV mode of travel: You needn't pay the cost of hotel rooms or restaurant meals. You'll eat out occasionally, of course; we'll cover that later in the chapter. But dining in is the key to saving money on your food budget. The trick is to make it fun rather than a discipline. But let's start with some basics, some nitty-gritty ways to save on day-to-day food shopping, then look at ways to make dining in fun and convenient as well.

Food-Shopping Basics

Shop in Supermarkets

Supermarkets buy in volume and sell in volume, with the resulting price break going to you, the consumer. Resist the temptation to stop by convenience stores or to rely on campground groceries. You can't beat the consistently low prices of major supermarkets. They're generally easy to find by nosing about the main street of any good-sized town. They also provide large parking lots that can easily accommodate RVs.

Shop in Membership Stores

Membership stores usually offer substantial discounts on staple items purchased in quantity. The quantities may be too large to take on the road, but you can divide them—take what you can carry and leave the rest at home. (See "Buy in Bulk," page 172.) Be sure to ask for a list of other locations of your membership store so you take advantage of the low prices while you travel.

Military? Shop at the Bases

Active-duty and retired military families are well aware of the savings available at their base commissary, but many neglect to seek out the same savings on the road. If a military base is convenient to your travel route, stop in and take advantage of the savings. A directory of services on military bases called *Guide to Military Installations* is sold at your base exchange, or for $13.50 from

Stackpole Books
P.O. Box 1831,
Harrisburg, Pennsylvania 17105

Avoid Convenience Foods

RV cooks sometimes fall prey to convenience-itis to save time or space in the kitchen. They pay for it. Convenience foods inevitably cost more. You pay for the packaging and the processing, plus they seldom provide the nourishment of fresh foods. The following are just a few examples of alternatives to so-called convenience foods:

Individual Juice Containers. You pay 30 percent more for the convenience of tiny portions of juice and a little plastic straw. Buy frozen or larger containers instead. Nonspill coffee mugs, baby cups,

---

$

Dollar-saving Tip

A large-capacity freezer can pay off in the long run.

or "sports" bottles provide the same convenience of on-the-drive sipping.

Salad Dressings.   Almost any cookbook offers delicious alternatives to bottled dressings, which are usually loaded with oil, sugar, and preservatives. Mix up your own before you go; most will last for weeks.

Boxed Mixes.   Again, consult a basic cookbook for biscuit, muffin, and cake recipes and mix your own. Store the mixes in labeled, airtight containers for a convenient and inexpensive source of fresh-baked goodies.

Spaghetti Sauces.   Market shelves are loaded with tempting bottled and powdered pasta sauces, but right next door are the canned tomato sauces and pastes. For the trouble of sautéing your own onions and mushrooms, you can prepare fresh sauces at a fraction of the cost, and freeze them for later. Roadside stands sell fresh tomatoes in the summer—a cheap and delicious source for fresh sauces.

Iced Tea.   Use tea bags in a large glass container and let the sun brew your iced tea, rather than paying more for a powdered mix or canned tea that never tastes as good as the real thing.

Breakfast Cereals.   Mix up your own granola, meusli, or oatmeal by buying rolled oats, other grains, raisins, and nuts. Be imaginative; nearly anything can be combined into hot or cold cereals, from prunes or chocolate syrup to dried banana chips, ginger, or cloves. You can add your own sweetener, or enjoy the natural sweetness of your mix—in any case, you save over processed cereals.

Frozen foods.   You pay about 300 percent more for commercial frozen meals. Nearly any dish you make from scratch can be divided into several meal-size portions and frozen, to be resurrected later in the oven or microwave at terrific savings. If you're to be on the road for a matter of weeks (and you have a large-capacity freezer), think ahead while at home, and prepare some of your favorite dishes for later. For inexpensive frozen-food containers, use folded-over milk cartons, meal-sealing devices, aluminum foil (reuse when possible), or plastic freezing bags.

Use Coupons, but Carefully

Coupons can certainly save you money, especially when stores compete with one another by offering double-coupon deals. But manufacturers tend to use coupons for some of their most expensive products; careful shopping can save you just as much. Also, coupons

You pay about 300 percent more for commercial frozen meals.

are often for processed and convenience foods for which you can easily find alternatives. Be alert for product coupons you use regularly, and keep a coupon file, alphabetized by product.

Some buyer's clubs offer coupon services, whereby you can order coupons for specific products, an excellent way to save on products you regularly use (see page 162).

Always check local papers (the weeklies that usually come out on Thursdays, or large Sunday papers) and free tabloids for local-market coupons. In addition, most supermarkets that print coupon ads in the papers distribute the coupon sections within the market. Many also maintain a rack of discount coupons; ask a clerk if you don't see them stacked inside the main door.

Use Lists

Making a list of needed items and sticking to it is the best way to avoid costly impulse buying. Maintain a list and keep it posted on or near the refrigerator, and you'll be more organized on your next trip to the market. You might also photocopy several copies of a checklist of foods you typically buy; then run down the list, ticking off the items you need at the time.

Plan Meals

Planning meals goes hand-in-hand with list making. Deciding just what you're going to prepare for the week saves trips to the market and reduces the temptation to buy at convenience stores. Try to plan either just the right amount for your family, or to make enough so another meal can be planned around the leftovers.

Check Unit Pricing

Most supermarkets today have unit pricing on the shelves; if you don't already make a practice of checking the per-ounce or per-unit price of products, begin doing so. It's among the most logical ways to save. After a few unit-pricing sessions, you'll begin to recognize the brands and sizes that save you money.

Dollar-saving Tip

Remember that old saw: Don't shop for food when you're hungry.

Buy Store Brands

Store and generic brands can save you up to 40 percent over name brands. Store brands are cheaper because they don't have big advertising budgets to be passed onto you, the consumer. In many cases, the products are virtually identical; in some cases, they're even made by the same manufacturer. Some products you can be certain are identical include sugar and some spices, baking soda, lemon juice, coffee, nonfat cooking oil, powdered milk, flour, vinegar, and honey.

Buy Fresh Foods in Season

On a year-round basis, frozen and canned foods may be less expensive than fresh foods, but if you buy fresh foods as they come into season, you'll save. And you'll eat more healthily. When you buy fresh fruits and vegetables, buy them loose rather than in packages, so you can inspect each item. The boxed copy on pages 172–173 includes some seasonal best buys. These are generally, but not always, the case, so allow for some regional differences. Also, certain items are almost always good buys; these include carrots, celery, onions, and potatoes.

Keep Your Fresh Foods Fresh

There's nothing more discouraging than having to throw out wilted vegetables or fruits and leftovers that have transmogrified into mysterious life forms. Refrigerate fruits when ripe. Refrigerate most vegetables in plastic bags or sealed plastic containers. Wrap meats in waxed paper. Freeze leftovers you don't intend to use right away. Naturally, you should be vigilant about leveling your rig to prevent your refrigerator from shutting off and perhaps losing all your fresh and frozen foods.

Watch for Day-Old Baked-Goods Outlets.

Many towns have day-old bread stores with great bargains on almost-fresh baked goods. If you have room, freeze the bargains for later consumption.

Pay Attention at the Checkstand

Checkers do make errors. So do scanners. Many stores will give you an item free if its price scans for more than what is indicated on the sticker or shelf label or if they fail to give you a receipt.

Buy Nonfood Items at Discount Stores

Grocery stores put high markups on items such as paper goods, shampoo, garbage bags, and toothpaste to make up for the low markups on fresh foods. Buy these things at discount or membership stores and save.

T ry to plan either just the right amount for your family, or to make enough so another meal can be planned around the leftovers.

Dollar-saving Tip

M enu planning reduces the temptation to make expensive impulse buys.

Buy in Bulk

Buying in bulk may not be practical for fulltimers and RVers on long trips, but everyone can keep in mind that larger quantities usually mean lower unit prices. Many supermarkets and health-food stores have bulk bins containing everything from muffin mixes to nuts to pastas. These allow you to scoop out just the quantities you need—you get the bulk rate because you're not paying for expensive packaging, but you don't have to buy more than you need.

One way to take advantage of bulk savings is to buy in bulk before leaving home, then divide the products into travel-size containers. For example, buy a large bag of flour, and take along a couple of pounds in an airtight container. Buy bulk hamburger, divide it into patties, and take some of it on the road, leaving the rest at home in the freezer. Transfer portions of mayonnaise and mustard to small plastic containers. Fulltimers and snowbirds can also purchase bulk purchases, divvy them up among themselves, and share the savings as well.

Liquor and meat tend to be the most expensive items on most RVers' shopping lists.

Seasonal Best-Buys

The following is a month-by-month list of seasonal best buys:

JANUARY	MARCH	Lamb	Summer squash
Apples	Apples	Lemons	Tomatoes
Beef	Artichokes	Pineapple	
Broccoli	Beef	Pork	JUNE
Brussels Sprouts	Broccoli	Rhubarb	Apricots
Chicken	Chicken	Summer squash	Asparagus
Eggs	Eggs	Turkey	Beans
Grapefruit	Fish		Beef
Oranges	Grapefruit	MAY	Beets
Pork	Lamb	Asparagus	Berries
Rhubarb	Oranges	Beans	Cherries
Turnips	Pineapple	Beef	Corn
	Rhubarb	Broccoli	Cucumbers
FEBRUARY	Scallops	Corn	Eggs
Apples	Turnips	Cucumbers	Fish
Broccoli		Eggs	Lemons
Chicken	APRIL	Fish	Melons
Fish	Artichokes	Lamb	Peas
Oranges	Asparagus	Lemons	Plums
Oysters	Broccoli	Peas	Radishes
Rhubarb	Chicken	Pineapple	Rhubarb
Scallops	Eggs	Pork	Salmon
Turnips	Fish	Rhubarb	Summer squash
	Grapefruit	Strawberries	Tomatoes

Cut Down on Costly Items

Liquor and meat tend to be the most expensive items on most RVers' shopping lists. Cutting back on both will reduce your food bills and will be good for your health as well. If you're accustomed to meat every night, cut back to two or three nights, and serve vegetable casseroles, pasta, salads, and rice dishes for alternative main courses.

Save Those Samples

Any time you receive sample-size versions of products in the mail (food, cosmetics, and cold remedies, for example), set them aside for your RV travels. They'll come in handy. Many discount stores offer a bin of sample-size products for sale at reasonable prices.

JULY
Apricots
Beans
Beets
Berries
Cherries
Corn
Cucumbers
Fish
Grapes
Lemons
Limes
Melons
Nectarines
Peaches
Peas
Peppers
Plums
Salmon
Summer squash
Tomatoes
Watermelon

AUGUST
Beans
Beets
Chicken
Corn
Eggplant
Fish

Grapes
Lemons
Melons
Nectarines
Peaches
Pears
Peppers
Plums
Salmon
Summer squash
Tomatoes
Watermelon

SEPTEMBER
Beans
Beef
Beets
Broccoli
Cauliflower
Chicken
Clams
Corn
Eggplant
Fish
Grapes
Peaches
Pears
Peppers
Plums
Scallops
Tomatoes

OCTOBER
Apples
Beans
Beef
Beets
Broccoli
Brussels sprouts
Cauliflower
Chestnuts
Cranberries
Parsnips
Pears
Pork
Pumpkin
Scallops
Sweet potatoes
Turkey
Turnips
Winter squash

NOVEMBER
Apples
Beef
Broccoli
Brussels sprouts
Cauliflower
Chestnuts
Cranberries
Fish
Lamb

Oranges
Oysters
Pears
Pumpkin
Sweet potatoes
Tangelos
Tangerines
Turkey
Turnips
Winter squash

DECEMBER
Apples
Broccoli
Brussels sprouts
Chicken
Cranberries
Grapefruit
Lamb
Oranges
Oysters
Pork
Sweet potatoes
Tangelos
Tangerines
Turkey
Turnips
Winter squash

Having Fun

Saving on food needn't be a matter of severe austerity. There are ways to take advantage of your RV lifestyle, save money, and have fun in the process. The following are some suggestions.

Use RV Cookbooks

Newcomers to an RV kitchen sometimes feel claustrophobic and uncreative. Many have gone your way before and overcome the challenges, and a few have shared their secrets in excellent cookbooks that take into account the priorities and circumstances of RV cooks. Here are three excellent books:

> ***The Good Sam RV Cookbook***
> Over 250 Recipes from Good Sam Club Members and Staff
> Beverly Edwards, editor
> Trailer Life Books, $14.95
> P.O. Box 4500
> Agoura, California

> ***The Great American RV Cookbook***
> William & Loretta Marshall
> Johnson Publishing Company, $12.95
> 1880 South 57th Court
> Boulder, Colorado 80301

> ***RV Cookery***
> Bonnie Webb
> Bonnie Webb, publisher $6.95
> Route 3, P.O. Box 680
> Holderness, New Hampshire 03245

Shop at Roadside Stands

Almost any area that raises fresh produce also offers you the opportunity to pick the produce yourself and save even more money.

One of the great delights of traveling rural America is finding roadside produce stands with delicious fresh fruits, juices, ciders, vegetables, preserves, honey, syrup, and nuts at great prices. Be spontaneous and willing to stop at these stands—they're part of the travel experience, as well as a way to save money.

Shop at Farmers' Markets

More and more communities are staging farmers' markets at least once a week, with fresh produce, baked goods, and often some entertainment as well. If farmers' markets aren't listed in information you've received from tourism bureaus, contact local visitors' bureaus or the county agriculture agency.

Pick Your Own

Almost any area that raises fresh produce also offers you the opportunity to pick the produce yourself and save even more money. Most states can provide lists of pick-your-own farms and orchards, but more likely, you'll simply encounter handwritten signs advertising the opportunity to pick cherries, berries, apples, and other goodies. The kids will especially enjoy these stops.

Also be on the lookout for wild berries and other wild edibles, such as watercress, sunflowers, and rose hips. Many RVers go as far as putting up their own preserves, juices, and syrups. Bookstores and libraries have volumes on the proper process for sanitary canning.

Grow Your Own

Really, as an RVer, you can't be much of a farmer, but you can easily raise your own sprouts as you travel. Seeds and sprouting jars are available in any health-food store. All you do is soak the seeds and rinse them occasionally; they sprout in a few days, providing a delicious addition to salads or sandwiches, or an excellent solo snack.

Catch Your Own

Few fishing enthusiasts really think of their pastime as a money saver, but once they've invested in all that gear, they may as well put some bounty on the table. Don't overlook clamming and crabbing possibilities along the coasts. Be very careful about where you do your catching: many waters are polluted; check with local authorities about local water safety and the legality of fishing and clamming.

Buy Regional Specialties

Equally a part of the travel experience are the many regional specialties you'll encounter on the road. You don't have to dine out to enjoy them. Many roadside stands sell prepared specialties such as cider, juices, honey, syrup, and pies. Fish markets sell local catches and seafood specialties, such as lobster in New England, catfish in the South, salmon in the Northwest, and crayfish in Louisiana. Watch for ham in Virginia, cheese in Wisconsin and Utah, and Cornish pasties in Michigan's Upper Peninsula. Very often, stores and stands

Very often, stores and stands selling local specialties will also sell or give away recipes.

selling local specialties will also sell or give away recipes. Or, you can pick up regional-cuisine cookbooks in bookstores (*The Great American RV Cookbook* has some excellent regional recipes) and learn to cook like a local.

Tour Food Plants and Canneries

A corollary to the process of buying regional specialties is to take advantage of tours through food-processing companies. You might visit a chocolate factory, a dairy, a winery, or a beverage-bottling plant. State or regional tourism offices can give you information on tours available in any area. These places are interesting, and most offer samples. As a general rule, they don't sell their products at a discount, because that would be competing with their retailers. Some, though, offer the opportunity to buy "bents and dents"—products with slightly damaged packaging that are otherwise undamaged. I recall touring the Ben & Jerry's ice-cream plant in Waterbury, Vermont, and purchasing "defective" ice cream. The problem was, the chunks of chocolate in a particular flavor were too large. I decided that was a defect I could live with!

Barbecue

Getting creative with barbecuing is a great way to enjoy summer evenings and delicious repasts that you couldn't buy at any price in a restaurant. Almost anything can be barbecued; don't be stuck with steaks, burgers, and chicken. Barbecue fish, shellfish, vegetables, and potatoes. Create creative kebabs. Portable propane grills make barbecuing clean and quick without the need to buy charcoal, lighter fluid, or firewood, and you don't have to clean those inevitably filthy campground grills.

Barbecuing is another way to "get regional," both in the method of grilling and the choice of what to grill. An excellent guide to regional barbecuing is *The All-American Barbecue Book* by Rich Davis and Shifra Stein (Vintage Books Division of Random House, New York).

Picnics

RVers are almost always in delightful places to picnic. Even though you have your own dining room, creative picnicking is a wonderful way to enliven your travel meals. With local fresh breads, cheeses, jams, cold cuts, juices, and a gingham tablecloth, you can prepare memorable repasts in settings no restaurant can match. Trade off the duties of picnic chef among partners—involve the kids, too. Have picnic dinners as well as lunches. Even when you splurge on gourmet picnic fodder, you're not paying nearly what you would for a restaurant meal.

DINING OUT

There's no question that you will generally pay much more to dine out than to dine in. But there's also no question that you will want or need to eat out from time to time. It's possible to do so without completely depleting your food budget.

One way to accommodate dining out is to use it as a reward to yourself for a week of well-budgeted dining in. Another way is to dine out for lunch rather than dinner. Expensive restaurants often have lunch menus with very reasonable prices. You can enjoy a great lunch as the day's main meal, and have a light meal—soup or salad—for dinner. The following are some additional suggestions for holding down the costs of dining out:

Ask about Senior Citizens' Specials. If you're in the right age category, you can often save as much as 20 percent on your meals out. Some restaurants offer special seniors' dishes rather than a discount; quantity might be a little less, but so will the price. Always ask; sometimes the sign advertising seniors' discounts may be hard to spot.

Take advantage of early-bird specials. RVers are usually early birds anyway; stopping for dinner before 6:00 P.M. or 7:00 P.M. can often save you up to 30 percent. Many chain restaurants offer such specials. Again, it's always worth asking if you don't happen to see a sign.

Use Resources to Find the Best Places to Eat. A bad meal out is a waste of money, and because RVers are generally strangers to the areas they visit, they run a high risk of finding poor or mediocre meals that still cost a bundle. Any type of recommendation can reduce those risks significantly. Campground managers and rangers almost always know of good, reasonably priced places to eat. Many campgrounds have sample menus from local restaurants. Weekly entertainment papers often carry restaurant listings with reviews, descriptions of cuisine, and prices. The chamber of commerce or visitors' bureau in any area can provide restaurant listings. These won't be actual reviews, but will still give you an idea of cuisine and prices.

One excellent book that covers interesting eateries around the country is *Roadside Food* by LeRoy Woodson (Stewart, Tabori & Chang, Publishers; $14.95).

If you're going to splurge, you might as well do so on good food. One way I've found excellent restaurants is by looking through dining guides in local bookstores. Such guides are often published for a

Dollar-saving Tip

You don't have to buy alcoholic drinks to enjoy restaurant "happy hours," where you can "graze" among delicious, free hors d'oeuvres.

I figure that anyone willing to put his or her name on a place takes a measure of pride in the food.

If you're going to splurge, you might as well do so on good food. One way I've found excellent restaurants is by looking through dining guides in local bookstores. Such guides are often published for a city, county, or state. If I'm just passing through, I don't actually buy the guide; I just make a mental note of the name of a place that interests me, then phone for a reservation. Some travelers contend that real-estate agents always know the best places to eat. It makes sense that they'd be more tuned in to the culinary highlights of the area than the kid who checks your oil in a service station.

Still, discovery can be part of the pleasure. Another trick of mine is to seek out the older part of any community, rather than the suburban fringe where neon and fast food reign. Once there, I look for places called Joe's, Mom's, or Betty's; I figure that anyone willing to put his or her name on a place takes a measure of pride in the food. It's far from foolproof, but it often works. I also look for signs such as "World Famous Cherry Pie," or, "homemade" anything. And, of course, I look for places advertising regional specialties.

William Least Heat Moon, in his book *Blue Highways: A Journey Into America,* has a unique formula for finding "honest" food:

> There is one almost infallible way to find honest food at just prices in blue-highway America: count the wall calendars in a cafe.
>
> No calendar: Same as an interstate pit stop.
> One calendar: Preprocessed food assembled in New Jersey.
> Two calendars: Only if fish trophies present.
> Three calendars: Can't miss on the farm-boy breakfasts.
> Four calendars: Try the ho-made pie too.
> Five calendars: Keep it under your hat, or they'll franchise.
>
> One time I found a six-calendar cafe in the Ozarks, which served fried chicken, peach pie, and chocolate malts, that left me searching for another ever since. I've never seen a seven-calendar place. But old-time travelers—road men in a day when cars had running boards and lunchroom windows said AIR COOLED in blue letters with icicles dripping from the tops—those travelers have told me the golden legends of seven-calendar cafes.

Seek Out Smorgasbords and All-You-Can-Eat Restaurants. These are seldom award-winning establishments, but can really be a boon for families. An all-you-can-eat stop usually suffices as the main meal of the day. Some all-you-can-eat salad bars provide reasonably priced, filling, healthy fare.

Participate in Potlucks. Potlucks are a fixture of RV lifestyle, especially at RV rallies and in snowbird parks. But many campgrounds have weekly potlucks in which anyone can participate. Check the campground bulletin board or the flyers you're handed when you check in. You risk overdosing on gelatin molds, but you can also have some excellent meals, make friends, and share recipes.

Watch for Local Fund-raising Meals.   Especially in summer, most communities have fund-raising meals hosted by churches, service groups, lodges, or youth groups. You may find a pancake breakfast, a fish-fry, clambake, barbecue, or potluck dinner. You're almost certain to find good, reasonably priced food. Check local bulletin boards, signs in store windows, and local papers for notices.

Attend Local Festivals.   Using the calendars of events you've collected from tourism bureaus (see pages 250–253), you can plan your travels to include local festivals, many of which are oriented around food. Those that aren't still include food booths and dinners. They take place everywhere, year-round: festivals honoring everything from garlic to catfish to frogs. The food and the atmosphere will be memorable treats no restaurant could equal.

Check Local Literature for Discounts.   Quite often, brochures you pick up at chambers of commerce, in campgrounds, or at state welcome centers include discount coupons for local restaurants. It's their way of luring in visitors, your way of saving money.

Buy Entertainment Coupon Books.   Entertainment books, which you're probably familiar with in your own community, offer lots of two-for-one dining specials, among many other money-saving coupons. The books cost money, and don't make sense for constant travelers. But if you're a snowbird or in a region for several months, such a book can be a great money saver. Inquire at the local chamber of commerce.

Everyone develops their own "tricks of the trade" when it comes to eating on the road, whether it's preparing simple, elegant meals, or seeking out interesting eateries. You'll no doubt develop some tricks of your own; it's all part of the discovery-filled way of life on the RV road. And because this is the case, making friends with the folks next door is often the best way to find good food. It may be in the form of a suggestion, a recipe, or an invitation to dinner. You might reciprocate the next night, and the cycle, the grapevine, spreads and continues. There's no reason ever to become bored, to fall into repetition, or to spend a lot of money. Eating on the road should always be a pleasant adventure.

CHAPTER SEVENTEEN

Your Health on the Road

■ ■ ■ ■ ■ ■ ■ ■ ■ ■ ■ ■ ■ ■

Count RVing as among the healthiest of activities. Away from the stresses of jobs and cities, surrounded by beauty, with time to be as active or relaxed as one could wish, RVers on the road often enjoy the most health-filled days of their lives. But RVers nonetheless must be aware of their health while they travel. As beneficial as RVing can be, it, like any pastime, presents certain challenges, not the least of which is finding and paying for health care away from home.

The mere fact that an RV vacation is so different from home life presents some health stresses for some: unusual chores to handle; long hours spent sitting; or conversely, the temptation to overdo certain activities; and possible changes of diet. The fact that you're often far from your ordinary medical providers can be a concern. And, if you camp in remote locations, you might be far from medical care of any kind. Persons with chronic conditions may be concerned about obtaining prescriptions out of state.

These and other topics will be addressed in this chapter. They should not daunt anyone from participating in the RV lifestyle. Hundreds of thousands of RVers who have genuine health concerns travel extensively, even full time. Many handicapped RVers enjoy active RV vacations. Travel itself is such an elixir: For most RVers, it's the best medicine they could take.

In This Chapter:

- *How can I stay healthy during my travels?*
- *What medical records and supplies should I carry?*
- *How do I find good medical care on the road?*
- *What do I need to know about health insurance? Medicare? Medigap?*
- *How can I save on medications and prescriptions?*
- *What resources exist for disabled RVers?*

STAYING HEALTHY

Whether you're on the road or at home, the best way to save on health-care costs (which, as everyone knows, are escalating dramatically) is to stay healthy. A recent study supported that fact. Stanford

University researchers compared the insurance claims of 5,680 retirees. Part of the group participated in a wellness program that emphasized these basic health tenets: don't smoke; limit alcohol; avoid saturated fat; exercise regularly; wear seat belts. The difference in costs—doctor's visits and hospital stays—was an average of $385 per person the first year.*

Another study, conducted by San Jose State University, showed that if people over sixty-five who smoked, drank, and were overweight and sedentary cut out all those bad habits, they could save at least $4,500 a year in medical costs.†

It's beyond the scope of this book to cover in detail all the ways to maintain or improve your health. Most of them are common sense and well known to intelligent adults anyway. The trick is to incorporate them into your RV travels so that you either maintain your healthy regimen of home life, or, better, utilize your RV travels to *improve* your health habits. After all, if you're not healthy, you're not getting your money's worth from your RVing, no matter how many money-saving suggestions you've gleaned from this book.

Following are some suggestions for staying healthy on the road. Not all of them apply to everyone. And by all means, if age or a chronic condition affect your health and lifestyle, *consult with your physician before embarking on your travels or making any changes in your health regimen*. Getting a clean bill of health or health-care suggestions specific to your needs before you take to the road will help you to enjoy your activities fully and obviate the need for urgent or emergency care on the road.

Stay Active

It's certainly not news that an active life with adequate exercise (within reasonable limits prescribed by your physician) is a key to good health. Most RVers have no trouble finding ways to stay active, but some give in to a sedentary way of traveling. Ironically, the very complaints they cite to avoid exercising are generally alleviated *by* exercising. See the boxed copy on the opposing page for some suggestions for staying fit and active.

Eat Sensibly

Vacationing often brings a temptation to splurge, to violate your diet, to eat convenience foods laden with salt and preservatives. But considering most RVs have a refrigerator and a full kitchen, there's really no excuse for succumbing to such temptations. Instead, enjoy the opportunity to buy good farm-fresh vegetables and fruits. Cut down on meat, fried foods, and white-flour products and eat more whole

> **A**nother study . . . showed that if people over sixty-five who smoked, drank, and were overweight and sedentary cut out all those bad habits, they could save at least $4,500 a year in medical costs.

**Changing Times, January 1991, 84.
† Ibid.

grains. An excellent basic primer for healthy eating is available free (with a $1 service charge) from the U.S. government:

Dietary Guidelines for Americans
Consumer Information Center
P.O. Box 100
Pueblo, Colorado 81002

Other booklets from the same center include *Eating for Life* ($1), *Eating to Lower Your High Blood Cholesterol* ($2), *Eating Better When Eating Out* ($1.50), and *Food News for Consumers* (four issues a year for $5).

Seven Tips for Keeping RV-Active

The following are some suggestions to help you keep active.

1. **Stop early in the day.** If you're between destinations, you're often tempted to push hard and drive until at least dinnertime. Stopping early in the day gives you time to be active every day. After all, life is short; why should one day be less important than another?

2. **Go for walks.** Dr. Bruce Barnett, the Good Sam Club's *Highways'* "Healthy Traveler" columnist, contends that walking is the healthiest of all exercises. Research shows that it reduces weight, lowers blood pressure, and alleviates depression. Any walk is better than none, but walking to lose weight and improve your health means brisk walking, within your health limitations. Dr. Kenneth Cooper's popular book, *Aerobics* (Bantam Books), emphasizes the importance of elevating your heart rate during walking or any type of exercise. The book is a very useful reference (to be used in conjunction with your doctor's advice), which shows how regular, nonstressful exercise can improve your health.

   Be alert for notices of group walks posted on the campground bulletin board. Some private campgrounds offer them, and most public campgrounds have occasional ranger-led hikes.

   Setting aside time each day for a brisk walk (not just a saunter to drain the poodle and to check out your neighbors) is a wonderful way to stay healthy and to fully enjoy the beauty of wherever your travels take you.

3. **Swim.** So many campgrounds have pools, and so many others are on lakes—don't just turn the water over to the kids; it's for you, too. Swim whenever you have the chance.

4. **Ride a bike.** Bicycling is an excellent way to run errands when you're all hooked up in a campground, and another way to enjoy the countryside wherever you're camped. Be sure to wear a helmet. Many RVers enjoy the stability and upright position of mountain bikes, which also provide a wide range of gears for pedaling up hills. As with walking, bicycling is only beneficial if you get your heart rate up a bit, best accomplished by briskly spinning the pedals in a reasonably low gear. This is why single-speed bikes aren't recommended for exercise; the fixed gear is too high to permit spinning.

5. **Dance.** Many RV parks, especially in snowbird areas, offer square dancing and ballroom dancing, both excellent forms of exercise.

6. **Stretch.** Slow, gentle stretches keep you limber and enhance your circulation. Stretch both before and after exercise, and before you go to bed. During a long drive, stop every couple of hours and spend ten minutes or so stretching. Take advantage of roadside rest areas, which are conveniently spaced, for stretching and a short, brisk walk. Many campgrounds offer morning stretching or yoga sessions.

7. **Join a recreation program.** Especially if you intend to stay in one area for a while, check into programs offered by local parks and recreation departments or the YMCA.

Maintain a Healthy Environment

The confined interior of a recreational vehicle can present various health hazards. As anyone who has purchased a new rig knows, the fumes emanating from carpet dyes and wood-paneling preservatives can be noxious. It's important to keep the rig well ventilated while these fumes are still present. Some RVers are particularly sensitive and develop respiratory difficulties, teary eyes, and even drowsiness.

If you travel with a smoker, ask him or her to smoke outside. The Surgeon General's office and the National Academy of Science have affirmed a link between passive smoking and both lung cancer and heart disease. A study published by the American Heart Association in 1991 called passive smoking the nation's third-leading cause of preventable death.

Tight quarters also call for diligence in maintaining a tidy ship. Keep floors clear of items one can trip on, keep knives secured in a drawer; in general, think safety as well as cleanliness.

If you don't have a smoke detector, get one (two, for a larger rig). Be sure everyone who travels in the RV knows the location of the fire extinguisher and how to use it. Everyone should also know an alternative way out of the rig should fire prevent access to the main door.

Be alert for LP-gas leaks, especially if you don't have a leak detector. If you catch a whiff of the telltale rotten-egg odor, ventilate the rig, turn off the cylinder supply valve, and check for leaks with soapy water at all LP-line connections.

Keep a First-Aid Kit on Board

All sorts and sizes of first-aid kits are available, but the most thorough and economical version is one you put together yourself and keep in a small box or bag. Dr. Paul G. Gill, an emergency physician from Vermont writing in *Trailer Life* magazine, recommended including the following items:

Antiseptic solution	Emetrol (for nausea and vomiting)
Adhesive bandages	First-aid manual
Adhesive tape	Ice packs (instant-type)
Antibiotic ointment	Kling or Kerlix gauze (a few rolls)
Aspirin, acetaminophen, or ibuprofen tablets	Maalox or Mylanta
Benadryl antihistamine tablets	Safety pins
Calamine lotion	Scissors
Cortisone cream	Solarcaine or Bactine
Cotton swabs	Sunscreen
Cough syrup	Triangular bandage
Donnagel (for diarrhea)	Tweezers
Dramamine (for motion sickness)	Vaseline
Elastic bandages	

Learn First Aid and CPR

First-aid classes are taught frequently at Red Cross centers, as are cardiopulmonary resuscitation (CPR) classes. Both teach you basic skills that could save the life of someone you love and are especially important to RV travelers who are often away from immediate professional help. They should include the Heimlich maneuver to prevent someone from choking to death. CPR classes are also taught frequently at campgrounds, especially in snowbird areas. But don't wait for one to be offered; contact the Red Cross office nearest you and enroll in a CPR course. The cost is nominal, and the course takes but a few hours.

Take Care of Your Skin

RVers tend to be lovers of sunshine, but true sun worshipping can be hazardous to their health. Sun damage is cumulative; once a certain amount of damage has been done, skin cancer can occur. The most susceptible are people who are fair-skinned, tan poorly, have red or blonde hair, or are blue-eyed.

Any progressively growing skin lesion should be checked by a physician. Play close attention to changes in old spots or moles.

When in the sun, always wear a hat and protective clothing, and use a sun block with a high skin-protection factor, preferably 15 or greater.

Be aware that certain medications can make you even more sensitive to the sun, including tetracycline, diuretics, and tranquilizers.

How to Recognize the Symptoms of a Heart Attack

Heart attacks, which can come on without warning or history of heart disease, are not always severe and obvious. For this reason, it's important to recognize the symptoms of a heart attack:

- Persistent chest pain, usually under the sternum (breastbone). The pain may radiate to one or both shoulders or arms, or the neck, jaw, or both.
- Gasping and shortness of breath
- Extreme pallor or bluish discoloration of the lips, skin, and fingernail beds
- Extreme prostration (physical weakness or exhaustion)
- Shock
- Swelling of the ankles

The victim should be placed in a comfortable position, usually sitting up. If the victim is not breathing, begin artificial respiration. (*Know Your CPR!*) Have someone call for an ambulance. Don't transport the victim unless a physician advises you to do so. Don't administer liquids.

Take Care of Your Back

RVing entails many situations that can cause back strain. Driving, of course, is one of them. Stopping frequently to walk and stretch can be a big help. Many RVers use a small pillow to support the lumbar, or lower back. Hooking up a rig can also be a back-straining chore. Don't merely bend at the waist to hook up hoses and cables or to pick up objects; bend your legs to stoop low.

BEFORE YOU LEAVE

Before beginning any extended trip, visit your doctor for a checkup, for any immunizations you may require, to renew prescriptions for medications, and to obtain photocopies of your medical records, including X-ray, laboratory reports, and electrocardiograms. Or, your doctor can give you a compendium of your medical history, including current or chronic illnesses, medications, allergies, previous operations, family history, and the names, addresses and phone numbers of any specialists who have been involved in your care. This information can be critically important to a physician trying to evaluate you in an emergency or urgent-care situation.

Some experts recommend that you keep your own medical records. This is especially important if you're on the road full time, or you've moved a lot in the past and your records may be incomplete. Under any circumstances, it's a way of being responsible for your own health. Record every medical condition you and your family members have had in the past. From now on, also record every visit to a physician or dentist. Note all medications prescribed and taken, with dosages and side effects noted; all hospitalizations and lab tests; and the names and phone numbers of every doctor and facility that has treated you.

Also take a copy of your health-insurance policy with you; you might need to consult it to see what medical procedures require prior authorization from your carrier.

Also ask your optometrist for a copy of your eyeglass prescription, should you need an emergency replacement while traveling.

Keep all these important documents, along with others, such as your insurance policies and vehicle-registration papers, in a fire-proof box. Many RVers store the box in the refrigerator.

If you have a particular condition or allergy to medication that you would want an emergency physician or paramedic to know about, you can register it with:

Medic Alert Foundation
P.O. Box 1009
Turlock, California 95381
(800) 344-3226

Take a copy of your health-insurance policy with you; you might need to consult it to see what medical procedures require prior authorization from your carrier.

OBTAINING HEALTH CARE ON THE ROAD

If the situation appears to be an emergency, waste no time. Rush to the nearest hospital emergency room or phone for an ambulance. Every time you arrive at a campground, note the locations of telephones, usually by the entrance station and the campground store.

You should carry a card with you at all times that includes the toll-free number of your insurance company or health maintenance organization (HMO). Call the number as soon as possible before, during, or after obtaining care on the road. Document the call by noting the time and obtaining the name of the person you speak to. This can help greatly later when you file a claim.

If the situation isn't dire, but appears to be important, urgent-care centers, which are proliferating around the country, may save you a considerable amount of money compared to an emergency-room visit, on the average, a 50-percent savings. Such clinics, often located in shopping centers, are open twelve to twenty-four hours a day and require no appointment. They're listed in the Yellow Pages under "Emergency Medical and Surgical Service," or "Physicians." The campground attendant should be able to direct you to the nearest center.

Note: If time and the circumstances permit, always contact your family doctor before seeking treatment on the road.

If you need to see a doctor, but the situation isn't as urgent, there are a number of ways to locate one:

Dollar-saving Tip

If it's not a dire emergency, an urgent-care clinic saves you about 50 percent over an emergency room.

- Call the largest hospital in the area and ask for the hospital's referral service. If it doesn't have such a service, ask for the supervising nurse on duty, who should be able to make a well-informed referral.
- The campground manager may be able to refer you to a doctor who has agreed to see patients on short notice.
- If you have a "gold" credit card, you have among the benefits a toll-free number you can call for medical assistance or a referral.
- Call your preferred-provider organization to learn if there's a network doctor in the area.
- You can walk in to a hospital or clinic—showing up in person may get you in to a doctor sooner that an appointment made by phone.
- You can ask a pharmacist for a referral.
- You can call the local medical society or local hospital referral service, listed in the Yellow Pages under "Physicians and Surgeons Information Bureaus." These services can refer you to a specialist or a doctor who will take patients on short notice, but be aware that many fine doctors are not members of local medical societies.
- If you belong to a national RV club, lodge, or fraternal order

and you have a membership list with you, you can call a local member and ask for a referral. An example is the list of Standby Sams, available to Good Sam Club members. Standby Sams are Good Samers who have indicated a willingness to help members needing assistance on the road.

If you plan to stay in any area for an extended period of time, you should seek out a doctor *before* you need the doctor's services.

If a doctor proposes nonemergency surgery, you should always seek a second opinion. Most insurance companies will pay for the second opinion, and many require it. If the second doctor disagrees with the first, seek a third opinion. It's best not to obtain a referral from the doctor proposing the surgery; use another referral source.

QUESTIONS TO ASK A DOCTOR

Before you choose a physician, ask the following questions:

- Does the physician commonly treat patients in your age group?
- Does he or she have expertise in the particular medical problem or condition you have?
- How long has the physician been practicing?
- Is the doctor board certified?
- Does the physician have admitting privileges at a good local hospital?
- Will the doctor accept your insurance, or, if you're on Medicare, does the physician accept assignment? (*Assignment* means agreeing to accept the Medicare-approved charge as payment in full, except for the deductible and co-insurance amount that you must pay.)
- Does the doctor accept credit cards?
- Will you be informed of fees for routine visits and procedures *before* any procedure or test is performed? Not only is this important once you have selected a doctor, it allows you to make price comparisons among doctors you're considering.
- Does the office have X-ray equipment, a blood-testing laboratory, and other testing and diagnostic equipment? Charges for tests are less in a doctor's office than at a hospital.
- Is the doctor cost-conscious? Will he or she prescribe generic drugs whenever possible? Does he or she suggest alternatives to expensive tests and procedures?

Once you've selected a doctor, be willing to ask more questions, such as why he or she has come to a certain diagnosis, what exactly it means, why medication is being prescribed, and what you can expect from the condition and the treatment. Be sure to ask what you can do, apart from taking medication, to improve your condition. Ask for informational pamphlets on your illness or condition,

Dollar-saving Tip

Tests conducted in the doctor's office will cost less than in a hospital.

or obtain books on it from a library or book store. Your willingness to be a partner in your own health care is the best way to insure your health and to spend your health-care money wisely.

INSURANCE

Anyone the least bit familiar with the cost of medical care knows the necessity of good health insurance. You probably either have such insurance already, you're covered by Medicare, or you belong to an HMO (health-maintenance organization) or PPO (preferred-provider organization, such as Blue Cross/Blue Shield). Your main consideration before traveling is to ask exactly how claims are handled when you're away from your primary-care provider and the company's policies regarding emergency treatment.

HMOs work out well financially for most people compared to health insurance. You pay premiums, but no deductibles or copayments. Charges for prescriptions are usually nominal. However, if you travel frequently or full time and belong to an HMO, you may have difficulty in obtaining coverage for treatment outside the HMO's geographical area. Emergency treatment should be covered, but filing a claim and getting it paid can be time consuming. Check into the HMO's policies carefully; you may want to consider switching to health insurance or to a PPO.

If you belong to a PPO such as Blue Cross/Blue Shield, ask the organization for a directory of physician members and preferred hospitals for the areas you will be visiting. If you go to a non-preferred provider, the charges may exceed what the PPO will pay, and you will be responsible for the difference.

Medi-Vac Coverage

Because RVers are often in remote locations, away from specialized treatment centers, the likelihood of needing emergency air evacuation is greater. Insurance policies cover ambulance transportation, but most don't cover helicopter or airplane transportation. Bearing the cost yourself could be expensive—as much as $6,000.

If you want the extra peace of mind that results from such coverage, check with your insurance company or agent. Find out if you are already covered, or if not, if a rider can be attached to your policy. Compare the cost of the rider with the cost of a policy from a specialist in this type of insurance, such as:

Sky-Med
Tower Group International
P.O. Box 2387
Brentwood, Tennessee 37024
(615) 370-8802

> Anyone the least bit familiar with the cost of medical care knows the necessity of good health insurance.

Saving on Health Insurance

The following are some ways to save on health insurance:

■ Raise the deductible on your present policy. Deductibles of $1,000 and higher are available, at a savings of 35 percent to 45 percent over $150 or $200 deductibles. The risk you should be concerned about is not the first thousand dollars of a claim, but the hundreds of thousands of dollars a serious illness or accident could cost you.

■ Purchase insurance only from financially stable companies. You can investigate the financial standing (look for a rating of A or A+) of an insurance company by consulting *Best's Insurance Reports,* available in most insurance agencies and the reference departments of many libraries, or contact:

A. M. Best
Ambest Road
Oldwick, New Jersey 08858
(908) 439-2200

■ Buy a group health plan. Group plans are almost always less expensive than individual plans. Even if your employer doesn't offer health insurance, or if you're retired or self-employed, you might be able to obtain a group plan through your spouse's group plan, or through membership in a club, guild, union, or volunteer organization. Some credit-card companies offer group health benefits. If you don't belong to any such groups, you can join one that is open to anyone wishing to obtain health insurance:

Co-Op America
2100 M Street NW, Suite 403
Washington, D.C. 20063
(202) 872-5307

If you're over fifty and a member of the American Association of Retired Persons, you can obtain insurance at group rates. Contact:

AARP Group Health Insurance Program
P.O. Box 7000
Allentown, Pennsylvania 18175
(800) 523-5800

■ If you retire early or become unemployed, you can continue your group health plan under the terms of the Federal Consolidated Omnibus Budget Reconciliation Act of 1985 (COBRA).

The act requires employers to continue your coverage for eighteen months after you retire or become unemployed at a rate not to exceed the normal group rate plus two percent. This is especially important if you have a medical condition that could make health insurance expensive or difficult to obtain.

After the eighteen months, most group plans allow departing members to convert to an individual policy. The cost will be higher; you should compare costs to those of other plans on the market. But again, this conversion can be very important if you have a pre-existing condition.

- Contact your local Blue Cross/Blue Shield organization. Most Blue Cross/Blue Shield groups offer health insurance to individuals, and because the company is nonprofit, the rates are generally competitive.
- See an independent insurance agent for price quotations from for-profit insurance companies.
- If you have a health condition that precludes obtaining an individual policy, your state might have a risk pool. The insurance will be expensive, but at least you can get it. Contact the state insurance department in your state capital.

> If you have a health condition that precludes obtaining an individual policy, your state might have a risk pool. The insurance will be expensive, but at least you can get it.

Medicare

If you're sixty-five or older, you're eligible for federal health insurance—Medicare. You should be familiar with the basic coverages of Medicare. As you undoubtedly know, Medicare is divided into Parts A and B.

Part A is hospitalization insurance. It pays for medically necessary hospitalization for 60 days after you pay a deductible, $628 at the time of this writing. You are responsible for $157 a day for days 61 to 90, $314 a day for days 91 to 150, and all costs after the 90th day.

Part B is Medicare's medical insurance plan, which helps pay for physician services no matter where you receive them. You pay an annual deductible of $100, then Medicare covers 80 percent of the approved amount for covered services you receive the rest of the year. You or your private health-insurance plan are responsible for the other 20 percent.

Doctors who "take assignment" on a Medicare claim agree to accept the Medicare-approved charge as payment in full, except for the deductible and 20-percent copayment. It's important to ask when you go to a new doctor if he or she will take assignment on your Medicare claim; if not, you will have to pay the difference between the doctor's charge and the Medicare-approved charge. The *Medicare Participating Physician/Supplier Directory* lists physicians who accept assignment on all Medicare claims (other doctors accept assignment on a case-by-case basis). The directory is available at Social Security offices.

For more information about Medicare, you should consult these free booklets, available from your local Social Security Office, listed under "U.S. Government" in your telephone book: *Your Medicare Handbook, How to Fill Out a Medicare Claim Form,* and *Your Medicare Recordkeeper.*

Medigap Insurance

Medigap insurance is private health insurance that is designed to supplement the benefits of Medicare. A Medigap policy must include:

- Either all or none of the Medicare hospitalization deductible. Be sure to clarify this. If the Medigap insurance does not pay the deductible, you may be getting less insurance than you think.
- The co-insurance for hospitalization for the 61st through the 90th days
- Ninety percent of expenses for up to 365 days after Medicare hospital benefits are exhausted
- Three pints of blood per calendar year
- The Part B co-insurance amount: 20 percent, after the $100 deductible

Dollar-saving Tip

Compare Medigap prices and coverage against AARP and Good Sam policies.

Be aware that Medigap policies are almost always designed to fill benefit gaps, not coverage gaps. Medicare has significant coverage gaps—it will not, for example, pay for prescriptions or routine checkups. *What isn't covered by Medicare will remain uncovered by Medigap with possible rare exceptions.*

Shop for Medigap insurance as you would for any other; investigate the stability and reputation of the company. Don't buy multiple Medicare supplements; many provide overlapping coverage. Buy one comprehensive policy.

Do not be pressured or rushed into buying a policy. Do not believe claims or implications that any insurance to supplement Medicare is sponsored by the government; it is not, and such a claim is fraudulent. Compare benefits and rates; for example, some policies cover prescriptions and travel abroad.

Although numerous Medigap policies are available and you should certainly shop around, use the highly regarded policies offered by AARP and the Good Sam Club as indices for comparison. You should also obtain the free booklet:

Guide to Health Insurance for People with Medicare
Health Care Financing Administration
6325 Security Boulevard
Baltimore, Maryland 21207
(301) 966-3000

Another information source is:

The Consumer's Guide to Medicare Supplement Insurance
Health Insurance Association of America
1025 Connecticut Avenue NW, Suite 1200
Washington D.C. 20036
(800) 942-4242 or (202) 223-7780

VETERANS' BENEFITS

The U.S. Department of Veterans Affairs (VA) maintains a network of hospitals and clinics nationwide that provide medical care to veterans. The VA maintains toll-free numbers all over the country to answer questions about veterans' benefits. Look in the White Pages under "U.S. Government."

A useful booklet, available for $2.50, is:

Federal Benefits for Veterans
Consumer Information Center
P.O. Box 100
Pueblo, Colorado 81002

SAVING ON PRESCRIPTIONS AND MEDICATIONS

The best way to save on medications is to take only what is truly necessary for your health. You should always be a participating partner in your health. When a doctor prescribes medication, be sure to ask precisely *why* it is being prescribed, if it is truly necessary, if you have a nondrug option for treating the condition, what the effects and side effects will be, and whether the drug will interact with other drugs you're taking. (Keep a card with you that lists all the medications you are taking. It's also a good idea to take the medications themselves with you when you visit a doctor.) You may be wasting money on prescriptions you don't really need, or worse, for drugs that could cause you harm.

Drug interactions should always be a concern; this is why it is so important to inform the doctor who prescribes the medication and the pharmacist who fills it if you are taking other medications—*including over-the-counter medications*. Some medications have interactive effects that can damage your health.

Treat over-the-counter (OTC) drugs as powerful medicines. They are. The fact that they're offered for sale without a prescription does not mean they are automatically safe for everyone. Read the labels carefully; you might have a condition that could be damaged by an OTC. Always consult a doctor if you're taking an OTC for more than a brief period of time, or if you're already taking any kind of medication.

Dollar-saving Tip

Always compare prices on OTCs; prices can vary for chemically identical medications.

How to Save on Prescriptions and Medications

The following tips can help you save additionally on medicines:

■ Ask your doctor and pharmacist about generic drugs. New drugs are sold by brand name and are protected by patent for seventeen years. After that, other companies can sell the same drugs under their generic, or nonbrand, names. By law, generic drugs must be identical to the brand-name equivalent in every important way. Be sure to ask your doctor if the generic equivalent is *proven* to be equally effective. For a complete, free listing of all prescription tablets and capsules for which generic equivalents are available, write for:

> **A Consumer Guide to Generic Drugs**
> Generic Pharmaceutical Industry Association
> 200 Madison Avenue, Suite 2404
> New York, New York 10016

Other useful booklets available for a $1-handling fee (each) are:

> **Myths and Facts of Generic Drugs** and
> **Some Things You Should Know about**
> **Prescription Drugs**
> Consumer Information Center
> P.O. Box 100
> Pueblo, Colorado 81002

■ Compare prices. Prices can vary as much as 30 percent from pharmacy to pharmacy for the same prescription. Don't be bashful about asking upfront what the cost will be and checking more than one pharmacy. Also compare prices on over-the-counter medications. Many different brands are identical in composition; only the prices differ. Some stores have inexpensive store brands of items such as aspirin and throat lozenges.

■ Ask for a senior's discount. Many pharmacies offer discounts to seniors.

■ Order by mail. If you take any medications on an ongoing basis, you can save by ordering through the mail. Also, because most states do not allow pharmacists to fill prescriptions written by out-of-state doctors, mail-order makes it easy for travelers to get refills; mail-order companies can fill orders and send them nationwide, regardless of the location of the prescribing physician. It generally takes seven to ten days to receive an order (or you can pay for overnight delivery), so you need only know where you'll be at that time. Some mail-order sources:

> **AARP Pharmacy**
> P.O. Box 19229
> Alexandria, Virginia 22320

> **America's Pharmacy**
> P.O. Box 10490
> Des Moines, Iowa 50306

> **Getz Prescription Company**
> 200 Main Street
> Madrid, Iowa 50156

> **Bronson Pharmaceuticals**
> 4526 Rinetti Lane
> La Canada, California 91011-3359
> (vitamins, minerals, skin-care)

RESOURCES FOR THE DISABLED

Thousands of physically challenged RVers testify to the fact that disabilities needn't put an end to the enjoyment of RVing. Many find RVing not only possible, but therapeutic. Federal legislation signed into law in 1990 gave persons with disabilities more rights than ever, which means more and more public and private facilities will have to cater to disabled travelers.

In addition, many products are available for disabled RVers, from custom motorhomes to special driving controls. One RV club, the Handicapped Travel Club, provides information and fellowship to handicapped RVers. The following are resources for disabled persons interested in beginning or continuing RVing:

Handicapped Travel Club
667 J Avenue
Coronado, California 92118

Accent on Information
P.O. Box 700
Bloomington, Illinois 61702
(309) 378-2961

Publishes a quarterly magazine called *Accent on Living* and numerous booklets for the handicapped, such as *Single-Handed,* a guide to special services for the handicapped, and *Traveling Like Everybody Else,* a travel-resource guide.

Automobile Association of America

Local offices of AAA distribute a book to members called *Handicapped Driver's Mobility Guide.*

RVIA
1896 Preston White Drive
Reston, Virginia 22090
(703) 620-6003

The Recreation Industry Vehicle Association will refer you to van converters, manufacturers of trailers and motorhomes, and to companies that can retrofit RVs to accommodate disabled travelers.

Here's to your health—and to many healthy years on the RV road.

CHAPTER EIGHTEEN

Handling Your Finances on the Road

■ ■ ■ ■ ■ ■ ■ ■ ■ ■ ■ ■ ■ ■

The challenge of handling your finances on the road becomes trickier in direct proportion to the duration of your travels. For weekenders and two-week vacationers, it's hardly a problem. For those who travel for months at a time, or full time, it's a different story. You're usually far away from your bank and your mailbox, yet you need money regularly and you need to pay your bills.

Full-time and long-term travelers have special challenges that will be addressed in this chapter, but everyone who travels shares a number of on-the-road financial concerns: Each of us wants our money to be secure while still having easy access to it—and for this money to earn as much interest as possible.

Fortunately, modern services, such as automatic teller machines (ATMs), telephone banking, and the wonderful convenience of credit cards, make traveling more convenient than ever. However long you wish to travel, you should not be daunted by the prospect of handling your finances. You may want to consolidate things a bit: reduce the number of accounts you maintain, the number of credit cards you carry, the number of bills you pay. But once you do, you should be able to travel for long periods or forever and still manage your finances as easily as you would at home.

WHERE TO PUT YOUR MONEY

No matter how much you try to simplify your life, you need a relationship with a bank and a bank account. If you still maintain a home and roots in your community, a neighborhood bank is the best place

In This Chapter:

- *Where should I keep my money, and how do I access it while traveling?*
- *Are traveler's checks necessary anymore?*
- *How can I use credit cards to my advantage?*
- *What do I need to know about ATMs?*
- *How do I pay my bills while I'm on the road?*

to maintain a checking account—although not necessarily your savings (see the section on cash-equivalent savings, page 199). You'll almost certainly need a checking account to pay your bills.

Your Checking Account

Keep the following in mind as you decide where to maintain a checking account and how much money to put in it:

- Keep in your checking account the smallest amount of money necessary. What is necessary? Consider the money you need to pay for your month-to-month expenses and the minimum balance required to avoid stiff bank charges.
- Open a Negotiated Order of Withdrawal (NOW) account or a money-market checking account. Both these accounts pay interest on your balances. Money-market accounts pay higher interest, but require a higher minimum balance, often $2,500. NOW accounts require a certain amount to open, typically $1,000, but will pay interest on any balance you have. Watch out, though; high monthly charges can easily gobble up the interest you receive on a low balance. Check with several banks and savings-and-loan institutions to compare fees.
- Ask about senior-citizen benefits. Many banks offer free checking and other services to seniors. The minimum age may be anywhere from fifty-five to sixty-five.
- Be sure to apply for automatic-overdraft privileges. This is a nice peace-of-mind benefit for anyone, but especially for frequent travelers. Returned-check charges these days can be as high as twenty dollars per check. You'll pay high interest on overdrafts—18 percent or more—but it's worth having the protection against returned-check charges.
- When you shop for a bank, evaluate all the benefits offered and fees charged. Be sure to tell the new accounts manager your situation if you're a frequent or full-time traveler, and investigate the bank's services that can benefit you, such as automatic deposit of payroll or Social Security checks and automatic bill paying. You should certainly shop around for fees and services, but also consider the possible advantages of "relationship banking," that is, staying with your bank of many years and maintaining more than one account and perhaps a credit card there. Having a good relationship with a bank can facilitate obtaining a loan, a special line of credit, or personalized services when you need them.
- Telephone banking—being able to obtain your account balance over the phone, having checks paid, or having funds transfered from one account to another—can be crucial to frequent travelers. Many banks offer this as a twenty-four-hour service.

$

Dollar-saving Tip

Keep your money earning interest; access it only when you need it.

Many banks offer free checking and other services to seniors.

Cash-Equivalent Savings

Even if your checking account pays interest, it will be less than most savings opportunities. Passbook savings accounts are only slightly better. Whatever your financial picture, you should have some money in high-earning cash-equivalent savings—programs that allow you to earn market rates of return with a high degree of safety. Here is where you should place your emergency cash reserves—money you can easily access to meet your cash needs at any time. Most investors also choose to keep a portion of their investment portfolio in cash equivalents. It is beyond the scope of this book to advise readers on their other investments—bonds, stocks, mutual funds, or securities. The following are some cash-equivalent options to consider.

Returned-check charges these days can be as high as twenty dollars per check.

Bank Money-Market Accounts

These accounts pay higher interest—up to 1 percent more—than passbook savings. Bank money-market accounts are not to be confused with money-market mutual funds, which usually pay even higher interest. If the account is federally insured, it's a safe and practical way to save. Money-market accounts require a minimum balance and allow limited check-writing privileges.

Certificates of Deposit

If you're willing to tie up your money for several months, you can earn higher interest in certificates of deposit (CDs). CDs are typically sold in $1,000 units. Maturity dates and interest rates vary from

---

How Safe Is Your Bank?

With the great number of failures of savings-and-loan institutions and banks, the safety of your bank deposits is naturally a concern.

The best assurance of safety is the type of insurance your financial institution has on your accounts. If it is federally insured through the Federal Deposit Insurance Corporation (most banks and S&Ls now belong to FDIC), your accounts are insured up to $100,000 per depositor. If you belong to a credit union, you have identical coverage if the credit union belongs to the National Credit Union Share Insurance Fund.

If you're fortunate enough to have more than $100,000 on deposit, you can extend the limit by placing one account in your name, another in your spouse's, yet another in a joint account. Or you can open insured accounts in different institutions.

If your money is in a federally insured institution, you will be protected even if the bank or savings and loan were to fail. Should that happen, government regulators will arrange a takeover or merger. Most likely, your bank's doors would never even close; at worst, you might lose a couple of days' interest payments. Your loans, too, would be taken over at the same terms as before.

institution to institution. Be sure to ask about the penalty for early withdrawal; many banks are easing those penalties to attract investors. You can usually earn a little more interest by purchasing a CD from a brokerage house than a bank.

Unless you're really concerned about relationship banking, don't hesitate to invest in CDs or money-market accounts at another bank, even an out-of-state bank. Banks in certain parts of the county frequently offer considerably higher rates. Check publications like the *Wall Street Journal, Barron's,* or *Money* for the highest yields.

Money-Market Funds

Most financial experts are very strong on money-market funds, which pay more than bank money-market accounts. The interest rates are generally good, the risk low, and the liquidity high. If you're especially cautious, invest in funds that buy only government securities. But your money should be quite safe (although never as safe as in a federally insured bank account) investing in a regular money-market fund, as long as it is run by a reputable mutual-fund group or brokerage. Yields don't vary much from fund to fund. They do vary from year-to-year; interest rates were as high as 17 percent in 1981. Lately they have been around 8 percent or 9 percent, still much better than money-market bank accounts.

Treasury Securities

The safest place to put your money is in the hands of the federal government. For individual investors, this means Treasury bills (T-bills), notes, and bonds. T-bills are sold in minimum denominations of $10,000, in three-, six-, and twelve-month maturities.

Other options take much longer to reach maturity: Treasury notes are usually sold in minimum denominations of $5,000 when the maturities are less than four years and in minimums of $1,000 when maturities are four or more years. Bonds sell in minimums of $1,000 but have maturities of more than ten years.

Treasury yields are good, the investment as safe as the government itself, and you don't pay state or local taxes on your earnings. Nor do you pay federal taxes until the bills mature.

ACCESSING YOUR MONEY

No traveler should carry large amounts of cash around, whether on their person or in the RV. Nor is there any need to. The wonders of electronic banking and plastic money make it unnecessary to carry much cash. Credit cards are discussed in detail beginning on page

> Unless you're really concerned about relationship banking, don't hesitate to invest in CDs or money-market accounts at another bank, even an out-of-state bank.

203. The other two most popular ways of handling day-to-day expenses are with traveler's checks and cash obtained from automatic teller machines (ATMs). ATMs have virtually eliminated the traveler's headaches of yesteryear, such as trying to cash a personal check in an out-of-town bank (often downright impossible) or having money wired (expensive and inconvenient). The following are the comparative advantages of traveler's checks.

Traveler's Checks

The old standby of travelers for years, traveler's checks make less and less sense all the time. They have never been a good deal financially—you give money that could be earning you interest to some institution that, in turn, earns interest on your money. Worse, you often pay a 1-percent charge for that dubious privilege.

Most RVers like to have some money in traveler's checks as an emergency-cash stash. The convenience of traveler's checks is indisputable—they function as cash virtually anywhere. It's important, though, to select a major brand, such as American Express, Bank of America, or Visa traveler's checks, since off-brands might be unfamiliar to a clerk in remote corners of the world.

How much to carry in traveler's checks is up to the individual, but a rule of thumb is to carry just enough to cover a few days' expenses. That way you're covered if you can't locate an automatic teller machine, you lose your cash, or just neglect to obtain cash. Remember, you can always buy more traveler's checks wherever you are.

If you decide to carry traveler's checks, you can avoid paying the standard 1-percent charge. Many banks offer free traveler's checks as a checking-account benefit. The Good Sam Club offers free traveler's checks to members (a $3 charge applies on amounts under $500), and AAA offers traveler's checks free to its members. Good Sam's Bank of America traveler's checks are available by mail or can be charged over the phone to a credit card. AAA's American Express traveler's checks can be purchased at any AAA branch office. Some branches accept personal checks; others require an American Express card, money order, or cashier's check.

Remember, "free" is a misnomer. Traveler's checks cost you the money they would be earning in an interest-bearing account.

Be sure to take seriously the instructions given whenever you purchase traveler's checks: Always sign them right away, and keep the list of check serial numbers separate from the checks themselves. (Record or tick off the check numbers as you cash them.) If your checks are lost or stolen, they are much easier to replace if you have the serial numbers. Be sure you understand the procedure for replacement of lost checks. Also remember that once you countersign a traveler's check, it can be cashed. Don't countersign until you make a purchase.

I f you decide to carry traveler's checks, you can avoid paying the standard 1-percent charge.

Dollar-saving Tip

Using an ATM is the best way to reduce the cost of traveler's checks.

Automatic Teller Machines

ATMs are among the greatest boons to convenient traveling since the invention of the RV. Nearly every ATM machine is electronically linked to thousands of others through networks such as Cirrus and Plus. They make it possible for you to keep your money earning interest until the moment you need cash. With over 90,000 ATMs in operation in the United States and Canada, you're never far from a convenient source of cash.

Most ATMs also allow you to draw a cash advance from your MasterCard, Visa, Discover, or American Express card.

Shopping for an ATM

Keep in mind the following when you are shopping for a bank, because the bank's automatic teller services will be very important to you as you travel:

- Does the bank's ATM card gain you access to a national or international network of ATMs? If so, how many? Are there plenty of locations in the areas you travel? Most banks will give you a directory of ATM locations within the network or networks, as well as a toll-free number you can call at anytime to learn the nearest ATM location.
- Is there a charge for use of the ATM? Only 14 percent of banks charge for using the bank's own machines, but about three out of four charge for withdrawals from the ATM network. These charges range from 10¢ to $2. You're likely to be a frequent ATM user, so compare these charges when you are selecting a bank.

Using an ATM

Keep in mind the following as you use the automatic teller machines:

Don't write the [PIN] number anywhere in your checkbook or wallet.

- More and more businesses are accepting ATM cards for purchases and will also allow you to draw cash at the same time. This is true of many service stations, grocery stores, fast-food chains, and convenience stores, and undoubtedly more locations in the future.
- Be sure to record your ATM transactions in your checkbook or savings-account ledger. It's easy to foul up your personal accounting by failing to do so.
- Keep in mind that some banks update account balances only once per day, so you may not be able to immediately access cash you've transferred or deposited to your account.

■ Most issuers of ATMs allow you to select a personal identification number (PIN), and also allow you to change the PIN at any time. This way you can select a number that's easy for you to remember. Don't write the number anywhere in your checkbook or wallet. Don't select a number that may be evident, such as four numbers from the card itself, on another card you carry or from your license plate.

■ If you lose your card, or you note a suspect transaction on your statement, report it immediately. If a thief figures out how to use your card, your liability can mount quickly. If you notify the bank within the first two business days after you realize something is amiss, your liability is limited to $50. But if you wait, the liability is $500 for the next 60 days, and 100 percent after that.

■ If you feel an automatic teller machine has made a mistake—for example, not recording the full amount of a deposit, notify your bank right away. Phone immediately, and follow up with a written account of the error. The bank has forty-five days to resolve it. If it has not completed its investigation within ten days, it must provisionally credit your account for the amount you claimed you lost through error, plus interest on that amount. If you are unable to reach an agreement with the bank, you can file a grievance with the Division of Consumer and Community Affairs, Board of Governors of the Federal Reserve System, Washington, D.C. 20551. If your dispute is with a federally chartered credit union, write the National Credit Union Administration, Division of Consumer Affairs, 1776 G Street N.W., Washington, D.C. 20006.

> ATMs are among the greatest boons to convenient traveling since the invention of the RV.

Credit Cards

Credit cards are not only a great convenience to travelers, they can also be among the most practical of financial tools. Naturally, you must guard against abusing your credit by overextending yourself. But if you have your credit-card use under control—if you're able to curb impulsive purchases and pay off your balance regularly—credit cards can be extremely useful.

What Cards to Carry

Frequent travelers find it most practical to pare their wallet-bulging pile of charge cards down to just one or two. There's really no reason to carry several gas cards, for example, when virtually every service station except cash-only stations accepts Visa and MasterCard. If you feel you might need to make purchases at large department stores, you should carry one or two cards for stores with coast-to-coast locations. If you tend to run up exceptionally high monthly balances, you might want to carry an American Express card, which has no credit limit. American Express and other travel-and-entertainment cards, such as Diner's Club, charge a high annual fee, though. If you need a higher credit limit, Visa and MasterCard issuers will usually raise it for the asking.

Most RVers do very well with just one MasterCard or Visa, but it's also a very good idea to have a backup card—either another Master-Card or Visa, or a Discover card. A backup card is useful should you exceed your credit limit or lose a card. With the availability of no-fee credit cards (see pages 205–206), a backup costs you nothing until you use it.

Consolidating your cards means consolidating your bills and rec-ordkeeping. That kind of streamlined simplicity adds to the peace of mind you no doubt want to enjoy while traveling.

The Advantage of Floating

Dollar-saving Tip

Float your charges while your money continues to earn interest.

Why use credit cards? The most obvious answer is to eliminate the need to carry a lot of cash. But there's an ancillary aspect to that fact: Credit cards allow you to "float" your money up to sixty days. During that time, your money can remain in an interest-bearing account. As long as you pay off your balance, the situation works to your advantage.

How does this work? Most credit cards have a twenty-five-day grace period. (If yours doesn't, get one that does.) That means you have twenty-five days to pay off the balance of your bill before any interest is charged. (Actually, most banks have an additional five-day grace period after the twenty-five days.) Plus, it may be thirty days from the time you make a charge before you receive the statement containing the charge. That means you can have as many as sixty interest-free days to pay your charges.

Be aware, though, that you must pay off your balance to enjoy the float. If a balance of any amount is carried over to the next month, most banks will begin to charge interest from the date of each new purchase; the interest charges begin accumulating even before you receive your monthly statement. In other words, if you carry a balance, you lose your grace period.

Cash Advances

Credit cards enable you to obtain a cash advance at banks and ATMs, a valuable backup service should you deplete the bank account or accounts that you draw upon with your ATM card. However, obtaining a cash advance usually costs money. The transaction fee is typically between 1 percent and 2½ percent of the transaction, up to

$10. There's generally no grace period; you're charged interest beginning the day of the transaction. The Good Sam Club Visa card is an exception. It allows members to draw $200 a day through ATMs with no fee and no interest charge during the grace period.

Purchase Protection

If you have a problem with a purchase you made by credit card, your credit-card issuer may stand behind you in your dispute. First you must attempt in good faith to resolve the dispute with the merchant. If this fails, write all the details of the dispute to your credit-card issuer. Send copies of the charge slip, your correspondence, and, if you returned merchandise, your return receipt. If the disputed charge is over $50 and was made within your home state or within 100 miles of your home, the process is most straightforward, and you stand a good chance of having the charge reversed.

However, any dispute is worth pursuing. Most bank-card issuers are willing to assist their customers whenever possible. Typical dispute scenarios include returning faulty merchandise and failing to receive a credit; merchandise or service not as advertised; or merchandise not received. The process can take longer if the charge was made out of state. Auto repairs can be particularly tricky and time consuming. But while the card issuer investigates (they usually deal more with the merchant's bank than the merchant), you can withhold payment for the disputed charge and you will not be responsible for finance charges during that period. You must, of course, pay the remainder of the balance on your account.

Eventually, assuming you win the dispute, the charge will be reversed. Or, if you already paid it, you will be issued a credit for the disputed amount.

How to Save on Credit-Card Rates

When was the last time you checked the annual fee and interest rate charged on your credit card? Most people tend to accept whatever their bank charges without realizing it's possible to find a better deal.

Card issuers generally charge $20 for conventional cards and $50 or more for premium (gold or platinum) cards. It's not unusual for interest rates to be 18 percent, 19 percent, or higher on top of the annual fee.

You can save on both annual fees and interest rates by obtaining lists of institutions currently charging low interest rates and no annual fees from the Bankcard Holders of America. At this writing, BHA's list included thirty or so banks offering no-fee credit cards. If you pay off your balances regularly, a no-fee card makes sense. BHA also lists banks offering interest rates as low as 11 percent. If you tend to carry a balance in your credit-card account, a low-interest card makes sense.

What *doesn't* make sense is a card with a high annual fee and a high rate of interest, which most banks are perfectly willing to offer you.

The lists of no-fee and low-interest cards are $1.50 each from:

Bankcard Holders of America
560 Herndon Parkway, Suite 120
Herndon, Virginia 22070.

A backup card is useful should you exceed your credit limit or lose a card.

(BHA is a membership organization representing the rights of credit-card users.)

Other possible sources of bargain credit cards are associations, clubs, and unions. Examples are cards sold by the Good Sam Club and AARP. In some cases, a small percentage of your transactions is donated to the association or charity. These "affinity-group" cards sometimes offer a good combination of low interest and low fee, but you should compare them to other available cards.

Another source of credit-card bargains is your own mail, which probably includes frequent promotions for Visa and MasterCard. It's a competitive business, so some of these credit card deals are very attractive. Many offer no annual fee the first year, and a few offer no annual fee for life—even for a gold card. Some might also offer exceptionally low interest the first year. Read these promotions carefully; you might otherwise be tossing away a real bargain.

One card that is always available for no annual fee is the Discover card. The interest rate is high, however, nearly 20 percent at this writing—not a concern, of course, if you pay off your monthly balance. Plus, if you make a lot of purchases, Discover's money-back program, a rebate of a small percentage of your charges, can offset the higher interest.

Gold Cards

Most credit-card issuers offer an option of a premium (gold) card that carries with it a higher annual fee and more fringe benefits than do standard cards.

The companies often stress the "prestige" of holding one of these cards, a marketing ploy that should not be a consideration for anyone contemplating one. Gold-card holders are not nearly as elite as advertising suggests. These cards are generally available to anyone with household income of $35,000 to $40,000.

Gold cards do offer some benefits worth considering, but weigh them carefully before deciding to spend up to $100 a year for them. The following are some of the factors you should consider.

Fees and Interest Rate. You should compare these just as you would a standard card. Sometimes all the fringe benefits, the "bells and whistles," obscure the most important factors: how much the card costs per year and what the interest charges are. A list of the best deals in gold cards is available from Bankcard Holders of America (for address, see page 206).

Higher Credit Limit. Gold-card credit limits start at $5,000 and go up from there. However, if you need a higher credit limit, you should be able to get one from the issuer of your standard card, or you should be able to obtain a second standard card. If you have an American Express card, you already have unlimited credit, although you must pay it off every month.

Enhancements. Typical enhancements, or fringe benefits, offered with gold cards include:

1. *Discounts on car rentals, hotels, tours, and the services of a travel agency.* These are not of interest to many RVers.
2. *Emergency road assistance.* These programs can help you locate roadside assistance through a toll-free number, but they should not be confused with services like Good Sam's Emergency Road Service. The gold-card service does not *pay* for the assistance; it just locates help for you and allows you to charge it to your credit card. Good Sam's ERS locates help *and* covers the cost of the roadside assistance and/or towing.
3. *Travel-accident insurance.* This, too, is irrelevant to most RVers, as the insurance applies only to travel by plane, train, ship, or bus, and the tickets must have been purchased with the gold card.
4. *Lost or damaged baggage insurance.* This applies to airline, boat, bus, and train travel.
5. *Emergency medical assistance.* Most gold cards offer medical-referral service, even an interpreter if necessary. Some gold cards also offer a small amount of actual medical insurance, with a low deductible and emergency evacuation. These are benefits worth considering if you're not already well covered.
6. *Legal assistance.* This is a referral service that can be valuable in foreign countries.
7. *Purchase insurance and extended warranty.* Most gold cards offer free ninety-day protection on items purchased with the card against loss, theft, damage, or fire and will double the original manufacturer's warranty up to one additional year. However, this insurance is secondary to protection you may already have on your homeowner's or RV policy. The theft provision does not cover theft from a vehicle.
8. *Collision damage waiver insurance.* This is designed to cover the daily loss-damage waiver policy that car-rental firms generally try to get you to tack on to the cost of a rental. However,

Dollar-saving Tip

Many gold-card enhancements may overlap benefits you already have.

most vehicle-insurance policies cover this anyway, and the gold-card protection does not extend to RV rentals.

9. *Credit-card registration.* This provides you with a single toll-free number to call should you lose your credit cards. If you carry a number of them, this can save you looking up all the appropriate numbers and phoning them.

10. *Long-distance telephone discounts.* Some gold cards offer telephone discounts through long-distance phone service providers. If you make a lot of long-distance calls while traveling, this benefit might cover the expense of a gold card.

Credit-Card Fraud and Protection

If you have an American Express card, you already have unlimited credit, although you must pay it off every month.

It should go without saying that you must report a lost or stolen credit card immediately. Carry a list of the appropriate numbers (nearly all of them are toll-free) to call. While your liability is limited to $50 per card, it's nevertheless to your benefit to avoid the hassle of disputing a thief's purchases.

Some gold cards and other issuing organizations offer credit-card registration, which allows you to list all your credit cards, place a single toll-free call, and have the company notify all your credit-card issuers. This is a good fringe benefit, but hardly worth paying for; it's not too difficult to maintain your own list of card issuers and to notify them should the need arise.

Always guard against unauthorized persons obtaining any of your credit-card numbers. Always take the carbon as well as the carbon copy of any credit-card draft. Fortunately, the carbon is often laminated to the customer copy these days. Thieves will scour trash cans for carbons or copies, which enables them to make mail-order purchases on your card.

Many merchants require that you present a major credit card when you write a personal check. If the salesperson takes down your card number, it can fall into the wrong hands. The card number, along with your name, address, and phone number on the check, can be used to place a fake credit application. In other words, someone "steals" your personal information and applies for credit in your name, running up large bills on "your" account.

There's probably no harm in showing the merchant that you hold a major credit card, but the Bankcard Holders of America recommends against giving out your credit-card number when writing a personal check. If the merchant is adamant about writing down your credit-card number, BHA suggests you inform the merchant that:

1. Visa, MasterCard, and American Express strictly prohibit charging a consumer's credit card to cover a bounced check.

2. A credit-card number, in most cases, cannot be used to locate a consumer if there is a problem with his or her personal check. Merchants have all the information they need to locate the

consumer—name, address, phone number, and driver's license.

Ask your bank if it issues a check-guarantee card (such a card often doubles as your ATM-access card). It should eliminate the need to show a credit card when writing a check.

In addition, requiring phone numbers or addresses on credit-card sales slips can be an invasion of privacy. The policies of Visa, MasterCard, and American Express prohibit merchants from refusing a sale to a customer who is paying by bank card simply because he or she refused to provide a telephone number or address. In fact, some states have passed laws making it illegal to demand a phone number.

R̲equiring phone numbers or addresses on credit-card sales slips can be an invasion of privacy.

PAYING YOUR BILLS

If you're new to long-term or full-time travel, paying your bills back home may seem like an obstacle almost impossible to overcome. It's not. Thousands of full-time RVers prove that it's possible even in this complicated era to simplify life and to easily handle any such residual obligations as a few bills to pay. Here's how:

- If you're to be gone a couple of months—long enough to miss some bills, but not long enough to completely shut down operations on the home front—you can pay some bills in advance. Write a check for the amount you usually pay (for example, on your last phone bill), and ask to be credited that amount.
- Consolidate and simplify. Before you embark on long-term travel, try to reduce the number of bills you'll have to take care of. Use a Visa or MasterCard for all your gas purchases, and be rid of a stack of oil-company bills. Stop your newspaper and magazine subscriptions, and pay off the balances.
- Arrange to have your regular income source, such as paycheck, pension check, or Social Security, deposited directly to your checking or savings account. Contact your bank for specifics.

You'll still have some bills to pay. The following are ways to handle them:

- If you'll be away several months, but not full time, you can presign checks and leave them with a trusted friend or relative who will receive your mail and pay the bills.
- If you'll be away a very long time, or full time, you can open a joint checking account in your name and in the name of the friend or relative who will pay your bills.
- You can arrange to have the friend or relative forward your mail to you by phoning in or dropping a postcard with a forwarding address, then pay the bills yourself. Although most mail can be

forwarded through the postal service by crossing out the address and writing a new one on the envelope, many bills cannot be forwarded this way; have your mail handler repackage them. Actually, it's best to have all your mail repackaged because envelopes may arrive at different times, increasing the possibility of missing some mail.

■ You can have the post office forward your mail if you'll have a fixed address for several months.

■ You can have an accountant handle your bills and deposits—an expensive alternative, but if you have special needs, it might be worthwhile.

■ You can use your bank's bill-paying service, an extra-cost aspect of telephone banking. Banks charge a monthly fee and a small per-bill fee. Bills that are the same every month, such as loan payments, can be paid automatically. You also leave a list of your creditors. When you wish a bill to be paid, you phone into your bank, punch a number code for the creditor, then for the amount to be paid, and the bank will pay it. You may also have the bills sent directly to the bank. Computer users can also subscribe to services such as Check Free. They do their accounts on their computers, modem them to the service from a telephone, and the service then prints and mails the check.

Mail-Forwarding Service

Dollar-saving Tip

Avoid late charges on your bills with reliable mail forwarding.

A mail-forwarding service such as the one offered by the Good Sam Club is another way to handle bill paying. Other mail-forwarding services are listed in the classified advertising sections of RV magazines such as *Trailer Life.* Private mailbox companies also offer mail-forwarding service.

Most on-the-go fulltimers use a mail-forwarding service. This costs more than other forwarding methods, but you have the convenience of notifying the service day to day (usually by means of a toll-free number) of your newest forwarding addresses. The services are professional: they know about postal rates, they know how to package your mail, and they provide you with a fixed address to give all your correspondents. Your friend or relative may move or go on vacation; mail-forwarding services won't. You'll naturally want to be sure the service has been in business for some time; ask other RVers for referrals.

Mail-forwarding services always bundle your mail into larger envelopes, which helps account for the cost of the service, but also reduces the possibility of lost mail.

Incidentally, many of the mail-forwarding operations also offer telephone-message service at an extra cost.

Which forwarding address to use? General Delivery at a small-town post office is probably the safest and most convenient. It's a good idea to drop a postcard to that post office notifying them to expect your mail, and give them an estimated time of your arrival. Before giving out a campground address, be sure to check with the park manager regarding the park's mail receiving and distributing policy. Most are happy to accommodate travelers' mail.

All the services and conveniences are there for you, eliminating most of the would-be financial headaches associated with long-term travel and allowing you to go wherever the breezes take you and still maintain a tight rein on your pecuniary affairs.

CHAPTER NINETEEN

Earning (or Volunteering) Your Way

■ ■ ■ ■ ■ ■ ■ ■ ■ ■ ■ ■ ■

This may sound too good to be true: Traveling around the country in an RV full time or several months a year, going just where you please, camping in pristine settings among friends, living the good life, and making it pay, as well. Thousands of RVers do it. Many on fixed incomes—pensions and/or Social Security—supplement their retirement incomes by selling arts and crafts or performing various services. Others actually go into the workplace, working a part-time circuit of sorts in different places. Some leave their jobs and find ways to earn a full-time living on the road, while yet others derive satisfaction from doing volunteer work.

The possibilities are more varied than you may think. There are so many ways of supplementing or earning income on the road—all it takes is a little creativity, perhaps a dash of courage, and you can see RVing not as a pastime that drains money, but a lifestyle that presents unlimited possibilities for making money—and even for making a contribution to the world.

SIX WAYS TO SUPPLEMENT YOUR INCOME

Most people who earn income on the road do so just to bring in a little extra money to help pay for their travels. It's not hard to do. Chances are you have some skill or creative gift on which you can capitalize. It may be something you've always enjoyed for fun, like

In This Chapter:

■ *How can I supplement my income while I travel?*

■ *How can I make money at flea markets and swap meets?*

■ *What about working in campgrounds?*

■ *What information sources exist for working campers?*

■ *What are my tax obligations?*

■ *Can I write off my RVing expenses?*

■ *What volunteer opportunities exist for RVers?*

knitting or wood carving. It may be your profession, like auto repair or bookkeeping. Whatever it is, you can put your skills to work, help pay for your travels, and perhaps get a tax break as well.

The following are some ways RVers earn supplemental income:

Selling Arts or Crafts

You needn't be a fine artist, although certainly some RVers are talented enough to sell paintings and carvings to galleries and at art shows. But others simply come up with a clever craft idea or derive inspiration from seeing the work of others. Some examples include knitted pot holders, nylon-net dish scrubbers, personalized needlepoints, wood carvings, name plaques, jewelry, caricatures, and leather goods.

Hint: Keep in mind that in RVing circles, practical objects, useful in an RV, sell well. So do gifts for grandchildren, such as children's clothes, dolls, or wooden toys.

Most campgrounds in snowbird areas hold regular swap meets and arts and crafts shows during the winter months. Pick up a copy of *Clark's Flea Market USA* for a national listing of flea markets (see page 158). State calendars of events often include listings of major arts shows and local festivals. If you're serious about exhibiting at art shows, obtain a copy of the following publication, which compiles and rates art shows nationwide. It's available for $40, postage included:

> ***Harris Rhodes List of the Nation's Best
>   Arts and Crafts Festivals***
> Harris Rhodes
> P.O. Box 142
> LaVeta, Colorado 81055

Another way to sell arts and crafts is through consignment shops. You might even set up a network of such shops as you travel. You should always put up a sign on the bulletin board in campgrounds where you stay, perhaps with a photo of your craft. Include your site number so people can come by and see your wares. Most campgrounds frown on site-to-site solicitation, but if you show to a few campers, word often travels quickly.

Selling Other Items at Flea Markets

You don't need artistic talent to make money at flea markets. Just look around at the things being sold: everything from antiques to collectibles to pure junk. You can even sell someone else's crafts. One trick some savvy flea marketeers practice is to visit a swap meet during the final hour and offer a package price for someone's re-

---

Keep in mind that in RVing circles, practical objects, useful in an RV, sell well.

maining merchandise, then sell the merchandise for full price at another swap meet.

Because selling at flea markets is generally a two-day work week, RVers have time to comb junk stores, garage sales, and thrift shops for items to sell at swap meets. Most RVers naturally prefer lightweight, portable goods. Some that sell well at swap meets are tools; new, used, or handmade clothes; linens and fabrics; crystals; pet-shop products; dolls; clocks; sunglasses; coins and stamps; toys; flags and banners; small appliances; cosmetics and perfumes; jewelry; cameras; handbags and luggage; posters and prints; musical instruments; gloves, belts, hats, scarves, socks, and other accessories.

Dollar-saving Tip

Crafts magazines advertise mail-order sources for hobby materials.

Selling Fishing Flies

Anyone who can tie good flies can sell them wherever fly-fishers are found: tackle shops, marinas, or around the campground.

RV Maintenance and Repair

Again, a notice on a bulletin board and a little word of mouth can bring you business if you're mechanically skilled. Even if you're not, you could do exterior maintenance, such as washing and waxing. Be sure to clear such a service with the campground management.

Teaching Classes

Snowbird campgrounds, senior-citizen centers, and community recreation programs all offer classes in various skills and activities: dance, yoga, aerobics, crafts, foreign language. Many teachers volunteer their efforts, but if you have special expertise, the campground or center will usually allow you to charge and will take a percentage of your enrollment money. Even if you don't stay long in one place, you might have a skill that you can teach in one or two sessions. You could, for example, become a certified CPR instructor.

Get Serious about Selling Your Services

If you really want to supplement your income by selling a craft or a service, get serious about marketing yourself. Have a business card printed. Design a flyer on brightly colored paper to post on bulletin boards. You needn't limit yourself to the campground bulletin board. Self-service laundries, shopping centers, and recreation centers are other good places to advertise. If you're in an area long enough, run an ad in the local newspaper. You can also paint a sign on your RV, or have a banner made that you can drape on the rig: "Mac's RV Detailing," or "Betty's Scrumptious Strudel." That way you won't need to solicit site-to-site; the folks will come to you.

Cooking or Baking

You've probably noticed that RVers love to eat. Some talented RV chefs make arrangements with campground owners to sell baked goods—usually breakfast items such as cinnamon rolls, doughnuts, or coffee cake. If the campground has a group barbecue area, you could arrange to stage a weekly barbecue, for which the campground would take a percentage. Any such arrangements must be cleared with the campground management and probably will not be permitted in public parks.

WORKING IN CAMPGROUNDS

According to the editors of *Workamper News,* more jobs exist in campgrounds and resorts than do people to fill them.

Growing numbers of RVers are finding employment in the very places they most enjoy visiting: RV parks, resorts, and public campgrounds. Campground managers and supervising rangers appreciate the maturity and responsible nature of RV travelers, many of whom also bring special skills to their part-time or seasonal work. They also appreciate the availability of RVers, who can usually work a longer season than college students, for example.

Campground jobs include registering campers, typing, computer operation, patrolling, construction, maintenance, and guiding recreation programs. Additional opportunities in state and federal parks might include interpretation (nature hikes and campfire programs), dispatching, or campground hosting (see page 222 for more on the volunteer host programs). Larger public parks have concessions that offer even more opportunities: food service, store sales, tour guides, and hotel jobs.

According to the editors of *Workamper News*, more jobs exist in campgrounds and resorts than do people to fill them. Although pay is generally rather low, employers are learning how to make a situation attractive, such as offering a discount in the campground store, a choice full-hookup campsite, and even a bit more money.

Private Campgrounds

Some private campgrounds are staffed almost entirely by RVers. Many offer free campsites plus modest salaries for part-time work, and many have opportunities for couples. Fortunately, the seasonal requirements of campgrounds match the seasonal preferences of RVers. Northern campgrounds need summer help; Sun Belt campgrounds need winter help.

Joan Stanley, whose Sun 'n Fun Campground in San Benito, Texas, hires RVers from November 1 to April 1, suggests that RVers be familiar with a campground's peak season, and arrive a few weeks ahead of time to apply and to receive training. You can phone or write in advance, but Stanley won't hire anyone she hasn't met first.

She frequently rehires people from the previous season, people who also have an ongoing arrangement with a northern campground. Her employees must be willing to work the entire season.

The wages aren't high for seasonal work, often minimum wage or slightly above, depending on the job, but the work is usually stress-free and enjoyable, in delightful surroundings. And the fact that wages are low helps keep campground costs low—savings that can be passed on to campers.

Applying at your favorite campgrounds is one way to find employment, but to learn of opportunities nationwide, the best source of information is *Workamper News*. This bimonthly newsletter serves as a clearinghouse of information on campground and resort jobs.

The newsletter lists openings at RV parks and resorts, some federal campgrounds and concessions, as well as "situation wanted" classifieds. In the latter case, you advertise your skills to prospective employers. The following are some listings from *Workamper News:*

> **QUAINT FAMILY LAKESIDE RESORT** is offering seasonal employment opportunities from April through Oct. Positions available are: store clerks, restaurant cooks and wait staff, nanny, handyman, and campground maintenance and fee collections. Benefits include laundry and shower facilities, living accommodations (RV site), and employee discounts. A great opportunity for neat, friendly people who can spend a season with us.

> **COUPLES NEEDED** for part-time help at beautiful park. Duties include maintenance, groundskeeping, registration, and help with special events and social activities. Looking for mature responsible people who are people-oriented and enjoy the RV lifestyle. Short-term or year-round available. Three-day workweek in exchange for site plus $250/couple/month.

Other positions advertised in *Workamper News* include sales positions, such as representing an RV manufacturer in a certain region, and work in theme parks and ski areas.

Workamper News also runs a referral system, collecting résumés and job preference information from its subscribers and making them available to employers upon request. The service is free to subscribers.

At this writing, *Workamper News* subscriptions were $18 from:

Workamper News
HCR 34, Box 125
Heber Springs, Arkansas 72543
(501) 362-2637

State and Federal Parks

National parks, state parks, the forest service, and the Bureau of Land Management all hire seasonal employees to supplement their maintenance and visitor services staffs. Many of the positions available are volunteer (see page 222). Some of the better government seasonal jobs require a written Civil Service examination. The pay is often quite good, generally better than the rate for similar work in private parks (although the campsites are usually more rustic). This means you'll need to apply far in advance, usually between September 1 and January 15 for summer seasonal jobs.

General policy information is available through agency headquarters—state parks in the state capitals, federal parks in Washington, D.C. (for addresses, see pages 244–246.) More specific information on employment at any government park is available from district and regional offices of the agency, whether state parks, national parks, or forest service, or from the personnel office at the park itself. These offices can tell you how many seasonals the region hires, the nature of the jobs, and the exact procedure for application.

The agencies generally list their jobs with state offices of employment, located in most towns and cities. These state offices often handle the application process, with final hiring done by the park itself.

The U.S. Army Corps of Engineers operates differently from the other government agencies that operate campgrounds. The Corps relies on independent contractors for much of the maintenance and operation of its parks. The contractors bid for their positions.

If you're interested, you should visit a park where you'd like to work, talk to the park manager about the nature of the work, and ask to be put on the mailing list to receive an invitation for bids. It's also a good idea to ask for the last successful bid so you can be sure to make your bid competitive.

Again, *Workamper News* is probably the best central source of information on the U.S. Army Corps of Engineers' contract jobs. The newsletter also carries occasional listings for additional government park jobs.

National Parks Concessions

Concessioners in national parks are under private operation and do their own hiring. The range of jobs is very wide: front-desk clerks and hotel maids, store clerks, tour-bus drivers, outdoor-skills instructors. As hiring is done completely on a local basis, you should contact the personnel office of the concessioner in the park where you wish to work. A central source of information is the *National Parks Trade Journal* (Taverly-Churchill Publishing, $12.95 for the third edition), which lists the addresses and seasonal needs of the larger park concessions. It's available in bookstores or from:

National Parks Trade Journal
P.O. Box 2221
Wawona Station
Yosemite National Park, California 95389
(209) 375-6552

The journal also lists opportunities at some ski resorts and destination resorts. *Workamper News* also lists similar positions.

OTHER JOB OPPORTUNITIES

If you have a particular skill or profession, you probably know the procedure for finding temporary work as you travel. Many RVing nurses register with nurse registries. If you're a scuba instructor, go to a dive shop. If you're a laborer, check with a local union office. Skilled carpenters and other tradesmen can follow construction booms and find work wherever there's building going on.

Temporary employment agencies such as Kelly Services and Manpower hire people with all sorts of skills, including receptionists, secretaries, typists, and word processors, and many others without specific skills who are competent, intelligent, and able to reliably take on special projects. Some RVers get in with a particular agency that has nationwide offices, which facilitates finding work in other locations.

If you're strong, able-bodied, and a bit adventurous, you can follow fruit and vegetable harvests. Growers hire thousands of seasonals at harvest time to pick apples in Washington, cherries in Montana, strawberries in California, citrus in Texas and Florida. Go directly to a growers' co-op for a referral, or contact the state agricultural office. Most growers will allow you to park on the premises during the harvest.

An opportunity that appeals to some RVers is delivering RVs and trucks from factories to dealers. Craig Chilton has written *How to Get Paid $30,000 a Year to Travel,* explaining how to do so, with listings of companies in the United States and Canada, available for $27.95 from:

Xanadu Enterprises
P.O. Box 3147
Evansdale, Iowa 50707
(319) 234-0676

> If you're strong, able-bodied, and a bit adventurous, you can follow fruit and vegetable harvests.

Free-lancing

In professions that don't really require a fixed base, RVers can work from their rigs and sell their services wherever they happen to be.

Some simply work on a free-lance basis for their old employers. They convince the employer that the job can be performed on the road as well as in the office, with the use of the telephone, computer, modem, and fax machine.

Some RVing free-lancers are retired accountants or take tax-preparation courses in order to prepare tax returns, especially for other campers in snowbird areas. Some write for magazines and news-

Dollar-saving Tip

Consulting within your profession is a natural way to supplement retirement income.

papers, others sell photography. *Writer's Market* and *Photographer's Market* (Writer's Digest Books) list the opportunities and explain how to break into these fields. Other free-lance occupations include sewing, construction, computer programming, and consulting.

You shouldn't overlook any musical or thespian talents you have. RVers who are professional clowns, singers, square-dance callers, and magicians all earn money on the road.

The point is to assess your skills and to realize that just because you've retired or have committed to long-term travel is no reason to stop working. The challenge of having to work to keep traveling can be a real motivator, and the variety of locales you visit can make the working highly rewarding.

TAX CONSIDERATIONS

Dollar-saving Tip

A portion of your RV payment and travel expenses may be deductible if you use it to earn income.

Even if you're not making much money from your transitory travails, you're still subject to the tax laws. If you're self-employed—for example, selling arts and crafts, dealing at flea markets, free-lancing a service—you must file a return if you have net self-employed earnings of $400 or more for the year, even if your total earnings are below the filing threshold. (Filing thresholds, which vary by age, marital status, and other factors, are listed in the front of the IRS Form 1040 instructions.) You may or may not owe income tax, but you will probably owe self-employment tax.

If you're below the filing threshold but your employer filed a W-2 form declaring your wages and withholding federal taxes, you must file a tax return to get any refund due. If you're certain to be below the filing threshold, tell your employer you want to file a W-4 form, which will exempt you from withholding. Be careful here, though. You cannot file a W-4 form to avoid paying taxes. If the IRS determines that such was your intent, you're subject to a $500 penalty.

If you sell in flea markets or in art shows, you may be subject to state or local sales tax. Because the laws differ from state to state, you'll need to contact the local state sales tax authorities, listed in the White Pages under "State Government" offices.

There's also good news, tax-wise, for RVing workers. You might be eligible for some substantial tax deductions. For example, your travel expenses, or a portion of them, might be deductible if you use your RV to conduct business.

If you make a profit from your self-employment in three years out of five, it's considered a business. For example, if you make jewelry in your motorhome, not only are your supplies deductible, but so is a portion of your motorhome expenses, including depreciation. Your motorhome is effectively a home office. How much of it is deductible? You're able to deduct a percentage of expenses equal to the percentage of the motorhome that you use exclusively and regularly to conduct your business. This home-office deduction is subject to special limitations; be sure to read IRS Schedule C instructions carefully and/or consult a tax accountant. You'll also be able to deduct your advertising expenses, such as brochures and business cards.

If you move from place to place to take employment, your expenses in between might be considered the same as moving expenses, in which case you follow the rules for deducting moving expenses.

These are all general considerations. Circumstances will dictate the specifics. You should obtain all the appropriate IRS schedules and instructions. For example, if you have any self-employment income, obtain the instructions to Schedule C, "Profit of Loss from Business," and for Schedule SE, "Social Security Self-Employment Tax." Visit a local IRS office, or have the forms mailed to you.

For answers to your specific questions, you can ask the IRS, but it's better to meet with a tax accountant. Look in the Yellow Pages under "Accountants—Enrolled Agents." These are accountants who are registered to represent taxpayers against the IRS. They know the tax laws very well, and they're paid to represent *you*. You may not need an accountant to actually prepare your tax forms—you or a tax preparer might be able to do them—but it will be worthwhile to consult with an enrolled agent on exactly what is deductible under your circumstances.

Once you begin to work on the road, keeping accurate records of your income and expenses becomes very important. If you're not familiar with recordkeeping, your accountant or an enrolled agent can assist you. Also of use to anyone who free-lances is a book called the *Artists' Recordkeeping Book*. It contains explanations of recordkeeping terms, what transactions must be recorded and why, and just what can be called a business expense. It covers such topics as bartering, filing, insurance, and self-employment tax and has blank pages for recording income, expenses, and banking transactions. It's available for $14.50, including postage and handling, from:

Chicago Artists Coalition
5 West Grand Avenue
Chicago, Illinois 60610
(312) 670-2060

EXTRA INCOME AND SOCIAL SECURITY

If you're between sixty-two and sixty-nine years old, receiving Social Security benefits, and earning money from part-time work or free-lancing, having income above a certain figure can affect your benefits. The income thresholds change with every new federal budget. At the time of this writing, if you're between sixty-two and sixty-four, you can earn up to $7,080 extra income without jeopardizing your benefits. After that, you must pay back $1 for every $2 earned. The threshold for Social Security enrollees from age sixty-five through

> **I**f your employer files a W-2 form declaring your wages and withholding federal taxes, you must file a tax return.

If you're seventy or older, you can earn unlimited extra income without sacrificing Social Security benefits.

sixty-nine is $9,720, after which you must pay $1 for every $3 earned.

If you're an income-earning Social Security enrollee and fall into this age sixty-two to sixty-nine category, you must report that income to Social Security as well as to the IRS. If you exceed the income threshold, you can either pay what you owe with one check, or have it deducted from upcoming Social Security checks. You can also ask for partial withholding to cover the payments in advance.

If you're seventy or older, you can earn unlimited extra income without sacrificing Social Security benefits.

VOLUNTEERING

Maybe you do not need to earn your way as you travel, or even to supplement your income, but you still have skills and time you'd like to put to good use. No matter what your skills or talents, it's certain that some worthwhile organization can use them.

Volunteer Hosting

The volunteer host programs in the national parks, forest service, the BLM, and some state parks are the volunteer opportunities best known to RVers. Volunteer hosts usually trade their part-time services for a free campsite, and possibly for a small stipend. While rangers have a litany of duties and responsibilities to perform, campground hosts are primarily oriented to serving campground visitors.

Although some hosts are asked to collect fees (usually by maintaining self-pay boxes), register campers, or do light maintenance (such as cleaning toilets), their primary duties are in public relations. They distribute maps and brochures and answer thousands of questions: How's the fishing? Where's the nearest store? Is the lake too cold for swimming? How did you get such a great job as this?

The answer to the last question is to just contact the appropriate agency, and you can get one too. Volunteer assignments are generally made on the local level, so you should inquire at a regional office or at the park at which you'd like to work. The regional offices are listed on pages 244–246. Another way is to contact the Good Sam Club, which acts as a central clearinghouse to place members in national-park, national-forest, and some state-park volunteer programs. Also, many of the agencies in need of volunteers list their needs in *Workamper News*.

Other Volunteer Opportunities

If you're a snowbird, or you spend long periods of time in one area, it's a simple matter to find volunteer opportunities. Many RVers work as hospital assistants or as Red Cross volunteers. Some assist in adult literacy programs. Others work with school children, others in senior-citizen or community recreation programs.

On a national basis, the largest federal clearinghouse for volunteerism information is Action, whose programs include:

- The Foster Grandparent Program, for providing companionship and guidance to handicapped children, juvenile offenders, child-abuse victims, and children in foster care
- The Retired Senior Volunteer Program (RSVP), which places seniors in community service—in schools, crisis centers, nursing homes, libraries, and hospitals
- The Senior Companion Program, which provides care and companionship to other adults, mostly the frail and elderly
- The Volunteers in Service to America (VISTA), a year-long volunteer program placing volunteers in literacy programs, working with the homeless, fighting drug abuse and hunger, and working with young people

Information on all these programs is available from:

Action Programs
806 Connecticut Avenue N.W.
Washington, D.C. 20525

The American Association of Retired Persons publishes a booklet called *To Serve, Not to Be Served,* a guide to finding volunteer work. AARP also maintains a national Volunteer Talent Bank, which matches volunteers with opportunities in AARP and other programs. You should be over fifty, but do not need to be an AARP member to participate. Write:

AARP Volunteer Talent Bank,
AARP Fulfillment
1909 K Street N.W.
Washington, D.C. 20049

Another national clearinghouse is:

Volunteer—The National Center
1111 North 19th Street, Suite 500
Arlington, Virginia 22209

This group maintains information on volunteer programs throughout the country through a network of more than 400 affiliated centers.

Parks, museums, botanical gardens, and historical sites often need docents—volunteers who are trained to answer questions, take tickets, even lead tours and nature walks. Contact the park or museum directly.

All too often travelers reach a point where they tire of travel for the sake of travel.

The Good Sam Club has a partnership with the National Forest Service through which volunteers work in campground renovation projects. Contact the Good Sam Club for information (see page 247).

RVers with limited time might enjoy taking a volunteer vacation. Some you can arrange yourself—a wildlife refuge might need help with a bird count, for example. Or you can arrange one through a group like Earthwatch, which operates programs worldwide: archeological digs, wildlife surveys, flora studies. You might be unearthing ancient tombs, searching for dinosaur fossils, or observing behavior in a bear sanctuary. You'll work with other volunteers as well as experts. You pay for the privilege, but most volunteers do indeed find their work to be a privilege. For more on this program, write:

Earthwatch
680 Mount Auburn St.
Watertown, Massachusetts 02172
(617) 926-8200

Other volunteer vacation opportunities are listed in a book called *Volunteer Vacations* (Chicago, Chicago Review Press).

Most RV clubs are involved in charity work that requires volunteer labor. Local chapters have their own charities. On a national level, Good Sam is well known for its efforts on behalf of Dogs for the Deaf and the Special Olympics. If you're not a member of an RV club, see the list on pages 247–248. You'll find that club members are a dedicated lot—dedicated to a lot more than simply enjoying camping.

Any RVing volunteer learns how compatible volunteerism and travel can be. All too often travelers reach a point where they tire of travel for the sake of travel. Adding the dimension of service can bring a great sense of purpose to your life, keep you feeling active and useful, and, of course, help others who need you.

CHAPTER TWENTY

Free Attractions, Green RVing, and Other Ways to Save

■ ■ ■ ■ ■ ■ ■ ■ ■ ■ ■ ■

The best way to save money is not to spend it. At least, don't spend it when you don't have to. North America offers so many wonderful things to do and see costing little or no money that there's just no reason to spend much on day-to-day activities and sightseeing. Free and inexpensive attractions are often much more entertaining and certainly more educational than the expensive ones. A few hours spent learning about local history in a small historical-society museum, touring a cookie factory, visiting a Civil War site or a botanic garden can be much more rewarding than spending money to visit an amusement park or tourist trap, with all their concomitant overpriced souvenirs and refreshments.

TAKE ADVANTAGE OF
FREE ENTERTAINMENT AND ATTRACTIONS

The keys to taking advantage of free attractions are:

- Find out about them. Some resource suggestions follow on page 226.
- Be alert for those that just pop up along the way. Keep an eye out for less-than-obvious signs pointing the way to little attractions. For example, historic landmarks are almost always signed, even along main highways. Even if it's nothing you've ever heard of, you'll come to enjoy the serendipitous rewards that follow the pursuit of whim.

In This Chapter:

- *How can I avoid paying a lot of money for attractions and family entertainment?*
- *How can environmental awareness save me money?*
- *What are some ways to save on long-distance phone costs? Laundry costs?*
- *How can joining an RV club save money?*
- *What do I need to know about customs and border crossings?*
- *How do I select a home base for full-time travel?*

■ Cultivate a sense of fascination for things small, subtle, obscure, and aesthetic.
■ Don't be seduced by the expensive attractions that lure you in with billboard siren songs and tempt you (or the kids) to buy goofy hats, drinking mugs, or backscratchers boldly emblazoned with the logo of the tourist trap.

Free Attractions—Sources of Information

Many of the sources of information on free attractions are covered in the Chapter Fourteen, "Trip Planning." These include such logical outlets as state departments of tourism and chambers of commerce. When you contact or stop in at such agencies, be sure to mention specific interests. Many have specialized brochures on such things as factory tours, historic homes, covered bridges, and historic battlefields. Other information sources follow.

Examples of Free or Nearly Free Attractions

The following suggestions offer free and inexpensive alternatives to expensive sightseeing.

■ *Historical museums and sites.* These may be run by a local historical society, a county, or state. Anyone with a fascination for history will enjoy virtually any historical museum. Most ask for a modest donation.
■ *Factory tours.* The opportunities are extensive: manufacturing plants, auto-assembly plants, food-canning factories, wineries, distilleries, breweries, sugar houses (where maple syrup is made), and paper mills.
■ *State capitols.* Most offer tours, either guided or self-guided, historical exhibits, and perhaps the opportunity to watch a legislature in session.
■ *Public gardens.*
■ *Fairs and festivals.* These include county fairs, local harvest festivals, crafts festivals, and holiday celebrations.
■ *Architectural attractions.* These include covered bridges, historic homes, historic districts, and ancient ruins.
■ *Wildlife refuges.* Many require no admission fee.
■ *Crafts centers.* Most feature craftspeople at work.
■ *Sporting events.* Minor-league baseball tickets cost a fraction of what the big leagues charge. Local rodeos offer a lot of entertainment for a few dollars.

■ *Scenic drives.* For the majority, this is the essence of RVing—not so much bagging destinations as savoring the process of travel. Driving is never without cost, of course, but as long as you're traveling, you may as well enjoy the most scenic routes.
■ *College campuses.* Many larger colleges have tours, guided or self-guided, and most have museums, gardens, and research facilities of interest.
■ *Churches and cathedrals.* Many are of architectural and historic interest, as well as places to pause for rest or contemplation. Some monasteries, too, welcome visitors, as do missions.
■ *Game farms and fisheries.* State-operated facilities that provide stock for hunters and fishermen often welcome visitors.
■ *Military bases.* Check to see if free tours are offered.
■ *Libraries.* Some have historical displays, as well as sections on local history and natural history. For travelers on the go a lot, a library is a great place to catch up on magazines and newspapers.

Guides to Free Attractions.   *Don Wright's Guide to Free Attractions* is $14.95 from Cottage Publications, 24396 Pleasant View Drive, Elkhart, Indiana 46517. It's impossible for any one book to be all-inclusive, but Wright's book contains hundreds of gems in every state. There's the Daisy BB Gun Plant and Air Gun Museum in Rogers, Arkansas; the Accounting Hall of Fame in Columbus, Ohio; vineyards and wineries even where you wouldn't expect them (Pennsylvania and Missouri, for example); and even Smokey the Bear's Grave and Museum in Capitan, New Mexico.

AAA Tour Books.   Town-by-town listings include many free attractions. The books are free to AAA members. AAA maps also designate scenic routes.

National Forest Service and Bureau of Land Management.   While we await the creation of a national network of official scenic byways, both these agencies have already designated a number of such drives. (See addresses in Appendix, pages 244–246.)

State Welcome Centers.   Many states have welcome centers just inside their borders with lots of information on free attractions.

Guides to Annual Events.   A motherlode of happenings ranging from the ridiculous to the religious, *Chase's Annual Events* sells for $24.95 and is published by Contemporary Books, Inc., Chicago. Many libraries have copies for reference.

Bulletin Boards and Posters.   Often the best way to find out what's going on locally is to check campground or supermarket bulletin boards and store windows for posters advertising local events.

Local Papers.   Most have a weekly events-and-entertainment section, typically published on Saturday, Thursday, or Sunday for some.

RV Magazines.   *Trailer Life, MotorHome, Highways, Family Motor Coaching* and other magazines include calendars of upcoming events.

Dollar-saving Tip

Look for discount coupons in brochures and other tourist literature.

PRACTICE GREEN RVING

Environmental consciousness is changing the way we live. Most Americans are adopting habits at home that contribute to a cleaner, less wasteful way of life. A fortuitous side benefit of these practices: They are almost always in our financial self-interest, as well as in the interest of our planet and our future. It's quite simple to carry over these practices to your RV travels and to adopt some further RV-specific habits that will contribute to a cleaner environment. The following are some examples.

Recycling can bring in some extra money in states that require a deposit on beverage containers.

Recycling

Recycling can bring in some extra money in states that require a deposit on beverage containers. (The containers needn't have been purchased in those states.) They can generally be redeemed at any supermarket for five cents per container in most states, ten cents in Michigan, and two cents in California. Bottles, both glass and plastic, and aluminum cans can be redeemed for cash in California, Connecticut, Delaware, Iowa, Massachusetts, Michigan, New York, Oregon, and Vermont.

Don't limit your recycling only to these states, though. Others may not pay you for your efforts, but you can recycle almost anywhere. The simplest way is to save your glass, plastic, aluminum (foil, too), and newspapers and watch for the igloo-shaped containers in many supermarket parking lots. If you can't find a recycling outlet, phone the local department of public works, under the city listings of the White Pages in the phone book, or look under "Recycling Centers" in the Yellow Pages.

Many supermarkets recycle or reuse plastic and paper shopping bags. Better yet, carry your own reusable canvas or string shopping bags, usually available for purchase in supermarkets. At least, request paper for your groceries when asked; it's biodegradable.

When you arrive at campgrounds, public or private, always ask if they recycle. Although most don't, enough inquiries might encourage them to begin.

Informal Recycling

Informal, or indirect, recycling is another way to save money and resources. For example, buy products with minimal packaging and those that have the "recycled" symbol on the packaging. Reuse pieces of aluminum foil whenever possible. Substitute plastic vegetable bags for plastic wrap. Avoid using foam cups and plates; polystyrene foam does not readily biodegrade. For that matter, try to limit your use of disposable products in general. Every time you wash your dishes, you are recycling; every time you toss out paper plates and plastic tableware, you are spending extra money and using up resources.

Another way to recycle informally is to share your newspapers and magazines. Pass them on to friends, leave them in the laundry room or recreation hall, or donate magazines to a library.

Other Green Strategies

The following are additional ways to help save the environment (and money as well):

Use Ventilation, Spices, and Vinegar. Rather than using pump sprays, keep your RV fresh smelling by using ventilation and fans. To kill strong odors in the refrigerator or elsewhere, use an open box of baking soda. Boil cinnamon and cloves on the stove. Use vinegar for fish odors.

Use Baking Soda. Use it as toothpowder (mixed with a little salt and an essential oil), mouthwash, antacid, and deodorizer. Keep a supply handy for small electrical fires. Mix a half-cup of soda with equal amounts of borax and white vinegar in a gallon of water for an all-purpose cleaner that you can transfer to a spray bottle. A quarter-cup added to a load of wash helps to freshen it. And should you ever be so unfortunate as to encounter a skunk, soak affected clothing in a baking-soda solution. Others swear by tomato juice, claiming it eliminates skunk odors effectively. Of course, then you have to clean out the juice.

Use Alternative Cleaning Products. An excellent source of information on home-remedy-style alternatives to caustic (or expensive) concoctions is *The Natural Formula Book for Home & Yard* by Dan Wallace, published by Rodale Press. The book tells how to create cleaning agents (such as the baking-soda solution above), body lotions, toothpaste, and remedies for pets such as herbal flea powder.

If you prefer commercial products, use one all-purpose cleaner rather than several different ones. Or use brands such as Eco Save, made from natural ingredients and available in health-food stores, some supermarkets, or from one of the mail-order sources listed on page 230.

Avoid Using Pesticides. If you must use such products, do so sparingly. Avoid breathing pesticide mist emitted from pump sprays or aerosol containers. When nearly empty, add a little water to a pump spray and continue to use; enough pesticide will remain to be effective for at least two such rinsings. Avoid solid pesticides, which emit small amounts of toxic fumes that may endanger children and pets. Pesticide alternatives include scrupulous cleanliness for prevention, a sponge and hot water to wipe out an ant invasion, or sprinkling powdered red chili, paprika, or borax where they come in.

Treat spent containers of pesticide as toxic waste. Do not throw them into the trash. Contact the local city offices or an environmental organization to learn how to dispose of toxic waste.

Use Insect Repellent Sparingly. Be aware that the active ingredient in most insect repellents, called "Deet," is toxic and has been linked to serious illness in children. Use very sparingly and always in non-aerosol form (to avoid breathing the mist). Some alternatives include the following: Inside, keep screens closed. Outside, cover arms and legs. Burn a citronella candle. Don't use sweet perfumes

Should you ever be so unfortunate as to encounter a skunk, soak affected clothing in a baking-soda solution.

Use [insect repellent] sparingly and always in nonaerosol form.

> You'll save in the long run with rechargeable batteries and a charger. . . .

and oils that may attract insects. One repellent lotion, Natrapel, from the Tender Corporation, Littleton, New Hampshire, uses citronella oil instead of Deet. Many swear by Avon's Skin-So-Soft bath oil as an insect repellent, although the company does not market it as such. Or try old-fashioned remedies, such as taking brewer's yeast or garlic tablets.

Use No-Phosphate, Biodegradable Detergents. Phosphates in laundry detergents pass right through wastewater systems and into the water supply, where they pollute lakes and streams.

Avoid Using Bleach. Use bleach sparingly; it's toxic and can disrupt wastewater treatment. Try using borax instead.

Buy Rechargeable Batteries. Batteries are a hazardous waste; they contain mercury, a toxin that leaches into the ground water. Although initially more expensive, you'll save in the long run with rechargeable batteries and a charger; the batteries are available in most common sizes.

Recycle Motor Oil and Antifreeze. These are highly toxic to the environment. In sewers, they can disrupt waste-treatment plants, resulting in untreated waste being released into the environment. When simply dumped onto the ground or thrown out with garbage, they find their way into the water table and can contaminate drinking water. (More oil is dumped into sewers and gutters every year than spilled in the Exxon *Valdez* accident in Alaska.) Always catch your oil and antifreeze, pour into clean containers (such as one-gallon water bottles), and take to a service station (there may be a charge). From there, they can be recycled.

Service stations may turn down your used waste oil or antifreeze. They can't allow their storage barrels to be contaminated with sol-

---

Mail-Order Sources for Environmentally Sensitive Products

The following sources can provide some of the environmentally sensitive products discussed in this chapter:

Eco Source
380-F Morris Street
Sebastopol, California 95472
(800) 274-7040

Real Goods
966 Mazzoni Street
Ukiah, California 95482
(800) 762-7325

Planetary Solutions
P.O. Box 1049
Boulder, Colorado 80306
(800) 488-2088

Seventh Generation
49 Hercules Drive
Colchester, Vermont 05446
(800) 456-1177

vents, or the whole barrel will be rejected by the recycler. If a service station won't take your waste, call the local recycling center or community environmental organization for a referral.

Avoid Using Charcoal Lighter Fluid. Most charcoal lighter fluids are highly toxic and pollute the air, although a new fluid from Kingsford is cleaner burning and odorless. Still, if you barbecue on the road, the cleanest way to do so is with a portable propane grill. An adapter available at RV-supply stores allows you to use propane from your RV tank. A clean way to start charcoal is with a cylindrical charcoal starter, available in supermarkets or barbecue/patio shops; it uses just a couple sheets of newspaper to light the charcoal.

Don't Burn Wood Excessively. A roaring campfire is a delight, but it does release particulate pollution into the air. A smaller campfire is also a delight and not nearly as polluting.

Avoid Using Toxic RV Cleaners. Many products designed to clean awnings and RV exteriors contain solvents, phosphoric acid, or petroleum distillates, toxins that wash into the ground or the sewer system. Either way, they harm the environment. Try using nylon netting with soap or a Simple Green solution to scrub RV exteriors.

Use Environmentally Safe Holding-Tank Chemicals. Don't purchase holding-tank formulas that contain formaldehyde (or any other aldehyde) or chlorine compounds. These toxins may not only kill bacteria in your tank, but also in the wastewater treatment system after you flush your tank. Wastewater plants operate biologically; any time you release one of these compounds into a sewer system, you potentially jeopardize lifeforms in the sewage plant—you kill a population that's doing a public service. This can knock out a municipal treatment plant and result in discharges of untreated sewage into our rivers, lakes, and oceans.

Products that use enzymes, such as RV Trine, or aerobic bacteria, such as Kilodor, are biodegradable and environmentally safe. These should not be mixed with formaldehyde or chlorine-containing products because the latter will destroy the biological action of the enzymes or bacteria. Flush out your tank thoroughly before switching to biodegradable products. The helpful bacteria and enzymes will build up over time, so these products become more effective with extended use.

Dispose of Toxic Wastes Properly. Batteries, aerosol cans, and partially full containers of solvent, paint, and insecticides are all hazardous wastes that endanger refuse workers as well as the environment. Contact a local environmental agency about disposing of such items if possible. Many communities sponsor special days for collection of household hazardous wastes.

If you barbecue on the road, the cleanest way to do so is with a portable propane grill.

Check Your Air-Conditioning System. Coolants in air conditioners contain chlorofluorocarbons (CFCs), the compounds linked to depletion of the earth's ozone layer. Have your air conditioner inspected for leaks and recharged by a professional who captures and recycles CFCs.

Keep Your Engine Well Tuned. Keep your tire pressure up as well. A properly tuned engine and tires inflated to the maximum recommended pressure can increase your mileage by as much as 10 percent, thereby reducing harmful emissions into the air.

Reduce Indoor Pollution. Industrial polluters spewing ugly gunk from smokestacks get the publicity, but according to the Environmental Protection Agency, sources in your own home or RV may present the greater risk to your health. The boxed copy below lists some common sources of indoor pollution.

SAVE ON TELEPHONE COSTS

Most people understand that phoning at night or on weekends—that is, outside of prime business hours—is the most logical way to save on long-distance calls. The low-rate hours are generally between 11:00 P.M. and 8:00 A.M. on weekdays, and from 5:00 P.M. Friday to 5:00 P.M. Sunday. The next lowest rates are between 5:00 P.M. and 11:00 P.M., Sunday through Thursday.

It's also common knowledge that limiting the duration of your

---

Some Common Sources of Indoor Pollution

Check for the following sources of indoor pollution:

■ *LP-gas.* The strong smell of LP-gas in an RV should alert you to inspect for a leak in your LP lines. (See page 53.)
■ *Second-hand tobacco smoke.* Tobacco contains a number of toxic compounds. Studies indicate that nonsmoking spouses of smokers may increase their risk of lung cancer by 30 percent. Ask smokers to light up outside.
■ *Formaldehyde.* Formaldehyde is used in pressed-wood products common in RV interiors. It has been shown to cause cancer in animals. A pungent-smelling gas, it causes watery eyes, burning sensations in the eyes and throat, nausea, and can trigger asthma attacks. Formaldehyde emissions generally decrease as products age. High temperature and high humidity can release formaldehyde. Keep a new RV cool when possible, and always well ventilated.
■ *Dry cleaning.* If you wear dry-cleaned clothes that have a strong chemical odor, they're emitting perchloroethylene, which has been shown to cause cancer in animals. Do not accept them from the dry cleaner if they smell strongly.
■ *Mothballs.* Mothballs contain a pesticide that causes cancer in animals. Avoid breathing their vapors. Instead, use cedar chips or cedar blocks as an alternative.

calls saves money. Some frugal folks use an egg timer or the count-down feature on their watches to time their calls.

These aren't the only ways to save on long-distance calls, though. In general, if you dial direct, you save, compared to operator-assisted or credit-card calls. However, this entails using a lot of change. Also, a pay phone may be presubscribed to a long-distance company with high rates. Deregulation of long-distance services brought about many new companies called Alternative Operator Services (AOS). The rates some of them charge, whether for direct-dial or credit-card calling, may be high. It might pay to gain access to your own long-distance carrier and use your telephone credit card.

Here's an important fact to know: Even if you use an AT&T calling card on one of these AOS phones, you pay the AOS rates, not AT&T's rates, and you'll see a charge on your phone bill from a long-distance company you may never have heard of. Here's how to avoid expensive surprises on your phone bill:

Dollar-saving Tip

You can ask the operator in advance for the rates on any long-distance call.

1. Check for a sign on or around the pay phone stating the name of the long-distance carrier.
2. If no sign is visible, call "0" and ask the operator who he or she works for. If it is not the company you're used to dealing with, ask the operator for the rate of the call you're placing. If it seems high, ask the operator how to reach the long-distance company of your choice.
3. Better yet, know how to reach your long-distance company yourself. Carry your long-distance credit card(s) and use the access codes that are printed on the back of the cards. These are either toll-free 950 numbers or five-digit access codes. The codes for the major companies:

    AT&T: 10288
    MCI: 950-1022 or 10222
    Metromedia: 950-0488 or 10488
    U.S. Sprint: 10333

    Note: Each of these companies, with the exception of Metro-media, charges an access fee every time you use their credit card. The access charges for domestic calls are: AT&T, 80 cents; MCI, 75 cents; U.S. Sprint, 75 cents.
4. If you use an AOS and feel you have been billed an unjust rate, call the company and ask for a refund or a credit. What constitutes an unjust rate? Call AT&T, (800) 222-0300, tell them the details of your call—from where to where, time of day, duration—and ask for their charge. If the AOS charged you signifi-cantly more, you should demand a credit for the difference.
5. If you receive no satisfaction, complain to the state public utility commission for a call within the state, or to the FCC for an interstate call. Write with the details and copy of your bill to:

If you dial direct, you save, compared to operator-assisted or credit-card calls.

Enforcement Division
Common Carrier Bureau
Federal Communications Commission
Washington, D.C. 20554.

E ven if you use an
AT&T calling card on
one of these Alternative
Operator Services (AOS)
phones, you pay the
AOS rates. . . .

If you're a fulltimer, you should still have no problem obtaining a telephone credit card. All you need is a billing address, and, in the case of U.S. Sprint, a contact phone number—a friend or message service will suffice.

Be sure to compare rates and discount programs available from these long-distance carriers. It may pay to switch carriers if one offers a program that suits your calling pattern. For example, at this writing, the companies offered these discounts:

- AT&T's Universal Card, which is also a MasterCard: a 10-percent discount on long-distance calls made on AT&T lines.
- AT&T's Reach Out America: one hour of night and weekend calling for $10.70, with no calling-card charge on those calls.
- MCI's Friends & Family program: a 20-percent discount to pre-registered numbers that are also MCI customers.
- U.S. Sprint: a 5-percent discount on all phone-card calls once you total $20 in long-distance charges in a month.

If you carry a gold bank card, check to see if discounts on long-distance calling are among your benefits.

For questions and advice regarding away-from-home calling, contact the Teleconsumer Hotline: (800) 332-1124.

SAVE ON LAUNDRY COSTS

The cost of doing laundry on the road can add up. Here are some ways to save:

- Campground laundromats are usually less expensive than those in town. For the campground operator, laundry is more a service than a profit center, so you might save fifty cents or more per load.
- Buy concentrated detergent. You pay less for packaging, and it's easier to store in an RV. Look for store brands to save more.
- Cut fabric-softener sheets in half for small loads.
- Carry a clothesline and clothespins and use nature as a dryer.

JOIN AN RV CLUB

The many ways that membership in one or more RV clubs can save you money are referred to throughout this book. Three clubs in particular offer tangible financial benefits to their members: the

Good Sam Club, the Family Motor Coaching Association (FMCA), and the Escapees (see Appendix, page 247, for addresses).

Good Sam is well known for providing access to many discounts—10 percent off on camping in Good SamParks, 10 percent off on service and supplies in affiliated RV centers, discounts on magazines and books, attractive rates on vehicle insurance and Emergency Road Service, group rates on supplemental health insurance, a low-cost Visa card, free trip routing, traveler's checks, mail-forwarding, and caravans and rallies, among other benefits.

FMCA also offers caravans and tours, as well as reduced insurance rates, mail-forwarding, and a monthly magazine.

The Escapees Club is an excellent resource for snowbirds and fulltimers. Affiliated with the club are low-cost cooperative campgrounds and boondocking retreats. The club's newsletter always offers practical money-saving advice on RV products and "tricks of the trade" for fulltimers and snowbirds. Club founders Joe and Kay Peterson are savvy, experienced RVers who understand the concerns of budget-conscious RVers.

Every RV club has a strong social aspect. For many club members, the primary reason for joining is the contact with other RVers. But this social aspect has an extra dimension: RV club members are almost always eager to share information with each other—information that can save a lot of money. Once you're a club member, you can call on other members for referrals to RV dealers and service centers, for suggestions on inexpensive places to camp, for hard-to-find parts for your RV (brand-name clubs are especially valuable in this department), for a place to park overnight (many clubs publish rosters of members willing to provide a "campsite" to visiting members), or for a referral to a doctor or dentist.

Even if you join two or three clubs, you can easily make up the cost of joining by the added savings from club benefits, plus enjoy the rallies, tours, and general camaraderie that go along with membership.

> Campground laundries are usually less expensive than those in town.

SELECT THE BEST HOME BASE

Every RVer, even the full-time RVer, needs a home base—even if it's not actually home. Many full-time RVers completely give up any permanent residence. "Why pay rent or make mortgage payments when our home is on the road?" they reason. Others find it more convenient to maintain a physical home base as a place to store things and occasionally return to sort out their financial and personal affairs.

Most home-base decisions are purely personal: Do you need a physical home base? Do you want to be near friends or family? Can you really commit to full-time travel?

From a purely financial point of view, being willing to sacrifice a physical home base is clearly the most practical way to be able to afford long-term or full-time travel. You avoid the need to make mortgage or rent payments, and you can use income from the sale of your home to finance your RV travels.

Nevertheless, you still need a home base because you're still responsible for taxes, voting, bills, and other matters of the business of living. Your home-base options include the home of a friend or family member, a post-office box, a campground or membership resort, a mobile home, an apartment, or a condominium.

If you do give up your physical home, you can locate your home base anywhere. If it will be a place where you intend to spend a lot of time, personal factors such as weather and proximity to family affect your decision. But if it's just a matter of having some place to legally call home, your decision should be based on the following considerations:

- *Taxes.* Is there a state income tax? What is the state sales tax?
- *Licenses and registration.* You should investigate the cost of a driver's license, vehicle and RV registration, and whether an annual safety and/or smog inspection is required.
- *Voting requirements.* Most states require that you have a physical address in order to vote.
- *Insurance rates.* Because most insurance companies use territorial ratings, insurance rates can vary significantly depending upon where your RV is registered. Urban areas, for example, generally have higher rates than rural areas. Rates in any one area vary from company to company, so it's important to consider not only your company's rates for a potential home-base location, but also to compare them with the rates of other companies. In other words, compare rates among both home bases and insurance companies.

A booklet called *Selecting a Home Base: State Tax & Registration Information* is available for $4.95 from:

Trailer Life Books
P.O. Box 4500
Agoura, California 91301

Another useful source of home-base information is the book *Full-time RVing: A Guide to Life on the Open Road,* by Bill and Jan Moeller, also from Trailer Life Books, for $14.95.

KNOW CUSTOMS AND BORDER-CROSSING LAWS

Because RVers naturally feel they are honest and law abiding, they are often taken aback by border searches.

RVers unaware of restrictions and duties imposed at border crossings may have to sacrifice certain goods or pay high import fees when they cross into Canada or Mexico or upon return to the United States. However, with foreknowledge of the purpose and procedures of customs and some advance preparation, you can breeze through customs without any unexpected expenses or hassles.

This doesn't mean you might not be detained during a border crossing for an inspection. Courts have upheld the rights of customs officials to search vehicles and RVs. They do not need a warrant, nor do they need to establish probable cause to justify a search.

Because RVers naturally feel they are honest and law abiding, they are often taken aback by border searches. But RVs have been used to smuggle illicit goods across borders. A Canadian customs official once told me, "There have been cases of Americans and Canadians in RVs with drugs—and the people were very senior in years. In some cases, they were inadvertent carriers, in others, they were very purposely carrying out an action. Smugglers of drugs will go to any length to introduce their product to Canada or the U.S."

There is nothing RVers can do to guarantee they will not be searched. But officials from the United States, Canada, and Mexico all agree that courtesy and honesty certainly help. To this end, it's important to understand just why the customs services exist.

The U.S. Customs informational booklet *Know Before You Go* cites the following purposes of customs: "To end the devastating impact of illicit drugs; maintain the integrity of our economy by protecting U.S. products, trademarks, and immigration laws; support a healthy economy by depositing in the national treasury duties levied on foreign goods; and guard our agricultural well-being from contaminated products." The same reasons account for the customs laws of any country.

The following are the regulations for the Canadian, United States, and Mexican borders that most affect RVers.

Customs Regulations

Canada

Most U.S.-Canada crossings are quick and trouble-free. No passport is required, though travelers should carry some identification showing their citizenship, such as a birth, baptismal, or voting certificate. You should also be sure to have your vehicle registration and a letter from the owner if the vehicle is borrowed. United States insurance is valid in Canada.

Firearms. Canada has strengthened its enforcement of gun laws in recent years; pistols and revolvers are strictly prohibited.

If you do have a pistol, you should declare it at the border. If you're returning the same way, Canadian Customs' officials will hold it for you at no charge. If you plan to return a different way, the border officials can direct you to the nearest U.S. gun shop, where arrangements can be made to ship it legally to your home. If you fail

> Courts have upheld the rights of customs officials to search vehicles and RVs. They do not need a warrant, nor do they need to establish probable cause to justify a search.

to declare your weapon, and it is found during a search, you will be arrested by the federal police. You may be jailed pending a court appearance, and your RV will be confiscated until you pay a penalty.

Legitimate hunting rifles and shotguns are permitted in Canada but must be declared at the border. Firearms are not allowed in national parks unless they are dismantled, carried in a closed case, or wrapped and tied securely.

Other Regulations.   Apart from firearms, visitors can bring into Canada ordinary personal baggage and recreational equipment without duty or tax. Extra gas and oil that exceeds the normal capacity of your vehicle is subject to duty. Canada used to restrict duty-free food supplies to two days' worth. A new regulation permits "reasonable quantities, consistent with the purpose, nature, and duration of the visit—however, agricultural and quota restrictions remain unchanged." These restrictions include:

- 40 ounces (1.1 liters) of liquor or wine per person of legal drinking age, or 24 12-ounce (355-ml) cans or bottles of beer.
- Additional liquor, up to 2 gallons (9 liters) may be imported (except to the Northwest Territories) on payment of duty and taxes.
- Persons sixteen or older may bring 50 cigars, 200 cigarettes, and 2.2 pounds (1 kg) of manufactured tobacco.
- Up to 10 kg (22 pounds) of meat and meat products of U.S. origin are allowed.
- Up to $30 worth of dairy products, if clearly of U.S. origin, are allowed. All animals, plants, vegetables, fruit, and meat must be declared to Canadian Customs.
- Dogs and cats may be brought into Canada provided you carry a certificate of rabies vaccination from a veterinarian that certifies that the pet has been vaccinated against rabies during the past thirty-six months. Up to two pet birds may be brought in provided they have not been in contact with other birds for ninety days. Exotic pets may require special permits; contact:

Chief of Imports
Animal Health Division
Food Production and Inspection Branch
Agriculture Canada
Ottawa, Ontario, Canada K1A 0Y9.

━━━━━ **$** ━━━━━
Dollar-saving Tip
Save your receipts in Canada for a 7-percent tax rebate.

Canada's Goods and Services Tax.   The Goods and Services Tax (GST) implemented in Canada in 1991 is a 7-percent tax levied on almost all goods and services in Canada. The tax is charged in addition to any provincial sales tax. Nonresidents must pay the tax at the time of purchase but may obtain a rebate later.

The GST is rebated on most items and services paid for in Canada, but GST is not rebated for camping fees, RV rentals, and car rentals.

Mexico

The subject of border crossings into Mexico, like the subject of Mexican travel in general, is laden with misconceptions. The truth is, crossing into Mexico is a very straightforward process. But it is different from crossing into Canada or returning to the United States in several respects.

Tourist Card and Vehicle Permit.   Motorists crossing into Mexico and intending to stay more than seventy-two hours must obtain both a tourist card and a vehicle permit. Passengers must also obtain the tourist card. The tourist card is available in advance from Mexican consulates, the Mexican Government Tourism Office, automobile clubs, and from Sanborn's Mexico Insurance Service. It can also be obtained from Mexican immigration offices at the border. It requires proof of citizenship in the form of a birth certificate or passport, military I.D., or a notarized affidavit of citizenship.

The tourist card is issued free of charge; if anyone asks you to pay for one, protest immediately or simply go elsewhere. Tourist cards are valid for a maximum of ninety days.

The vehicle permit is also issued free of charge. It is available only from the Mexican customs office at the border. To obtain a vehicle permit, you'll need proof of ownership: the title, registration, or notarized bill of sale. You'll also need a current driver's license.

Note: You cannot drive an RV into Mexico, leave it, and fly back without it, unless you make special arrangements. Certain RV parks are authorized to act as agents for the government, but be sure to make arrangements in advance if you wish to leave an RV in Mexico.

It is important to stress that these documents are free. Many travelers have the misguided notion that it costs $30 or $40 to cross the border into Mexico. It doesn't. However, seasoned travelers know that despite claims of the Mexican government to the contrary, a small tip at the border can facilitate a crossing.

> Tipping at the border is a practice I neither condone or endorse.

Tipping.   "Tipping" at the border is a practice I neither condone nor endorse. However, border guards often make it clear, as one fills out forms, another gives you a window sticker, another inspects your vehicle, that they expect a tip for these "services." John Howells, author of *RV Travel in Mexico* (no relation to this author), suggests a $1 tip to each guard who "assists" you.

Another expert on travel in Mexico who has led tours and made hundreds of RV crossings explains: "The reality is that an appropriate tip is customary. But if somebody doesn't feel they want to pay anything, they don't have to. They will get their permits and get across with no major hassles. It's a tip for service."

This traveler said that if you want to tip, have the money (no more than $5) folded in your hand when you encounter the customs official. Occasionally, according to this source, you may be asked for a tip.

"You know you're being asked for a tip if the inspector sort of hems and haws, and says, 'Well, there's a lot of stuff in here. We'll have to unload everything. It'll take a lot of time.' (Virtually all Mexican border guards speak English.)

"The wise person will say, 'Is there an easier way to handle this?' I'd pull out $5 at this point and say, 'Maybe this will pay for your time,' or, 'Why don't you buy some coffee for your friends?'"

A spokesperson for the Mexican government didn't deny that the tipping practice takes place. She said, "I can only advise that people cross in the legal way."

Firearms. As in Canada, firearms are a major concern of Mexican customs officials. Handguns are flatly prohibited in Mexico and being caught with one is one of the surest ways to get into serious trouble. Rules for hunting rifles vary from state to state. Some permit hunting rifles only when the traveler is accompanied by a licensed Mexican hunting guide. Check with your nearest Mexican consulate or the Mexico Government Tourism Office for state regulations.

Other Restrictions. Pets must have had a rabies vaccination within the last six months and a veterinarian's certificate to prove it.

Adults may bring in 50 cigars, 200 cigarettes, or up to 9 ounces (250 grams) of tobacco. Adults may also bring in up to about 2½ gallons (3 liters) of wine or liquor.

United States auto insurance is not valid in Mexico. RVers should obtain Mexican insurance in advance or at the border.

United States

Keeping track of your purchases and declaring them at the border when you return is the best way to facilitate your passage through U.S. Customs. Returning United States residents can each bring back, duty-free, $400 worth of articles purchased abroad. The tobacco allowance for each adult is not more than 100 cigars or 200 cigarettes. The liquor allowance is 33.8 ounces (1 liter). Certain hard-goods items, such as switchblade knives and fireworks, are prohibited. You must declare all your purchases. If one of your purchases happens to be a restricted item, you'll be given a choice of returning it or leaving it with U.S. Customs to be destroyed.

Foreign-made goods that you take over the border are subject to duty every time you return to the United States, unless you have the original bill of sale, an insurance policy, or some proof of prior ownership. Typical items for which you could be assessed include tailored suits and jewelry. Other items, such as watches and cameras that can be identified by a serial number or permanent markings, can be registered with U.S. Customs before you leave the country.

It's a good idea to stop in at the U.S. Customs Office at the border before leaving the country. The *Know Before You Go* pamphlet is

---

Foreign-made goods that you take over the border are subject to duty every time you return to the United States.

very helpful. The office also will have a variety of pamphlets on specific subjects, including the Agriculture Department's current list of banned foodstuffs, the category under which RVers are most frequently found in violation.

For example, you cannot bring chicken or eggs in from Mexico unless the eggs are hardboiled and the chicken is cooked. Pork is prohibited, but beef is permitted. Mangoes are prohibited, but papayas are permitted. Potatoes are prohibited, but other vegetables are permitted.

Customs officials suggest that travelers always obtain receipts for their more expensive purchases. Agents have a pretty good sense of the value of items, so it's wise to declare the value you actually paid.

Customs and Border Crossings

Contact the following for more information on customs and border crossings:

U.S. Customs District Directors
Chicago, Illinois 60607; (312) 353-6100
Houston/Galveston, Texas 77029; (713) 671-1000
New York, New York 10048; (212) 466-5817
San Diego, California 91288; (619) 557-5360
Seattle, Washington 98104; (206) 553-0554

Canada Customs
360 Coventry Road
Ottawa, Ontario, Canada K1K 2C6
(613) 993-0040

Mexican Government Tourism Office
10100 Santa Monica Boulevard, Suite 224
Los Angeles, California 90067
(213) 203-8191

Passing through customs without unexpected costs is a simple matter of being informed and prepared. Those are the keys, really, to saving money in every aspect of your RV travels. Being informed, prepared, and maintaining a money-saving consciousness becomes habitual. It's really nothing like penny-pinching. It's more like penny-diverting. You channel your hard-earned money to paying for the things that truly bring you pleasure—seeing the beauty of the world, enjoying the company of people you love, savoring the most precious resource we have: the time we are allotted to live.

Passing through customs without unexpected costs is a simple matter of being informed and prepared.

Appendix

■■■■■■■■■

Automobile Clubs

Allstate Motor Club
P.O. Box 3094
Arlington Heights, Illinois 60006
(800) 347-8880

Amoco Motor Club
P.O. Box 9040
Des Moines, Iowa 50369
(800) 334-3300

American Automobile Association
1000 AAA Drive
Heathrow, Florida 32746
(800) 336-4357

Canadian Automobile Association
2525 Carling Avenue
Ottawa, Ontario, Canada K2B 7Z2
(613) 820-1890

Chevron Travel Club
P.O. Box P
Concord, California 94524
(800) 243-8766

Mobil Auto Club
200 Martingale
Schaumburg, Illinois 60193
(800) 621-5581

Montgomery Ward Auto Club
P.O. Box 4781
North Suburban, Illinois 60197
(800) 621-5151

Shell Motorist Club
P.O. Box 60199
Chicago, Illinois 60660
(800) 852-0555

Bureau of Land Management Offices (alphabetical by state or region)

Bureau of Land Management
U.S. Department of the Interior
18th and C Streets N.W.
Washington, D.C. 20240
(202) 208-5261

Alaska State Office
222 West Seventh Avenue, #13
Anchorage, Alaska 99513-7599
(907) 271-5555

Arizona State Office
3707 North Seventh Street
Phoenix, Arizona 85011
(602) 640-5504

California State Office
2800 Cottage Way, E-2841
Sacramento, California 95825
(916) 978-4746

Colorado State Office
2850 Youngfield Street
Lakewood, Colorado 80215-7076
(303) 239-3669

Eastern States Office
350 South Pickett Street
Alexandria, Virginia 22304
(703) 461-1365

Idaho State Office
3380 Americana Terrace
Boise, Idaho 83706
(208) 334-1406

Montana State Office
222 North 32nd Street
Billings, Montana 59107
(406) 255-2913

Nevada State Office
850 Harvard Way
Reno, Nevada 89520
(702) 785-6586

New Mexico State Office
Joseph M. Montoya Federal Building
South Federal Place
Santa Fe, New Mexico 87504-1449
(505) 988-6316

Oregon State Office
1300 Northeast 44th Avenue
Portland, Oregon 97208-2965
(503) 280-7287

Utah State Office
324 State Street, Suite 301
Salt Lake City, Utah 84111-2303
(801) 539-4021

Wyoming State Office
P.O. Box 1828
Cheyenne, Wyoming 82003
(307) 775-6011

National Forest Service Offices (alphabetical by region)

U.S.D.A. Forest Service
U.S. Department of Agriculture
201 14th Street S.W.
Washington, D.C. 20090
(202) 655-4000

Alaska Region
P.O. Box 21628
Juneau, Alaska 99802-1628
(907) 586-8863

Eastern Region
310 West Wisconsin Avenue, Room 500
Milwaukee, Wisconsin 53203
(414) 297-3693

Intermountain Region
Federal Building
324 25th Street
Ogden, Utah 84401
(801) 625-5352

Northeastern Area
5 Radnor Corporate Center
100 Matsonford Road, Suite 200
Radnor, Pennsylvania 19087
(215) 975-4111

Northern Region
Federal Building
P.O. Box 7669
Missoula, Montana 59807
(406) 329-3511

Pacific Northwest Region
319 Southwest Pine Street
Portland, Oregon 97208
(503) 326-2971

Pacific Southwest Region
630 Sansome Street
San Francisco, California 94111
(415) 705-2870

Rocky Mountain Region
11177 West Eighth Avenue
Lakewood, Colorado 80225
(303) 236-9431

Southern Region
1720 Peachtree Road N.W.
Atlanta, Georgia 30367
(404) 347-2384

Southwestern Region
Federal Building
517 Gold Avenue S.W.
Albuquerque, New Mexico 87102
(505) 842-3292

National Park Service Offices (alphabetical by region)

National Park Service
U.S. Department of the Interior
P.O. Box 37127
Washington, D.C. 20013-7127
(202) 208-4747

National Parks *(continued)*

Alaska Region
National Park Service
2525 Gambell Street
Anchorage, Alaska 99503-2892
(907) 257-2696

Mid-Atlantic Region
National Park Service
143 South Third Street
Philadelphia, Pennsylvania 19106
(215) 597-3679

Midwest Region
National Park Service
1709 Jackson Street
Omaha, Nebraska 68102
(402) 221-3448

National Capital Region
National Park Service
1100 Ohio Drive, S.W.
Washington, D.C. 20242
(202) 619-7222

North Atlantic Region
National Park Service
15 State Street
Boston, Massachusetts 02109
(617) 223-5199

Pacific Northwest Region
National Park Service
83 South King Street, Suite 212
Seattle, Washington 98104
(206) 442-5622

Rocky Mountain Region
National Park Service
P.O. Box 25287
Denver, Colorado 80225
(303) 969-2504

Southeast Region
National Park Service
Richard B. Russell Federal Building
75 Spring Street S.W.
Atlanta, Georgia 30303
(404) 331-4998

Southwest Region
National Park Service
P.O. Box 728
Santa Fe, New Mexico 87501
(505) 988-6375

Western Region
National Park Service
600 Harrison Street, Suite 600
San Francisco, California 94107
(415) 744-3929

RV Buyers Guides

Trailer Life's RV Buyers Guide
TL Enterprises
29901 Agoura Road
Agoura, California 91301
(800) 234-3450

Woodall's RV Buyer's Guide
Woodall Publishing Company
P.O. Box 5000
Lake Forest, Illinois 60045
(708) 362-6700

RV Campground Directories

Camping Canada Directory
2585 Skymark Avenue, #306
Missassuaga, Ontario, Canada L4W 4L5
(416) 624-8218

***Trailer Life Campground &
RV Services Directory***
29901 Agoura Road
Agoura, California 91301
(800) 234-3450

Wheelers RV Resort & Campground Guide
1310 Jarvis Avenue
Elk Grove Village, Illinois 60007
(708) 981-0100

Woodall's Campground Directory
P.O. Box 5000
Lake Forest, Illinois 60045
(800) 323-9076

RV Clubs

Alpenlite Travel Club
P.O. Box 9152
Yakima, Washington 98909
(509) 452-3524

American Clipper Owners Club
514 Washington Street
Marina Del Rey, California 90292
(213) 823-8945, (213) 821-6433

Avion Travelcade Club
P.O. Box 236
DeBary, Florida 32713
(407) 668-6219

Barth Ranger Club
State Road 15
Milford, Indiana 46542
(219) 658-9401

Beaver Ambassador Club
20545 Murray Road
Bend, Oregon 97701
(503) 389-1144

Carriage Travel Club
P.O. Box 246
Millersburg, Indiana 46543
(219) 642-3622

Champion Fleet Owners Association
5573 East North Street
Dryden, Michigan 48428
(313) 796-2211

Cortez National Motorhome Club
11022 East Daines Drive
Temple City, California 91780
(818) 444-6030

El Dorado Caravan
15012 Johansson Avenue
Hudson, Florida 34667
(813) 868-6700

Escapee Club
Route 5, Box 310
Livingston, Texas 77351
(409) 327-8873

Family Motor Coach Association
8291 Clough Pike
Cincinnati, Ohio 45244
(800) 543-3622, (513) 474-3622

Fireball Caravaner
4100 South Eagleson Road
Boise, Idaho 83705
(208) 362-9314

First Xplorer
3950 Burnsline Road
Brown City, Michigan 48416
(313) 346-2771

Foretravel Motorcade Club
1221 Northwest Stallings Drive
Nacogdoches, Texas 75961
(409) 564-8367

Good Sam RV Owners Club
29901 Agoura Road
Agoura, California 91301
(800) 234-3450

Handicapped Travel Club
667 J Avenue
Coronado, California 92118
(619) 435-5213

Holiday Rambler RV Club
400 Indiana Avenue
Wakarusa, Indiana 46573
(219) 862-7330

International Coachmen Caravan Club
P.O. Box 30
Middlebury, Indiana 46540
(219) 825-8245

International Country Coach Country Club
P.O. Box 207
Junction City, Oregon 97448
(800) 537-0622, (503) 998-3712

RV Clubs *(continued)*

International Family Recreation Association
P.O. Box 6279
Pensacola, Florida 32503
(904) 477-2123

International Skamper Camper Club
P.O. Box 338
Bristol, Indiana 46507
(219) 848-7411

Jayco Jafari
P.O. Box 192
Osceola, Indiana 46561-0192
(219) 258-0591

Lazy Daze Caravan Club
4303 East Mission Boulevard
Pomona, California 91766
(714) 627-1219

Loners on Wheels
P.O. Box 1355
Poplar Bluff, Missouri 63901
(314) 785-2420

National Campers and Hikers Association
4804 Transit Road, Building 2
Depew, New York 14043
(716) 668-6242

National RV Owners Club
P.O. Drawer 17148
Pensacola, Florida 32522-7148
(904) 477-2123

North American Family Campers Association
P.O. Box 730
Dracut, Massachusetts 01826

Rockwood Travel Club
P.O. Box 191
Osceola, Indiana 46561-0191
(219) 258-0591

Serro Scotty Club
450 Arona Road
Irwin, Pennsylvania 15642
(412) 863-3407

Silver Streak Trailer Club
226 Grand Avenue, # 207
Long Beach, California 98083
(213) 433-0539

Sportscoach Owners International
3550 Foothill Boulevard
Glendale, California 91214
(818) 249-4175

Starcraft Camper Club
P.O. Box 176
Osceola, Indiana 46561-0176
(219) 258-0612

Streamline Royal Rovers
808 Clebud Drive
Euless, Texas 76040
(817) 267-2167

Wally Byam Caravan Club International
803 East Pike Street
Jackson Center, Ohio 45334
(513) 596-5211

Wings of Shasta Travel Club
P.O. Box 912
Middlebury, Indiana 46540
(800) 234-5571

Winnebago-Itasca Travelers
P.O. Box 268
Forest City, Iowa 50436
(515) 582-6874

RV Industry Associations

American Membership Campers Union
9753 South Orange Blossom Trail, Suite 203
Orlando, Florida 32821-9832
(800) 755-5777

Canadian Recreation Vehicle Association
670 Bloor Street West, Suite 200
Toronto, Ontario
Canada M6G 1L2
(416) 533-7800

Canadian Recreation Vehicle Dealers Association
19623 56th Avenue, #201
Langley, British Columbia
Canada V3A 3X7
(604) 533-4200

National Campground Owners Association
11307 Sunset Hills Road, Suite B-7
Reston, Virginia 22090
(703) 471-0143

Recreation Vehicle Dealers Association
3251 Old Lee Highway, Suite 500
Fairfax, Virginia 22030
(703) 591-7130

Recreation Vehicle Industry Association
1896 Preston White Drive
Reston, Virginia 22090
(703) 620-6003

Recreation Vehicle Rental Association
3251 Old Lee Highway, Suite 500
Fairfax, Virginia 22030
(703) 591-7130

RV Insurance Specialists

AARP Insurance
P.O. Box 2905
Hartford, Connecticut 06104
(800) 541-3717

Alexander & Alexander
700 Fisher Building
Detroit, Michigan 48202
(800) 521-2942
(800) 624-7539 (Michigan)

Caravanner Insurance
14805 North 73rd Street
Scottsdale, Arizona 85260
(800) 423-4403, (602) 991-2645

Foremost Insurance Company
P.O. Box 2450
Grand Rapids, Michigan 49501
(800) 545-8608, (616) 942-3000

Good Sam VIP Insurance
(National General Insurance Company)
P.O. Box 66937
St. Louis, Missouri 63166-6937
(800) 847-2886, Ext. 5784

Good Sam Emergency Road Service
P.O. Box 700
Agoura, California 91301
(800) 234-3450

Prudential Mechanical Breakdown Insurance
1250 South Parker Road, #205
Denver, Colorado 80231
(800) 638-8001

Sanborn's (for Mexican travel)
P.O. Box 310
McAllen, Texas 78502
(512) 686-3601

RV Magazines

Camping Canada
2585 Skymark Avenue, #306
Missassuaga, Ontario, Canada L4W 4L5
(416) 624-8218

Escapees
Escapees Club
Route 5, Box 310
Livingston, Texas 77351
(409) 327-8873

Family Motor Coaching
Family Motor Coach Association
8291 Clough Pike
Cincinnati, Ohio 45244
(800) 543-3622

Highways
Good Sam RV Owners Club
29901 Agoura Road
Agoura, California 91301
(800) 234-3450

RV Magazines (continued)

MotorHome
TL Enterprises
29901 Agoura Road
Agoura, California 91301
(800) 234-3450

Trailer Life
TL Enterprises, Inc.
29901 Agoura Road
Agoura, California 91301
(800) 234-3450

State Tourism Offices

Alabama Bureau of Tourism and Travel
532 South Perry Street
Montgomery, Alabama 36104
(800) 252-2262

Alaska Division of Tourism
P.O. Box 110801
Juneau, Alaska 99811-0801
(907) 465-2010

Arizona Office of Tourism
1100 West Washington Avenue
Phoenix, Arizona 85007
(602) 542-8687

Arkansas Department of Parks and Tourism
1 Capital Mall
Little Rock, Arkansas 72201
(800) 828-8974, (501) 682-1511

California Office of Tourism
801 K Street, Suite 1600
Sacramento, California 95814
(916) 322-1397

Colorado Department of Tourism
1625 Broadway, Suite 1700
Denver, Colorado 80202
(800) 255-5550, (303) 592-5510

Connecticut Tourism
865 Brooks Street
Rocky Hills, Connecticut 06067
(800) 282-6863, (203) 258-4355

Delaware Tourism Office
99 Kings Highway
Dover, Delaware 19901
(800) 441-8846

**Florida Department of Commerce
Division of Tourism**
107 West Gaines Street, Suite 566
Tallahassee, Florida 32399
(904) 488-7598

Georgia Department of Tourism
P.O. Box 1776
Atlanta, Georgia 30301
(800) 847-4842

Hawaii Visitors Bureau
2270 Kalakaua Avenue, Suite 801
Honolulu, Hawaii 96815
(808) 923-1811

**Idaho Department of Commerce
Tourism Division**
700 West State Street
Boise, Idaho 83720
(800) 635-7820, (208) 334-2470

Illinois Bureau of Tourism
310 South Michigan Avenue, Suite 108
Chicago, Illinois 60604
(800) 223-0121

Indiana Tourism
One Hoosier Dome, Suite 100
Indianapolis, Indiana 46225
(800) 289-6646

Iowa Division of Tourism
200 East Grand Avenue
Des Moines, Iowa 50309
(800) 345-4692, (515) 242-4705

Kansas Department of Commerce
400 West Eighth Street, 5th Floor
Topeka, Kansas 66603
(800) 252-6727, (913) 296-2009

Kentucky Department of Travel
Capitol Plaza Towers, 22nd Floor
500 Mero Street
Frankfort, Kentucky 40601
(800) 225-8747, (502) 564-4930

Louisiana Office of Tourism
P.O. Box 94291
Baton Rouge, Louisiana 70840
(800) 334-8626, (504) 342-8119

Maine Publicity Bureau
P.O. Box 2300
Hallowell, Maine 04347
(800) 533-9595, (207) 582-9300

Maryland Tourism
217 East Redwood Street
Baltimore, Maryland 24233
(800) 543-1036

Massachusetts Office of Travel and Tourism
100 Cambridge Street, 13th Floor
Boston, Massachusetts 02202
(800) 447-6277, (617) 727-3201

Michigan Travel Bureau
P.O. Box 30226
Lansing, Michigan 48909
(800) 543-2937, (517) 373-0670

Minnesota Office of Tourism
250 Skyway Level
375 Jackson Street
St. Paul, Minnesota 55101
(800) 657-3700, (612) 296-5029

Mississippi Division of Tourism
P.O. Box 22825
Jackson, Mississippi 39205-2825
(800) 647-2290, (601) 359-3297

Missouri Division of Tourism
P.O. Box 1055
Jefferson City, Missouri 65102
(800) 877-1234, (314) 751-4133

Travel Montana
1424 Ninth Avenue
Helena, Montana 59620
(800) 548-3390, (406) 444-2654

Nebraska Division of Travel and Tourism
P.O. Box 94666
Lincoln, Nebraska 68509
(800) 228-4307

Nevada Commission on Tourism
5151 South Carson Street
Carson City, Nevada 89710
(800) 237-0774, (702) 687-4322

New Hampshire Travel
P.O. Box 856
Concord, New Hampshire 03302-0856
(603) 271-2343

New Jersey Travel and Tourism
20 West State Street, CN 826
Trenton, New Jersey 08625
(800) 537-7397, (609) 292-2470

New Mexico Tourism
1100 St. Francis Drive
Santa Fe, New Mexico 87501
(800) 545-2040, (505) 827-0291

New York State Division of Tourism
1 Commerce Plaza
Albany, New York 12245
(800) 225-5697, (518) 474-4116

North Carolina Tourism
430 North Salisbury Street
Raleigh, North Carolina 27603
(800) 847-4862, (919) 733-4171

North Dakota Tourism
604 East Boulevard
Bismark, North Dakota 58505
(800) 437-2077, (701) 224-2525

Ohio Division of Tourism
P.O. Box 1001
Columbus, Ohio 43216
(800) 282-5393

Oklahoma Tourism
500 Will Rogers Building
Oklahoma City, Oklahoma 73105
(800) 652-6552, (404) 521-2406

State Tourism (continued)

Oregon Tourism Division
775 Summer Street N.E.
Salem, Oregon 97310
(800) 547-7842

Pennsylvania Travel
453 Forum Building
Harrisburg, Pennsylvania 17120
(800) 847-4872, (717) 787-5453

Rhode Island Tourism Division
7 Jackson Walkway
Providence, Rhode Island 02903
(800) 556-2484, (401) 277-2601

South Carolina Department of Tourism
P.O. Box 71
Columbia, South Carolina 29201
(803) 734-0235

South Dakota Department of Tourism
Capitol Lake Plaza
Pierre, South Dakota 57501
(800) 843-1930, (605) 773-3301

Tennessee Tourist Development
P.O. Box 23170
Nashville, Tennessee 37202
(615) 741-2158

Texas Department of Commerce
P.O. Box 12728
Austin, Texas 78711
(512) 462-9191

Utah Travel Council
Capitol Hill
Salt Lake City, Utah 84114
(801) 538-1030

Vermont Travel Division
134 State Street
Montpelier, Vermont 05602
(802) 828-3236

Virginia Division of Tourism
1021 East Cary Street, 14th Floor
Richmond, Virginia 23219
(804) 786-4484

Washington D.C. Convention & Visitors Association
1212 New York Avenue
Washington, D.C. 20015
(202) 789-7000

Washington State Tourism
101 General Administration Building, AX-13
Olympia, Washington 98504
(206) 586-2088

West Virginia Department of Commerce
Capitol Complex, Building 6, #564B
1900 Kanawha Boulevard East
Charleston, West Virginia 25305
(800) 225-5982

Wisconsin Department of Tourism
123 West Washington Avenue
Madison, Wisconsin 53702
(800) 432-8747, (608) 266-2161

Wyoming Division of Tourism
I-25 and College Drive
Cheyenne, Wyoming 82002
(800) 225-5996, (307) 777-7777

Tourism Offices, Canadian Provincial

Alberta Tourism
City Centre Building
10155 102nd Street
Edmonton, Alberta
Canada T5J 4L6
(800) 661-8888

Newfoundland and Labrador
Department of Development
P.O. Box 8730
St. John's, Newfoundland
Canada A1B 4K2
(800) 563-6353

Northwest Territories
Travel Arctic
Box 1320
Yellowknife, Northwest Territories
Canada X1A 2L9
(800) 661-0788

Nova Scotia Department of Tourism and Culture
P.O. Box 456
Halifax, Nova Scotia
Canada B3J 2R5
(800) 565-0000, (902) 424-5000

Ontario Travel
Queen's Park
Toronto, Ontario
Canada M7A 2E5
(800) 668-2746

Prince Edward Island
Department of Tourism and Parks
Visitor Services Division
P.O. Box 940
Charlottetown, Prince Edward Island
Canada C1A 7M5
(800) 565-0267

Tourism British Columbia
Parliament Buildings
Victoria, British Columbia
Canada V8V 1X4
(800) 663-6000

Tourism New Brunswick
P.O. Box 12345
Fredericton, New Brunswick
Canada E3B 5C3
(800) 561-0123

Tourism Saskatchewan
1919 Saskatchewan Drive
Regina, Saskatchewan
Canada S4P 3V7
(800) 667-7191

Tourism Yukon
P.O. Box 2703
Whitehorse, Yukon
Canada Y1A 2C6
(403) 667-5340

Tourismé Québec
C.P. 20-000
Quebec, Quebec
Canada G1K 7X2
(800) 363-7777

Travel Manitoba
155 Carlton Street, Department 20, #7
Winnipeg, Manitoba
Canada R3C 3H8
(800) 665-0040

Tourism Offices, Mexican Government

Mexican Government Tourism Office
70 East Lake Street, Suite 1413
Chicago, Illinois 60610
(312) 565-2786

Mexican Government Tourism Office
10100 Santa Monica Boulevard, Suite 224
Los Angeles, California 90067
(213) 203-8191

Mexican Government Tourism Office
405 Park Avenue, Suite 1002
New York, New York 10022
(212) 755-7261

U.S. Army Corps of Engineers Offices (alphabetical by region)

Lower Mississippi Valley Division
Attn: CELMC-CO-R
P.O. Box 80
Vicksburg, Mississippi 39181-0080
(601) 634-5885

Missouri River Division
Attn: CEMRD-CO-R
P.O. Box 103
Omaha, Nebraska 68101-0103
(402) 221-7284

North Atlantic Division
Attn: CENAD-CO-OP
90 Church Street
New York City, New York 10007-2979
(212) 264-7534

Corps of Engineers (continued)

North Central Division
Attn: CENCD-CO-O
111 North Canal Street, 14th Floor
Chicago, Illinois 60606-7205
(312) 353-7762

New England Division
Attn: CENED-OD-P
424 Trapelo Road
Waltham, Massachusetts 02254-9149
(617) 647-8107

North Pacific Division
Attn: CENPD-CO-O-R
P.O. Box 2870
Portland, Oregon 97208-2870
(503) 326-3780

Ohio River Division
Attn: CEORD-CO-OR
P.O. Box 1159
Cincinnati, Ohio 45201-1159
(513) 684-3192

South Atlantic Division
Attn: CESAD-CO-R
77 Forsyth Street SW
Atlanta, Georgia 30335-6807
(404) 331-6746

South Pacific Division
Attn: CESPD-CO-O
630 Sansome Street, #720
San Francisco, California 94111-2206
(415) 705-1443

Southwestern Division
Attn: CESWD-CO-R
1114 Commerce Street
Dallas, Texas 75242-0216
(214) 767-2435

Select Bibliography

■ ■ ■ ■ ■ ■ ■ ■ ■

ALDERMAN, BILL JR., AND ELEANORE WILSON. *Recreational Vehicles: Finding the Best Buy.* Chicago: Bonus Books, 1989.

BIRACREE, TOM, AND NANCY BIRACREE. *Over Fifty: The Resource Book for the Better Half of Your Life.* New York: Harper Perennial, 1991.

BOARDMAN, JOHN. *Living on Wheels: The Complete Guide to Motorhomes.* Blue Ridge Summit, Pennsylvania: TAB Books, 1987.

BOTTOM LINE PERSONAL. *The Book of Inside Information.* New York: Boardroom Classics, 1989.

BREITBARD, STANLEY H., AND DONNA SAMMONS CARPENTER. *The Price Waterhouse Book of Personal Financial Planning.* New York: Henry Holt and Company, 1990.

ELLIS, JUNIUS, ed. *Money* magazine's *Smart Money Moves for the '90s.* Birmingham, Alabama: Oxmoor House, 1990.

ESTES, BILL. *The RV Handbook.* Agoura, California: Trailer Life Books, 1991.

FARIELLO, SAL. *Mugged by Mr. Badwrench.* New York: St. Martin's Press, Inc., 1991.

GILLIS, JACK. *The Car Book.* New York: Harper Perennial, 1990.

GIVENS, CHARLES J. *Financial Self-Defense.* New York: Simon & Schuster, Inc., 1990.

———. *Wealth Without Risk.* New York: Simon & Schuster, Inc., 1988.

GROENE, GORDON, AND JANET GROENE. *Living Aboard Your Recreational Vehicle.* Merrillville, Indiana: ICS Books, 1986.

HOWELLS, JOHN. *RV Travel in Mexico.* San Francisco: Gateway Books, 1989.

IDS FINANCIAL SERVICES. *Money Matters: Your IDS Guide to Financial Planning.* New York: Avon Books, 1990.

LACROIX, RICHARD. *Exposed: History of the Membership Resort Campground Industry.* Longwood, Florida: Gary Publishing, 1990.

LIVINGSTON, BOB, ed. *RV Repair & Maintenance Manual.* Agoura, California: Trailer Life Books, 1989.

LOEB, MARSHALL. *Marshall Loeb's 1991 Money Guide.* Boston: Little, Brown & Company, 1991.

MCCULLOUGH, BONNIE. *Bonnie's Household Budget Book.* New York: St. Martin's Press, Inc., 1987.

MOELLER, BILL, AND JAN MOELLER. *Trailer Life's Full-time RVing.* Agoura, California: Trailer Life Books, 1986.

NADER, RALPH, AND WESLEY SMITH. *Winning the Insurance Game.* New York: Knightsbridge Publishing Company, 1990.

PALDER, EDWARD L. *The Retirement Sourcebook.* Rockville, Maryland: Woodbine House, 1989.

PETERSON, JOE, AND KAY PETERSON. *Survival of the Snowbirds.* Livingston, Texas: RoVers Publications, 1990.

———. *The Revised Encyclopedia for RVers.* Livingston, Texas: RoVers Publications, 1989.

PORTER, SYLVIA. *New Money Book for the 80s.* New York: Avon Books, 1979.

PORTNOY, J. ELIAS. *Let the Seller Beware!* New York: Collier Books, 1990.

THE PRINT PROJECT. *The Wholesale-by-Mail Catalog.* New York: HarperCollins Publishers, 1991.

RODALE PRESS. *Cut Your Bills in Half.* Emmaus, Pennsylvania: Rodale Press, 1989.

ROSS, JAMES R. *How to Buy a Car.* New York: St. Martin's Press, Inc., 1989.

SUTTON, REMAR. *Don't Get Taken Every Time.* New York: Penguin Books, 1991.

TAVERLY CHURCHILL PUBLISHING. *National Parks Trade Journal.* Wawona Station, Yosemite National Park: Taverly Churchill Publishing, 1989.

THOMPSON, JOHN. *Secrets of Successful RVing.* Agoura, California: Trailer Life Books, 1981.

WALLACE, DAN, ed. *The Natural Formula Book for Home & Yard.* Emmaus, Pennsylvania: Rodale Press, 1982.

WRIGHT, DON. *Guide to Free Attractions.* Elkhart, Indiana: Cottage Publications, 1989.

Index

Money-Saving Coupons

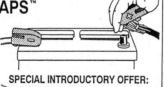
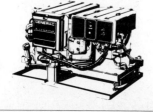

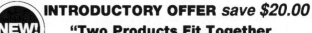

Money Saving Coupons From Camping World

SAVE $150.00
#7299,7891,7965,7966,9455 HWH Hydraulics

Coupon is valid on regular price merchandise only. Offer is not retroactive and cannot be used in combination with any other offer on this item except regular President's Club member 10% discount. Limit one coupon per item.

Offer good through December 31, 1992.

CAMPING WORLD.

2822

SAVE $30.00
#6224,7656,8864,8865 Dahon Classic or StowAway

Coupon is valid on regular price merchandise only. Offer is not retroactive and cannot be used in combination with any other offer on this item except regular President's Club member 10% discount. Limit one coupon per item.

Offer good through December 31, 1992.

CAMPING WORLD.

2820

SAVE $1.50
#4160 Aqua-Kem 6 Pak

Coupon is valid on regular price merchandise only. Offer is not retroactive and cannot be used in combination with any other offer on this item except regular President's Club member 10% discount. Limit one coupon per item.

Offer good through December 31, 1992.

CAMPING WORLD.

2813

SAVE $30.00
#1631,7284,8980 Fantastic Fan Vent

Coupon is valid on regular price merchandise only. Offer is not retroactive and cannot be used in combination with any other offer on this item except regular President's Club member 10% discount. Limit one coupon per item.

Offer good through December 31, 1992.

CAMPING WORLD.

2821

SAVE $5.00
#7346-48 Classy Chrome Chair

Coupon is valid on regular price merchandise only. Offer is not retroactive and cannot be used in combination with any other offer on this item except regular President's Club member 10% discount. Limit one coupon per item.

Offer good through December 31, 1992.

CAMPING WORLD.

2815

SAVE $5.00
#6632 Elastomeric Roof Coating

Coupon is valid on regular price merchandise only. Offer is not retroactive and cannot be used in combination with any other offer on this item except regular President's Club member 10% discount. Limit one coupon per item.

Offer good through December 31, 1992.

CAMPING WORLD.

2817

SAVE $10.00
#5958 Leisure Table

Coupon is valid on regular price merchandise only. Offer is not retroactive and cannot be used in combination with any other offer on this item except regular President's Club member 10% discount. Limit one coupon per item.
5994 Parasol sold separately

Offer good through December 31, 1992.

CAMPING WORLD.

2818

SAVE $1.50
#5340,7152 Slip Stop

Coupon is valid on regular price merchandise only. Offer is not retroactive and cannot be used in combination with any other offer on this item except regular President's Club member 10% discount. Limit one coupon per item.

Offer good through December 31, 1992.

CAMPING WORLD.

2814

SAVE $15.00
#6849,4537,4553 Foldaway Recliner

Coupon is valid on regular price merchandise only. Offer is not retroactive and cannot be used in combination with any other offer on this item except regular President's Club member 10% discount. Limit one coupon per item.

Offer good through December 31, 1992.

CAMPING WORLD.

2819

SAVE $5.00
#1476,5004,5014,5045,5060,7794 Tyre Gards

Coupon is valid on regular price merchandise only. Offer is not retroactive and cannot be used in combination with any other offer on this item except regular President's Club member 10% discount. Limit one coupon per item.

Offer good through December 31, 1992.

CAMPING WORLD.

2816

Money Saving Coupons From Camping World

Coupon may be redeemed at any Camping World location, or call **1-800-626-5944**.

ARIZONA • Mesa • **CALIFORNIA** • Anaheim, El Cajon, Fairfield, Rocklin, San Bernardino, San Martin *(Opening Soon)*, Valencia
COLORADO • Denver *(Opening Soon)*
FLORIDA • Fort Myers, Kissimmee, Tampa
ILLINOIS • Bolingbrook • **KENTUCKY** • Bowling Green
MICHIGAN • Belleville • **OHIO** • Cleveland *(Opening Soon)*
OREGON • Wilsonville • **SOUTH CAROLINA** • Myrtle Beach
TENNESSEE • Nashville • **TEXAS** • Denton, Mission
WASHINGTON • Fife

Coupon may be redeemed at any Camping World location, or call **1-800-626-5944**.

ARIZONA • Mesa • **CALIFORNIA** • Anaheim, El Cajon, Fairfield, Rocklin, San Bernardino, San Martin *(Opening Soon)*, Valencia
COLORADO • Denver *(Opening Soon)*
FLORIDA • Fort Myers, Kissimmee, Tampa
ILLINOIS • Bolingbrook • **KENTUCKY** • Bowling Green
MICHIGAN • Belleville • **OHIO** • Cleveland *(Opening Soon)*
OREGON • Wilsonville • **SOUTH CAROLINA** • Myrtle Beach
TENNESSEE • Nashville • **TEXAS** • Denton, Mission
WASHINGTON • Fife

Coupon may be redeemed at any Camping World location, or call **1-800-626-5944**.

ARIZONA • Mesa • **CALIFORNIA** • Anaheim, El Cajon, Fairfield, Rocklin, San Bernardino, San Martin *(Opening Soon)*, Valencia
COLORADO • Denver *(Opening Soon)*
FLORIDA • Fort Myers, Kissimmee, Tampa
ILLINOIS • Bolingbrook • **KENTUCKY** • Bowling Green
MICHIGAN • Belleville • **OHIO** • Cleveland *(Opening Soon)*
OREGON • Wilsonville • **SOUTH CAROLINA** • Myrtle Beach
TENNESSEE • Nashville • **TEXAS** • Denton, Mission
WASHINGTON • Fife

Coupon may be redeemed at any Camping World location, or call **1-800-626-5944**.

ARIZONA • Mesa • **CALIFORNIA** • Anaheim, El Cajon, Fairfield, Rocklin, San Bernardino, San Martin *(Opening Soon)*, Valencia
COLORADO • Denver *(Opening Soon)*
FLORIDA • Fort Myers, Kissimmee, Tampa
ILLINOIS • Bolingbrook • **KENTUCKY** • Bowling Green
MICHIGAN • Belleville • **OHIO** • Cleveland *(Opening Soon)*
OREGON • Wilsonville • **SOUTH CAROLINA** • Myrtle Beach
TENNESSEE • Nashville • **TEXAS** • Denton, Mission
WASHINGTON • Fife

Coupon may be redeemed at any Camping World location, or call **1-800-626-5944**.

ARIZONA • Mesa • **CALIFORNIA** • Anaheim, El Cajon, Fairfield, Rocklin, San Bernardino, San Martin *(Opening Soon)*, Valencia
COLORADO • Denver *(Opening Soon)*
FLORIDA • Fort Myers, Kissimmee, Tampa
ILLINOIS • Bolingbrook • **KENTUCKY** • Bowling Green
MICHIGAN • Belleville • **OHIO** • Cleveland *(Opening Soon)*
OREGON • Wilsonville • **SOUTH CAROLINA** • Myrtle Beach
TENNESSEE • Nashville • **TEXAS** • Denton, Mission
WASHINGTON • Fife

Coupon may be redeemed at any Camping World location, or call **1-800-626-5944**.

ARIZONA • Mesa • **CALIFORNIA** • Anaheim, El Cajon, Fairfield, Rocklin, San Bernardino, San Martin *(Opening Soon)*, Valencia
COLORADO • Denver *(Opening Soon)*
FLORIDA • Fort Myers, Kissimmee, Tampa
ILLINOIS • Bolingbrook • **KENTUCKY** • Bowling Green
MICHIGAN • Belleville • **OHIO** • Cleveland *(Opening Soon)*
OREGON • Wilsonville • **SOUTH CAROLINA** • Myrtle Beach
TENNESSEE • Nashville • **TEXAS** • Denton, Mission
WASHINGTON • Fife

Coupon may be redeemed at any Camping World location, or call **1-800-626-5944**.

ARIZONA • Mesa • **CALIFORNIA** • Anaheim, El Cajon, Fairfield, Rocklin, San Bernardino, San Martin *(Opening Soon)*, Valencia
COLORADO • Denver *(Opening Soon)*
FLORIDA • Fort Myers, Kissimmee, Tampa
ILLINOIS • Bolingbrook • **KENTUCKY** • Bowling Green
MICHIGAN • Belleville • **OHIO** • Cleveland *(Opening Soon)*
OREGON • Wilsonville • **SOUTH CAROLINA** • Myrtle Beach
TENNESSEE • Nashville • **TEXAS** • Denton, Mission
WASHINGTON • Fife

Coupon may be redeemed at any Camping World location, or call **1-800-626-5944**.

ARIZONA • Mesa • **CALIFORNIA** • Anaheim, El Cajon, Fairfield, Rocklin, San Bernardino, San Martin *(Opening Soon)*, Valencia
COLORADO • Denver *(Opening Soon)*
FLORIDA • Fort Myers, Kissimmee, Tampa
ILLINOIS • Bolingbrook • **KENTUCKY** • Bowling Green
MICHIGAN • Belleville • **OHIO** • Cleveland *(Opening Soon)*
OREGON • Wilsonville • **SOUTH CAROLINA** • Myrtle Beach
TENNESSEE • Nashville • **TEXAS** • Denton, Mission
WASHINGTON • Fife

Coupon may be redeemed at any Camping World location, or call **1-800-626-5944**.

ARIZONA • Mesa • **CALIFORNIA** • Anaheim, El Cajon, Fairfield, Rocklin, San Bernardino, San Martin *(Opening Soon)*, Valencia
COLORADO • Denver *(Opening Soon)*
FLORIDA • Fort Myers, Kissimmee, Tampa
ILLINOIS • Bolingbrook • **KENTUCKY** • Bowling Green
MICHIGAN • Belleville • **OHIO** • Cleveland *(Opening Soon)*
OREGON • Wilsonville • **SOUTH CAROLINA** • Myrtle Beach
TENNESSEE • Nashville • **TEXAS** • Denton, Mission
WASHINGTON • Fife

Coupon may be redeemed at any Camping World location, or call **1-800-626-5944**.

ARIZONA • Mesa • **CALIFORNIA** • Anaheim, El Cajon, Fairfield, Rocklin, San Bernardino, San Martin *(Opening Soon)*, Valencia
COLORADO • Denver *(Opening Soon)*
FLORIDA • Fort Myers, Kissimmee, Tampa
ILLINOIS • Bolingbrook • **KENTUCKY** • Bowling Green
MICHIGAN • Belleville • **OHIO** • Cleveland *(Opening Soon)*
OREGON • Wilsonville • **SOUTH CAROLINA** • Myrtle Beach
TENNESSEE • Nashville • **TEXAS** • Denton, Mission
WASHINGTON • Fife